OpenCV for Secret Agents

Use OpenCV in six secret projects to augment your home, car, phone, eyesight, and any photo or drawing

Joseph Howse

[PACKT] open source✳
PUBLISHING   community experience distilled

BIRMINGHAM - MUMBAI

OpenCV for Secret Agents

First published: January 2015

Production reference: 1230115

Published by Packt Publishing Ltd.
Livery Place
35 Livery Street
Birmingham B3 2PB, UK.

ISBN 978-1-78328-737-6

www.packtpub.com

Cover image by Jeremy Segal (info@jsegalphoto.com)

Credits

Author

Joseph Howse

Reviewers

Karan Kedar Balkar

Michael Beyeler

Demetris Gerogiannis

Kevin Hughes

Ganesh Iyer

Andrew Colin Kissa

Lihang Li

Ryohei Tanaka

Commissioning Editor

Sam Birch

Acquisition Editors

Sam Birch

Richard Brookes-Bland

Content Development Editor

Arwa Manasawala

Technical Editor

Aman Preet Singh

Copy Editor

Neha Vyas

Project Coordinator

Sageer Parkar

Proofreaders

Simran Bhogal

Ameesha Green

Paul Hindle

Clyde Jenkins

Indexer

Monica Ajmera Mehta

Graphics

Sheetal Aute

Abhinash Sahu

Production Coordinator

Arvindkumar Gupta

Cover Work

Arvindkumar Gupta

About the Author

Joseph Howse has four first-rate cats; yet, if his books sell well, he could build a menagerie fit for a pharaoh.

OpenCV for Secret Agents is Joseph's third book, following *OpenCV Computer Vision with Python* and *Android Application Programming with OpenCV*. When not writing books or grooming cats, Joseph is working to grow the augmented reality industry by providing software development and training services through his company, Nummist Media (http://nummist.com).

Acknowledgments

Many people, near and far, have guided this book to completion.

My parents, Jan and Bob, have given me nine full lives or so it seems. My four cats, Plasma Tigerlily Zoya, Sanibel Delphinium Andromeda, Lambda Catculus Puddingcat, and Josephine Antoinette Puddingcat, have provided constant supervision and contributed to testing the cat recognition software in *Chapter 3, Training a Smart Alarm to Recognize the Villain and His Cat.*

My readers and listeners have taken time to provide valuable feedback and ask questions about my previous books and presentations. Thanks to their loyalty and dedication to discovery, our shared exploration of OpenCV goes on!

My clients at Market Beat, in El Salvador, have inspired several of the book's topics, including detection, recognition, tracking, and the use of Raspberry Pi.

Thanks, Steven Puttemans, for the helpful discussion on Haar features. Thanks, Tanya Suhodolska, for icons used in the application bundles.

My editors at Packt Publishing have once again given me all the benefit of their skill, experience, and professionalism in the planning, polishing, and marketing of this book. Writing one of Packt's "Secret Agent" books has been a uniquely fun project! Thanks, Sam Birch, for suggesting Eulerian video magnification as the topic of *Chapter 6, Seeing a Heartbeat with a Motion Amplifying Camera.*

My technical reviewers have once again saved me from sundry errors and omissions. Read their biographies here! They are fine members of the OpenCV community.

Sam Howse, Bunny Moir, and dear old cats — you are remembered for the love, laughter, learning, and long journeys home.

About the Reviewers

Karan Kedar Balkar has been working as an independent Android application developer since the past 4 years. Born and brought up in Mumbai, he holds a bachelor's degree in computer engineering. He has written over 50 programming tutorials on his personal blog (`http://karanbalkar.com`) that covers popular technologies and frameworks.

At present, he is working as a software engineer. He has been trained on various technologies, including Java, Oracle, and .NET. Apart from being passionate about technology, he loves to write poems and travel to different places. He likes listening to music and enjoys playing the guitar.

> First, I would like to thank my parents for their constant support and encouragement. I would also like to thank my friends, Srivatsan Iyer, Ajit Pillai, and Prasaanth Neelakandan, for always inspiring and motivating me.
>
> I would like to express my deepest gratitude to Packt Publishing for giving me a chance to be a part of the reviewing process.

Michael Beyeler is a PhD student in the department of computer science at the University of California, Irvine, where he is working on large-scale cortical models of biological vision, motion, learning, and memory, as well as their implementation on GPGPUs and their applications for cognitive robotics. He received a bachelor's of science degree in electrical engineering and information technology in 2009 as well as a master's of science degree in biomedical engineering in 2011 from ETH Zurich, Switzerland.

Demetris Gerogiannis received his bachelor's of science, master's of science, and PhD degrees from the department of Computer Science & Engineering, University of Ioannina, Greece in 2004, 2007, and 2014, respectively. He is an active researcher of computer vision, and his research interests include image segmentation and registration, point set registration, feature extraction, pattern recognition, and autonomous navigation. His work has been presented in international conferences, and it has been published in international journals. He is an IEEE student member, and from October 2012 till June 2013, he was the interim chair at the IEEE student branch of the University of Ioannina. Since his early years in the university, he was interested in entrepreneurship. He was involved in several entrepreneurial technological ventures, and he has participated in several international business competitions. The most important one was the participation at the Startupbootcamp for NFC & Contactless, communication selection days, in Amsterdam in September 2013. His start-up was selected among 250 plus international start-ups that had applied for this accelerator project. He is also involved in the development of his local region start-up ecosystem. To that end, he has cofounded in 2014 a nonprofit team (StartupLake) with a view to provide mentorship to young ambitious people who want to have their own start-ups.

Ryohei Tanaka is a software engineer at Yahoo! Japan Corporation. His focus is now on machine learning, information extraction, and distributed computing. He has sound knowledge of image processing on web browser (HTML5/JavaScript). More details on his programming skills, interests, and experience about computer vision can be found at `http://rest-term.com`.

Congrats to the author and all those who worked on this book, and thanks to the editors and publishers who gave me a chance to work on the publication of this book.

www.PacktPub.com

Support files, eBooks, discount offers, and more

For support files and downloads related to your book, please visit www.PacktPub.com.

Did you know that Packt offers eBook versions of every book published, with PDF and ePub files available? You can upgrade to the eBook version at www.PacktPub.com and as a print book customer, you are entitled to a discount on the eBook copy. Get in touch with us at service@packtpub.com for more details.

At www.PacktPub.com, you can also read a collection of free technical articles, sign up for a range of free newsletters and receive exclusive discounts and offers on Packt books and eBooks.

http://PacktLib.PacktPub.com

Do you need instant solutions to your IT questions? PacktLib is Packt's online digital book library. Here, you can search, access, and read Packt's entire library of books.

Why subscribe?

- Fully searchable across every book published by Packt
- Copy and paste, print, and bookmark content
- On demand and accessible via a web browser

Free access for Packt account holders

If you have an account with Packt at www.PacktPub.com, you can use this to access PacktLib today and view 9 entirely free books. Simply use your login credentials for immediate access.

Table of Contents

Preface

Computer vision systems are deployed in the Arctic Ocean to spot icebergs at night.
They are flown over the Amazon rainforest to create aerial maps of fires, blights,
and illegal logging. They are set up in ports and airports worldwide to scan for
suspects and contraband. They are sent to the depths of the Marianas Trench to guide
autonomous submarines. They are used in operating rooms to help surgeons visualize
the planned procedure and the patient's current condition. They are launched from
battlefields as the steering systems of heat-seeking, anti-aircraft rockets.

We might seldom—or never—visit these places. However, stories often encourage
us to imagine extreme environments and a person's dependence on tools in these
unforgiving conditions. Perhaps fittingly, one of contemporary fiction's most popular
characters is an almost ordinary man (handsome but not too handsome, clever but
not too clever) who wears a suit, works for the British Government, always chooses
the same drink, the same kind of woman, the same tone for delivering a pun, and is
sent to do dangerous jobs with a peculiar collection of gadgets.

Bond. James Bond.

This book teaches seriously useful technologies and techniques with a healthy dose
of inspiration from spy fiction. The Bond franchise is rich in ideas about detection,
disguise, smart devices, image capture, and sometimes even computer vision
specifically. With imagination, plus dedication of learning new skills, we can
become the next generation of gadget makers to rival Bond's engineer, Q!

What this book covers

Chapter 1, Preparing for the Mission helps us to install OpenCV, a Python development environment, and an Android development environment on Windows, Mac, or Linux systems. In this chapter, we also install a Unity development environment on Windows or Mac.

Chapter 2, Searching for Luxury Accommodations Worldwide helps us to classify images of real estate based on color schemes. Are we outside a luxury dwelling or inside a Stalinist apartment? In this chapter, we use the classifier in a search engine that labels its image results.

Chapter 3, Training a Smart Alarm to Recognize the Villain and His Cat helps us to detect and recognize human faces and cat faces as a means of controlling an alarm. Has Ernst Stavro Blofeld returned with his blue-eyed Angora cat?

Chapter 4, Controlling a Phone App with Your Suave Gestures helps us to detect motion and recognize gestures as a means of controlling a guessing game on a smartphone. The phone knows why Bond is nodding even if no one else does.

Chapter 5, Equipping Your Car with a Rearview Camera and Hazard Detection helps us to detect car headlights, classify their color, estimate distances to them, and provide feedback to a driver. Is that car tailing us?

Chapter 6, Seeing a Heartbeat with a Motion Amplifying Camera helps us to amplify motion in live video, in real time, so that a person's heartbeat and breathing become clearly visible. See the passion!

Chapter 7, Creating a Physics Simulation Based on a Pen and Paper Sketch helps us to draw a ball-in-a-maze puzzle on paper and see it come to life as a physics simulation on a smartphone. Physics and timing are everything!

What you need for this book

This book supports several operating systems as development environments, including Windows XP or a later version, Mac OS X 10.6 or a later version, Debian Wheezy, Raspbian, Ubuntu 12.04 or a later version, Linux Mint 13 or a later version, Fedora 18 or a later version, CentOS 7 or a later version, and openSUSE 13.1 or a later version.

The book contains six projects with the following requirements:

- Four of these six projects run on Windows, Mac, or Linux and require a webcam. Optionally, these projects can use Raspberry Pi or another single-board computer that runs Linux.

- One project runs on Android 2.2 or a later version and requires a front-facing camera (which most Android devices have).

- One project runs on Android 2.3 or a later version and requires a rear-facing camera and gravity sensor (which most Android devices have). For development, it requires a Windows or Mac machine and approximately $75 worth of game development software.

Setup instructions for all required libraries and tools are covered in the book. Optional setup instructions for Raspberry Pi are also included.

Who this book is for

This book is for tinkerers (and spies) who want to make computer vision a practical and fun part of their lifestyle. You should already be comfortable with 2D graphic concepts, object-oriented languages, GUIs, networking, and command line. This book does not assume experience with any specific libraries or platforms. Detailed instructions cover everything from setting up the development environment to deploying finished apps.

A desire to learn multiple technologies and techniques and to integrate them is highly beneficial! This book will help you branch out to understand several types of systems and application domains where computer vision is relevant, and it will help you to apply several approaches to detect, recognize, track, and augment faces, objects, and motions.

Conventions

In this book, you will find a number of text styles that distinguish between different kinds of information. Here are some examples of these styles and an explanation of their meaning.

Code words in text, database table names, folder names, filenames, file extensions, pathnames, dummy URLs, user input, and Twitter handles are shown as follows: "You can edit /etc/modules to check whether bcm2835-v4l2 is already listed there."

A block of code is set as follows:

```
set PYINSTALLER=C:\PyInstaller\pyinstaller.py

REM Remove any previous build of the app.
rmdir build /s /q
```

```
rmdir dist /s /q

REM Train the classifier.
python HistogramClassifier.py
```

When we wish to draw your attention to a particular part of a code block, the relevant lines or items are set in bold:

```
<activity
  android:name="com.nummist.goldgesture.CameraActivity"
  android:label="@string/app_name"
  android:screenOrientation="landscape"
  android:theme="@android:style/Theme.NoTitleBar.Fullscreen">
<intent-filter>
<action android:name="android.intent.action.MAIN" />
<category android:name=
"android.intent.category.LAUNCHER" />
</intent-filter>
</activity>
```

Any command-line input or output is written as follows:

```
$ echo "bcm2835-v4l2" | sudo tee -a /etc/modules
```

New terms and **important words** are shown in bold. Words that you see on the screen, for example, in menus or dialog boxes, appear in the text like this: "Click on the link for **Bing Search API** (not any variant such as **Bing Search API – Web Results Only**)."

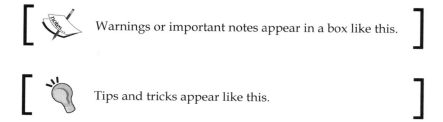

> Warnings or important notes appear in a box like this.

> Tips and tricks appear like this.

Reader feedback

Feedback from our readers is always welcome. Let us know what you think about this book—what you liked or disliked. Reader feedback is important for us as it helps us develop titles that you will really get the most out of.

To send us general feedback, simply e-mail feedback@packtpub.com, and mention the book's title in the subject of your message.

If there is a topic that you have expertise in and you are interested in either writing or contributing to a book, see our author guide at www.packtpub.com/authors.

Customer support

Now that you are the proud owner of a Packt book, we have a number of things to help you to get the most from your purchase.

Downloading the example code

You can download the example code files from your account at http://www.packtpub.com for all the Packt Publishing books you have purchased. If you purchased this book elsewhere, you can visit http://www.packtpub.com/support and register to have the files e-mailed directly to you. The latest and updated example code for this book is also available from the author's website at http://nummist.com/opencv/.

Errata

Although we have taken every care to ensure the accuracy of our content, mistakes do happen. If you find a mistake in one of our books—maybe a mistake in the text or the code—we would be grateful if you could report this to us. By doing so, you can save other readers from frustration and help us improve subsequent versions of this book. If you find any errata, please report them by visiting http://www.packtpub.com/submit-errata, selecting your book, clicking on the **ErrataSubmissionForm** link, and entering the details of your errata. Once your errata are verified, your submission will be accepted and the errata will be uploaded to our website or added to any list of existing errata under the Errata section of that title.

To view the previously submitted errata, go to https://www.packtpub.com/books/content/support and enter the name of the book in the search field. The required information will appear under the **Errata** section.

Piracy

Piracy of copyrighted material on the Internet is an ongoing problem across all media. At Packt, we take the protection of our copyright and licenses very seriously. If you come across any illegal copies of our works in any form on the Internet, please provide us with the location address or website name immediately so that we can pursue a remedy.

Please contact us at copyright@packtpub.com with a link to the suspected pirated material.

We appreciate your help in protecting our authors and our ability to bring you valuable content.

Questions

If you have a problem with any aspect of this book, you can contact us at questions@packtpub.com, and we will do our best to address the problem. You can also contact the author directly at josephhowse@nummist.com or you can check his website, http://nummist.com/opencv/, for answers to common questions about this book.

1
Preparing for the Mission

Q: I've been saying for years, sir, that our special equipment is obsolete. And now, computer analysis reveals an entirely new approach: miniaturization.

On Her Majesty's Secret Service (1969)

James Bond is not a pedestrian. He cruises in a submarine car, he straps on a rocket belt, and oh, how he skis, how he skis! He always has the latest stuff and he is never afraid to put a dent in it, much to the dismay of Q, the engineer.

As software developers in the 2010s, we are witnessing an explosion in the adoption of new platforms. Under one family's roof, we might find a mix of Windows, Mac, iOS, and Android devices. Mom and Dad's workplaces provide different platforms. The kids have three game consoles or five if you count the mobile versions. The toddler has a LeapFrog learning tablet. Smart glasses are becoming more affordable.

We must not be afraid to try new platforms and consider new ways to combine them. After all, most users do.

This book embraces multi-platform development. It presents weird and wonderful applications that we can deploy in unexpected places. It uses several of the computer's senses, but especially uses computer vision to breathe new life into the humdrum, heterogeneous clutter of devices that surround us.

Before Agent 007 runs amok with the gadgets, he is obligated to listen to Q's briefing. This chapter performs Q's role. This is the setup chapter.

By the end of this chapter, you will obtain all the tools to develop OpenCV applications in C++ or Python for Windows, Mac, or Linux, and in C++ or Java for Android. You will also be the proud new user of a Raspberry Pi single-board computer (this additional hardware is optional). You will even know a bit about Unity, a game engine into which we can integrate OpenCV.

If you find yourself a bit daunted by the extent of this setup chapter, be reassured that not all of the tools are required and no single project uses all of them in combination. Although Q and I live for the big event of setting up multiple technologies at once, you could just skim this chapter and refer back to it later when the tools become useful, one by one, in our projects.

> Where basic OpenCV setup and reference materials are concerned, this chapter includes excerpts from my introductory books, *OpenCV Computer Vision with Python* and *Android Application Programming with OpenCV*, published by Packt Publishing. All contents are retested, updated, and expanded to cover newer OpenCV versions and additional operating systems. Also, there are all new sections on the optional hardware and game engine used in this book.

Setting up a development machine

We can develop our OpenCV applications on a desktop, a notebook, or even the humble Raspberry Pi (covered later in the *Setting up a Raspberry Pi* section). Most of our apps have a memory footprint of less than 128 MB, so they can still run (albeit slowly) on old or low-powered machines. To save time, develop on your fastest machine first and test on slower machines later.

This book assumes that you have one of the following operating systems on your development machine:

- Windows XP or a later version
- Mac OS 10.6 or a later version
- Debian Wheezy or a derivative such as the following:
  - Raspbian
  - Ubuntu 12.04 or a later version
  - Linux Mint 13 or a later version
- Fedora 18 or a later version, or a derivative such as the following:
  - Red Hat Enterprise Linux (RHEL) 7 or a later version
  - CentOS 7 or a later version
- openSUSE 13.1 or a later version, or a derivative

Other Unix-like systems can also work but they are not covered in this book.

You should have a USB webcam and any necessary drivers. Most webcams come with instructions for installing drivers on Windows and Mac. Linux distributions typically include the **USB Video Class (UVC)** Linux driver, which supports many webcams, listed at `http://www.ideasonboard.org/uvc/#devices`.

We are going to set up the following components:

- A C++ development environment. On Windows, we will use Visual Studio 2010 or a later version. Alternatively, Windows users can follow Kevin Hughes' helpful tutorial on setting up OpenCV with MinGW and the Code::Blocks IDE at `http://kevinhughes.ca/tutorials/opencv-install-on-windows-with-codeblocks-and-mingw/`. On Mac, we will use Xcode. On Linux, we will use GCC, which comes as standard.

- On Mac, we will use a third-party package manager to help us install libraries and their dependencies. We will use either MacPorts or Homebrew.

- A Python 2.7 development environment. At the time of writing, the best option is to use version 2.7 as it is the most recent Python version supported by OpenCV's stable branch. (Python 2.6 is also supported by the stable branch.)

- Popular libraries such as NumPy (for numeric functions), SciPy (for numeric and scientific functions), Requests (for web requests), and wxPython (for cross-platform GUIs).

- PyInstaller, a cross-platform tool used for bundling Python scripts, libraries, and data as redistributable apps, such that users machines do not require installations of Python, OpenCV, and other libraries. For this book's purposes, building redistributables of Python projects is an optional topic. We will cover the basics in *Chapter 2, Searching for Luxury Accommodations Worldwide*, but you might need to do your own testing and debugging as PyInstaller (like other Python bundling tools) does not show entirely consistent behavior across operating systems, Python versions, and library versions. It is not well supported on Raspberry Pi or other ARM systems.

- A build of OpenCV with C++ and Python support plus optimizations for certain desktop hardware. At the time of writing, OpenCV 2.4.x is the stable branch and our instructions are tailored for this branch.

- Another build of OpenCV with C++ and Java support plus optimizations for certain Android hardware. Specifically, we will use the OpenCV build that comes with **Tegra Android Development Pack (TADP)**. At the time of writing, TADP 3.0r4 is the most recent release.

- An Android development environment, including Eclipse, ADT, Android SDK, and Android NDK. TADP includes these too.

- On Windows or Mac, a 3D game engine called Unity.

Eclipse has a big memory footprint. Even if you want to use Raspberry Pi for developing desktop and Pi apps, use something with more RAM for developing Android apps.

Let's break this setup down into three sets of platform-dependent steps, plus a set of platform-independent steps for TADP, and another set of platform-independent steps for Unity.

Windows

On Windows, we have the option of setting up a 32-bit development environment (to make apps that are compatible with both 32-bit and 64-bit Windows) or a 64-bit development environment (to make optimized apps that are compatible with 64-bit Windows only). Recent versions of OpenCV are available in 32-bit and 64-bit versions.

We also have a choice of either using binary installers or compiling OpenCV from source. For our Windows apps in this book, the binary installers provide everything we need. However, we will also discuss the option of compiling from source because it enables us to configure additional features, such as support for Kinect and Asus depth cameras, which might be relevant to your future work or to our projects in other books.

 For an OpenCV project that uses a depth camera, refer to my book *OpenCV Computer Vision with Python*, published by Packt Publishing.

Regardless of our approach to obtain OpenCV, we need a general-purpose C++ development environment and a general-purpose Python 2.7 development environment. We will set up these environments using binary installers.

As our C++ development environment, we will use Visual Studio 2010 or a later version. Use any installation media you might have purchased, or go to the downloads page at `http://www.visualstudio.com/en-us/downloads/download-visual-studio-vs.aspx`. Download and run the installer for one of the following:

- Visual C++ 2010 Express, which is free
- Visual Studio Express 2013 for Windows desktop, which is free
- Any of the paid versions, which have 90-day free trials

If the installer lists optional C++ components, we should opt to install them all. After the installer runs till completion, reboot.

If we plan to compile OpenCV from source (as described in the *OpenCV on Windows with CMake and Compilers* section), I recommend you use Visual Studio 2010 (and not any later version). At the time of writing, OpenCV and some of its optional dependencies do not compile easily with Visual Studio 2012 or Visual Studio 2013.

Installers for Python 2.7 are available at `http://www.python.org/getit/`. Download and run the latest revision of Python 2.7 in either the 32-bit variant or the 64-bit variant.

To make Python scripts run using our new Python 2.7 installation by default, let's edit the system's `Path` variable and append `;C:\Python2.7` (assuming Python 2.7 is installed in the default location). Remove any previous Python paths, such as `;C:\Python2.6`. Log out and log back in (or reboot).

Let's assume that we also want to use binary installers for NumPy, SciPy, and wxPython. Download and run the installers for the latest stable library versions that target Python 2.7. We can find these installers at the following locations:

1. **NumPy**: The official installers are 32-bit only and are located at `http://sourceforge.net/projects/numpy/files/NumPy/`. Unofficial 64-bit installers are available at `http://www.lfd.uci.edu/~gohlke/pythonlibs/#numpy`.

2. **SciPy**: The official installers are 32-bit only and are located at `http://sourceforge.net/projects/scipy/files/scipy/`. Unofficial 64-bit installers are available at `http://www.lfd.uci.edu/~gohlke/pythonlibs/#scipy`.

3. **wxPython**: This can be downloaded from `http://www.wxpython.org/download.php`. The apps in this book are successfully tested with wxPython 2.8, 2.9, and 3.0. If in doubt, choose version 3.0. However, if you choose version 2.8, get its Unicode variant.

Requests does not have a binary installer but we can download the latest source bundle from `https://github.com/kennethreitz/requests/archive/master.zip`. Unzip it to any destination, which we will refer to as `<unzip_destination>`. Open Command Prompt and run the following commands:

```
> cd <unzip_destination>
> python setup.py install
```

Next, we can put PyInstaller in any convenient location, since it is treated as a set of tools rather than a library. Let's download the latest release version from `http://www.pyinstaller.org/` and unzip it to `C:\PyInstaller` or any another location of your choice.

Now, we are ready to set up OpenCV and, optionally, other computer vision libraries.

OpenCV on Windows with binary installers

Download OpenCV as a self-extracting ZIP file from `http://opencv.org/downloads.html`. Choose the latest version, which should contain both 32-bit and 64-bit binaries. Double-click on the self-extracting ZIP file and, when prompted, enter any destination folder, which we will refer to as `<unzip_destination>`. A subfolder named `<opencv_unzip_destination>\opencv` is created.

Copy `<opencv_unzip_destination>\opencv\build\python\2.7\x86\cv2.pyd` (32-bit) or `<opencv_unzip_destination>\opencv\build\python\2.7\x64\cv2.pyd` (64-bit) to `C:\Python2.7\Lib\site-packages` (assuming Python 2.7 is installed to the default location). Now, Python 2.7 can find OpenCV.

You might want to look at the code samples in `<unzip_destination>/opencv/samples`.

At this point, we have everything we need to develop OpenCV applications for Windows. To also develop the same for Android, we need to set up TADP as described in the section *Tegra Android Development Pack*, later in this chapter.

OpenCV on Windows with CMake and compilers

OpenCV uses a set of build tools called CMake, which we must install. Optionally, we can install several third-party libraries in order to enable extra features in OpenCV. These libraries include OpenNI (for depth camera support), SensorKinect (to add Kinect support to OpenNI), and TBB (for Intel multiprocessing). After installing third-party libraries, we will configure and build OpenCV. Last, we will ensure that our C++ and Python environments can find our build of OpenCV.

> The binary installers for OpenCV do provide TBB support but do not provide OpenNI or SensorKinect support. Thus, for depth camera support on Windows, it is necessary to compile OpenCV from source. Although we do not use depth cameras in this book, we have used them in *OpenCV Computer Vision with Python* and you might want to use them in your future projects.

Here are the detailed steps to build OpenCV on Windows:

1. Download and install the latest stable version of CMake from `http://www.cmake.org/cmake/resources/software.html`. Even if we are using 64-bit libraries and compilers, 32-bit CMake is compatible. When the installer asks about modifying `PATH`, select either **Add CMake to the system PATH for all users** or **Add CMake to the system PATH for current user**.

2. Optionally, download and install the development version of OpenNI 1.5.4.0 (not any other version) from `http://www.nummist.com/opencv/openni-win32-1.5.4.0-dev.zip` (32 bit) or `http://www.nummist.com/opencv/openni-win64-1.5.4.0-dev.zip` (64 bit). Other versions besides OpenNI's 1.5.4.0 development version are not recommended. At least some of them do not work with OpenCV, in my experience.

3. Optionally, download and install SensorKinect 0.93 (not any other version) from `https://github.com/avin2/SensorKinect/blob/unstable/Bin/SensorKinect093-Bin-Win32-v5.1.2.1.msi?raw=true` (32-bit) or `https://github.com/avin2/SensorKinect/blob/unstable/Bin/SensorKinect093-Bin-Win64-v5.1.2.1.msi?raw=true` (64-bit). Other versions besides SensorKinect 0.93 are not recommended. In my experience, a few of them do not work with OpenCV.

4. Download OpenCV as a self-extracting ZIP file from `http://opencv.org/downloads.html`. Choose the latest version, which should contain both 32-bit and 64-bit binaries. Double-click the self-extracting ZIP file and, when prompted, enter any destination folder, which we will refer to as `<opencv_unzip_destination>`. A subfolder named `<opencv_unzip_destination>\opencv` is created.

5. Download the latest stable version of TBB from `https://www.threadingbuildingblocks.org/download`. It includes both 32-bit and 64-bit binaries. Unzip it to any destination, which we will refer to as `<tbb_unzip_destination>`.

6. Open Command Prompt. Create a folder to store our build:

    ```
    > mkdir <build_folder>
    ```

    Change the directory to the newly created build folder:

    ```
    > cd <build_folder>
    ```

7. Having set up our dependencies, we can now configure OpenCV's build system. To understand all the configuration options, we could read the code in `<opencv_unzip_destination>\opencv\sources\CMakeLists.txt`. However, as an example, we will just use the options for a release build that includes Python bindings, depth camera support via OpenNI and SensorKinect, and multiprocessing via TBB.

To create a 32-bit project for Visual Studio 2010, run the following command (but replace the angle brackets and their contents with the actual paths):

```
> cmake -D CMAKE_BUILD_TYPE=RELEASE -D WITH_OPENNI=ON -D OPENNI_LIB_
DIR="<openni_install_destination>\Lib" -D OPENNI_INCLUDE_DIR="<openni_
install_destination>\Include" -D OPENNI_PRIME_SENSOR_MODULE_BIN_
DIR="<sensorkinect_install_destination>\Bin" -D WITH_TBB=ON -D TBB_LIB_
DIR="<tbb_unzip_destination>\lib\ia32\vc10" -D TBB_INCLUDE_DIR="<tbb_
unzip_destination>\include" -G "Visual Studio 10" "<opencv_unzip_
destination>\opencv\sources"
```

Alternatively, to create a 64-bit project for Visual Studio 2010, run the following command (but replace the angle brackets and their contents with the actual paths):

```
> cmake -D CMAKE_BUILD_TYPE=RELEASE -D WITH_OPENNI=ON -D OPENNI_LIB_
DIR="<openni_install_destination>\Lib" -D OPENNI_INCLUDE_DIR="<openni_
install_destination>\Include" -D OPENNI_PRIME_SENSOR_MODULE_BIN_
DIR="<sensorkinect_install_destination>\Bin" -D WITH_TBB=ON -D TBB_LIB_
DIR="<tbb_unzip_destination>\lib\intel64\vc10" -D TBB_INCLUDE_DIR="<tbb_
unzip_destination>\include" -G "Visual Studio 10 Win64" "<opencv_unzip_
destination>\opencv\sources"
```

If OpenNI is not installed, omit `-D WITH_OPENNI=ON -D OPENNI_LIB_ DIR="<openni_install_destination>\Lib" -D OPENNI_INCLUDE_ DIR="<openni_install_destination>\Include" -D OPENNI_PRIME_SENSOR_ MODULE_BIN_DIR="<sensorkinect_install_destination>\Bin"`. (In this case, depth cameras will not be supported.)

If OpenNI is installed but SensorKinect is not, omit `-D OPENNI_PRIME_SENSOR_ MODULE_BIN_DIR="<sensorkinect_install_destination>\Bin"`. (In this case, Kinect will not be supported.)

If TBB is not installed, omit `-D WITH_TBB=ON -D TBB_LIB_DIR="<tbb_unzip_ destination>\lib\ia32\vc10" -D TBB_INCLUDE_DIR="<tbb_unzip_ destination>\include"` (32-bit) or `-D WITH_TBB=ON -D TBB_LIB_DIR="<tbb_ unzip_destination>\lib\intel64\vc10" -D TBB_INCLUDE_DIR="<tbb_unzip_ destination>\include"` (64-bit). (In this case, Intel multiprocessing will not be supported.)

CMake will produce a report on the dependencies that it did or did not find. OpenCV has many optional dependencies, so do not panic (yet) about missing dependencies. However, if the build does not finish successfully, try installing missing dependencies (many are available as prebuilt binaries). Then, repeat this step.

1. Now that our build system is configured, we can compile OpenCV. Open `<build_folder>\OpenCV.sln` in Visual Studio. Select **Release** configuration and build the project (you might get errors if you select another build configuration besides **Release**.)

2. Copy `<build_folder>\lib\RELEASE\cv2.pyd` to `C:\Python2.7\Lib\` `site-packages` (assuming that Python 2.7 is installed in the default location). Now, the Python installation can find part of OpenCV.

3. Finally, we need to make sure that Python and other processes can find the rest of OpenCV and its dependencies. Edit the system's `Path` variable and append `;<build_folder>\bin\RELEASE`. If we are using TBB, also append `;<tbb_unzip_destination>\lib\ia32\vc10` (32-bit) or `;<tbb_unzip_destination>\lib\intel64\vc10` (64-bit). Log out and log back in (or reboot).

You might want to look at the code samples in `<unzip_destination>/opencv/samples`.

At this point, we have everything we need to develop OpenCV applications for Windows. To also develop the same for Android, we need to set up TADP as described in the section *Tegra Android Development Pack*, covered later in this chapter.

Mac

Let's begin by setting up Xcode and the Xcode Command Line Tools, which give us a complete C++ development environment:

1. Download and install Xcode from the Mac App Store or `http://connect.apple.com/`. If the installer provides an option to install **Command Line Tools**, select it.

2. Open Xcode. If a license agreement is presented, accept it.

3. If the Xcode Command Line Tools were not already installed, we must install them now. Go to **Xcode | Preferences | Downloads** and click on the **Install** button next to **Command Line Tools**. Wait for the installation to finish. Then, quit Xcode. Alternatively, if you do not find an option to install the Command Line Tools from inside Xcode, open Terminal and run the following command:

```
$ xcode-select install
```

Next, we need a Python 2.7 development environment. Recent versions of Mac come with Python 2.7 preinstalled. However, the preinstalled Python is customized by Apple for the system's internal needs. Normally, we should not install any libraries atop Apple's Python. If we do, our libraries might break during system updates or worse, might conflict with preinstalled libraries that the system requires. Instead, we should install standard Python 2.7 and then install our libraries atop it.

For Mac, there are several possible approaches to obtain standard Python 2.7 and Python-compatible libraries such as OpenCV. All approaches ultimately require OpenCV to be compiled from source using Xcode Command Line Tools. However, depending on the approach, this task is automated for us by third-party tools in various ways. We will look at approaches using MacPorts or Homebrew. These two tools are package managers, which help us resolve dependencies and separate our development libraries from the system libraries.

I recommend MacPorts. Compared to Homebrew, MacPorts offers more patches and configuration options for OpenCV. Also, I maintain a MacPorts repository to ensure that you can get continue to get an OpenCV build that is compatible with all of my books. Particularly, my version includes support for depth cameras such as Kinect, which were used in *OpenCV Computer Vision with Python*.

Normally, MacPorts and Homebrew should not be installed on the same machine.

Regardless of the approach to set up our Python environment, we can put PyInstaller in any convenient location, since it is treated as a set of tools rather than a library. Let's download the latest release version from `http://www.pyinstaller.org/` and unzip it to `~/PyInstaller` or another location of your choice.

Our installation methods for Mac do not give us the OpenCV sample projects. To get these, download the latest source code archive from `http://sourceforge.net/projects/opencvlibrary/files/opencv-unix/` and unzip it to any location. Find the samples in `<opencv_unzip_destination>/samples`.

Now, depending on your preference, let's proceed to either the *Mac with MacPorts* section or the *Mac with Homebrew* section.

Mac with MacPorts

MacPorts provides Terminal commands that automate the process of downloading, compiling, and installing various pieces of **open source software (OSS)**. MacPorts also installs dependencies as needed. For each piece of software, the dependencies and build recipe are defined in a configuration file called a **Portfile**. A MacPorts **repository** is a collection of Portfiles.

Starting from a system where Xcode and its Command Line Tools are already set up, the following steps will give us an OpenCV installation via MacPorts:

1. Download and install MacPorts from `http://www.macports.org/install.php`.

2. If we want an OpenCV build that is fully compatible with all of my books, we need to inform MacPorts where to download some custom Portfiles that I have written. To do so, edit `/opt/local/etc/macports/sources.conf` (assuming MacPorts is installed in the default location). Just above the line `rsync://rsync.macports.org/ release/ports/ [default]`, add the following line:

   ```
   http://nummist.com/opencv/ports.tar.gz
   ```

   Downloading the example code

   You can download the example code fies from your account at `http://www.packtpub.com` for all the Packt Publishing books you have purchased. If you purchased this book elsewhere, you can visit `http://www.packtpub.com/support` and register to have the fies e-mailed directly to you. The latest and updated example code for this book is also available from the author's website at `http://nummist.com/opencv/`.

   Save the file. Now, MacPorts knows to search for Portfiles in my online repository first and then the default online repository.

3. Open Terminal and run the following command to update MacPorts:

   ```
   $ sudo port selfupdate
   ```

   When prompted, enter your password.

4. Now (if you are using my repository), run the following command to install OpenCV with Python 2.7 bindings, plus extras such as support for Intel TBB multiprocessing and support for depth cameras including Kinect:

   ```
   $ sudo port install opencv +python27 +tbb +openni_sensorkinect
   ```

   Alternatively (with or without my repository), run the following command to install OpenCV with Python 2.7 bindings, plus extras such as support for Intel TBB multiprocessing and support for depth cameras excluding Kinect:

   ```
   $ sudo port install opencv +python27 +tbb +openni
   ```

   Dependencies, including Python 2.7, NumPy, OpenNI, and (in the first example) SensorKinect, are automatically installed as well.

By adding +python27 to the command, we are specifying that we want the OpenCV variant (build configuration) with Python 2.7 bindings. Similarly, +tbb specifies the variant with support for Intel TBB multiprocessing, which can greatly improve the performance on compatible hardware. The +openni_ sensorkinect tag specifies the variant with the broadest possible support for depth cameras via OpenNI and SensorKinect. You can omit +openni_ sensorkinect if you do not intend to use depth cameras or you can replace it with +openni if you do intend to use OpenNI-compatible depth cameras but just not Kinect. To see the full list of available variants before installing, we can enter:

```
$ port variants opencv
```

Depending on our customization needs, we can add other variants to the install command.

5. Run the following commands to install SciPy, Requests, and wxPython:

```
$ sudo port install py27-scipy
$ sudo port install py27-requests
$ sudo port install py27-wxpython-3.0
```

6. The Python installation's executable is named python2.7. If we want to link the default python executable to python2.7, let's also run:

```
$ sudo port install python_select
$ sudo port select python python27
```

Now we have everything we need to develop OpenCV applications for Mac. To also develop the same for Android, we need to set up TADP as described in the section *Tegra Android Development Pack*, covered later in this chapter.

Mac with Homebrew

Like MacPorts, Homebrew is a package manager that provides Terminal commands to automate the process of downloading, compiling, and installing various pieces of open source software.

Starting from a system where Xcode and its Command Line Tools are already set up, the following steps will give us an OpenCV installation via Homebrew:

1. Open Terminal and run the following command to install Homebrew:

```
$ ruby -e "$(curl -fsSkLraw.github.com/mxcl/homebrew/go)"
```

2. Unlike MacPorts, Homebrew does not automatically put its executables in PATH. To do so, create or edit the file ~/.profile and add this line at the top:

```
export PATH=/usr/local/bin:/usr/local/sbin:$PATH
```

Save the file and run this command to refresh PATH:

```
$ source ~/.profile
```

Note that executables installed by Homebrew now take precedence over executables installed by the system.

3. For Homebrew's self-diagnostic report, run:

    ```
    $ brew doctor
    ```

    Follow any troubleshooting advice it gives.

4. Now, update Homebrew:

    ```
    $ brew update
    ```

5. Run the following command to install Python 2.7:

    ```
    $ brew install python
    ```

6. Now, we can install NumPy. Homebrew's selection of Python library packages is limited, so we will use a separate package management tool called pip, which comes with Homebrew's Python:

    ```
    $ pip install numpy
    ```

7. SciPy contains some Fortran code, so we need an appropriate compiler. We can use Homebrew to install the GFortran compiler:

    ```
    $ brew install gfortran
    ```

    Now, we can install SciPy:

    ```
    $ pip install scipy
    ```

8. Similarly, we can install Requests and wxPython:

    ```
    $ pip install requests wxpython
    ```

9. We need to install OpenCV from an optional repository called homebrew/science. Run the following commands:

    ```
    $ brew tap homebrew/science
    $ brew install opencv
    ```

10. Lastly, we must tell Python where to find Homebrew's installation of OpenCV. Edit your ~/.profile file to add the following line:

    ```
    export PYTHONPATH=/usr/local/Cellar/opencv/2.4.7/lib/python2.7/
    site-packages:$PYTHONPATH
    ```

Now we have everything we need to develop OpenCV applications for Mac. To also develop the same for Android, we need to set up TADP as described in the section *Tegra Android Development Pack*, later in this chapter.

Debian Wheezy and its derivatives, including Raspbian, Ubuntu, and Linux Mint

> For information on setting up the Raspbian operating system, refer to the section *Setting up a Raspberry Pi* covered later in this chapter.

On Raspbian, Ubuntu 13.04 and its later versions, and Ubuntu derivatives such as Linux Mint 15 and its later versions, a recent version of OpenCV is available in the standard repository. This OpenCV package includes support for many video codes and for Intel TBB multiprocessing, but it does not include support for depth cameras (as used in my other book, *OpenCV Computer Vision with Python*). To install OpenCV and SciPy, open Terminal and run the following commands:

```
$ sudo apt-get install python-opencv
$ sudo apt-get install python-scipy
```

On other systems, the standard repository contains OpenCV 2.3.1 but this version is old (from 2011) and lacks some of the functionality used in this book. Thus, we want to compile a newer version of OpenCV from source. Compiling from source is likewise a requirement if we want support for Asus and Kinect depth cameras. Because the dependencies are complex, I have written a script that downloads, configures, and builds OpenCV and related libraries. Here are the steps to obtain and use the script, and then install a few additional elements of our Python environment:

1. Download the script from `http://nummist.com/opencv/install_opencv_debian_wheezy.sh` and put it in any destination, say `<script_folder>`.

2. If you prefer Qt over GTK (for example, if you intend to build apps for KDE), then edit `<script_folder>/install_debian_wheezy.sh` and replace `WITH_QT=0` with `WITH_QT=1`. Save and close the file.

3. Open Terminal. Change the directory to `<script_folder>`:

    ```
    $ cd <script_folder>
    ```

Set the script's permissions so that it is executable:

```
$ chmod +x install_opencv_debian_wheezy.sh
```

Execute the script:

```
$ ./install_opencv_debian_wheezy.sh
```

When prompted, enter your password.

4. The script creates a folder named `<script_folder>/opencv` that contains downloads and built files that are temporarily used in the installation process. Once the script terminates, `<script_folder>/opencv` can safely be deleted; although first, you might want to look at the code samples in `<script_folder>/opencv/samples`.

5. SciPy is already installed by the script. Run the following commands to install Requests and wxPython:

```
$ sudo apt-get install python-requests
$ sudo apt-get install python-wxgtk2.8
```

6. Finally, we can put PyInstaller in any convenient location since it is treated as a set of tools rather than a library. Let's download the latest release version from `https://github.com/pyinstaller/pyinstaller/wiki` and unzip it to `~/PyInstaller` or another location of your choice.

If the script ran successfully, we now have a recent version of OpenCV configured to support C++, Python 2.7, and (on compatible systems) several extras such as video codecs, support for Intel TBB multiprocessing, and support for Kinect and Asus depth cameras. Not all the extras are relevant to our current projects but they might be useful in your future work.

 For an OpenCV project that uses a depth camera, refer to my book *OpenCV Computer Vision with Python*.

Now we have everything we need to develop OpenCV applications for Debian Wheezy or a derivative. To also develop the same for Android, we need to set up TADP as described in the section *Tegra Android Development Pack*, later in this chapter.

Fedora and its derivatives, including RHEL and CentOS

Recent versions of OpenCV, SciPy, Requests, and wxPython are in the standard repository. To install them, open Terminal and run the following commands:

```
$ sudo yum install opencv-python
$ sudo yum install scipy
$ sudo yum install python-requests
$ sudo yum install wxPython
```

Download the latest release version of PyInstaller from `http://www.pyinstaller.org/` and unzip it to `~/PyInstaller` or another location of your choice.

As an alternative to using the packaged build of OpenCV, the following official tutorial provides instructions to install OpenCV's dependencies and compile it from source: `http://docs.opencv.org/trunk/doc/py_tutorials/py_setup/py_setup_in_fedora/py_setup_in_fedora.html`.

For optional dependencies and additional compilation options, including depth camera support, refer to my Debian-compatible build script as a starting point: `http://nummist.com/opencv/install_opencv_debian_wheezy.sh`.

Now we have everything we need to develop OpenCV applications for Fedora or a derivative. To also develop the same for Android, we need to set up TADP as described in the section *Tegra Android Development Pack*, later in the chapter.

openSUSE and its derivatives

Recent versions of OpenCV, SciPy, Requests, and wxPython are in the standard repository. To install them, open Terminal and run the following commands:

```
$ sudo yum install python-opencv
$ sudo yum install python-scipy
$ sudo yum install python-requests
$ sudo yum install python-wxWidgets
```

Download the latest release version of PyInstaller from `http://www.pyinstaller.org/` and unzip it to `~/PyInstaller` or another location of your choice.

As an alternative to using the packaged build of OpenCV, the steps to install OpenCV from source should be similar to the steps on Fedora, though dependencies' package names might differ.

Next, we need to follow the cross-platform steps to set up an Android development environment.

Tegra Android Development Pack

Tegra Android Development Pack (**TADP**) contains a complete, preconfigured development environment for Android, OpenCV, and some other libraries. TADP builds apps that are optimized for NVIDIA's Tegra processors. Despite being optimized for Tegra, the apps are compatible with other hardware too.

> TADP's OpenCV is a third-party build of OpenCV. OpenCV's standard Android build does not offer the optimizations that are present in TADP. Moreover, TADP includes all components of an Android development environment and its setup process is simple. For these reasons, I recommend TADP.
>
> TADP also contains some extras that we do not require for this book. For a complete list of TADP's contents, refer to the official description at https://developer.nvidia.com/tegra-android-development-pack.

To set up TADP, we just need to download and install it from a secure section of NVIDIA's website. Here are the required steps:

1. Join the NVIDIA Registered Developer Program at https://developer.nvidia.com/user/register. (It is free.)

2. Log in at https://developer.nvidia.com/user/login.

3. Complete your user profile at https://developer.nvidia.com/user/me/profile/rdp_profile.

4. Apply to join the Tegra Registered Developer Program at https://developer.nvidia.com/rdp/applications/tegra-registered-developer-program (it is free, too!). Wait for NVIDIA to send you an acceptance e-mail. Normally, you might receive it a few minutes after applying.

5. Go to https://developer.nvidia.com/tegra-resources and find the download link for TADP's latest version. At the time of writing, the latest version of TADP is 3.0r4. There are installers for Windows (32-bit or 64-bit), Mac, and Ubuntu (32-bit or 64-bit). Download and run the appropriate installer. On Linux, run the installer from a sudoer account because the installer will prompt you to sudo at some stages.

TADP's Ubuntu installer depends on a more recent version of libc (the GNU C Library) than the version available in standard Debian Wheezy. However, on a Debian Wheezy system, we can upgrade libc to a newer version available in Debian Sid (Debian's unstable version) without upgrading the whole system to Debian Sid. Then, our Debian system will be compatible with the TADP Ubuntu installer.

Upgrading libc worked for me but it has the potential to break a lot of things. You do it at your own risk. The steps are as follows:

With root privileges, edit /etc/apt/sources.list. Add this line to the file:

```
deb http://ftp.debian.org/debian sid main
```

Save the file.

Run the following commands in Terminal:

```
$ sudo apt-get update
$ sudo apt-get -t sid install libc6 libc6-dev libc6-dbg
```

Edit /etc/apt/sources.list again to remove the line that we added. This way, we cannot accidentally upgrade anything else to Debian Sid. Save the file.

Now, proceed with running the TADP installer.

6. When the installer presents the **Installation Directory** step, we can enter any destination, which we will refer to as <tadp>. By default, <tadp> is C:\NVPACK (in Windows) or ~/NVPACK (in Mac and Linux).

7. When the installer presents the **Installation Options** step, we can select any option: **Complete**, **Express**, or **Custom**. Compared to an **Express** installation, a **Complete** or **Custom** installation might include additional versions of Android SDK and binary images of Tegra Android OS, which is NVIDIA's customization of Android. If in doubt, choose **Express**.

8. When the installer presents the **Proxy Configuration** step, we can leave all fields blank unless we are using a proxy server.

9. After finishing all of the installer's configuration steps, wait for TADP's content to be downloaded and installed.

That's all! Before proceeding, let's just take a note of the locations where TADP has installed certain components. For TADP 3.0r4 (the latest version at the time of writing), the locations are as follows:

- Android SDK is located at <tadp>/android-sdk-windows (in Windows), <tadp>/android-sdk-macosx (in Mac), or <tadp>/android-sdk-linux (in Linux). We will refer to this location as <android_sdk>.

- Android NDK is located at `<tadp>/android-ndk-r10c`. We will refer to this location as `<android_ndk>`.

- OpenCV is located at `<tadp>/OpenCV-2.4.8.2-Tegra-sdk`. We will refer to this location as `<opencv>`.

- Eclipse is located at `<tadp>/eclipse`. We will refer to this location as `<eclipse>`.

The TADP installer automatically edits the system's PATH to include `<android_sdk>/platform-tools` and `<android_sdk>/ tools`. Also, it creates an environment variable called NDKROOT, whose value is `<android_ndk>`.

Building OpenCV Android sample projects with Eclipse

By building and running a few sample applications, we can test our OpenCV installation. At the same time, we can practice using Eclipse.

Let's start by launching Eclipse. The Eclipse launcher should be located at `<eclipse>/eclipse.exe` (in Windows), `<eclipse>/Eclipse.app` (in Mac), or `<eclipse>/eclipse` (in Linux). Run it.

As shown in the following screenshot, we should see a window called **Workspace Launcher**, which asks us to select a workspace:

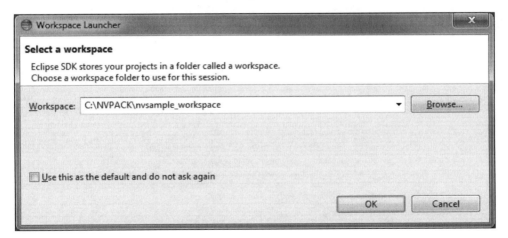

A workspace is the root directory for a set of related Eclipse projects. Enter `<tadp>/nvsample_workspace`, which is a workspace where the OpenCV library, samples, and tutorials are already set up as projects.

 We can return to **Workspace Launcher** anytime via the menu: **File** | **Switch Workspace** | **Other...**.

If the **Welcome to Eclipse** screen appears, click on the **Workbench** button.

Now, we should see a window with several panels, including **Package Explorer**. The OpenCV library, samples, and tutorials should be listed in **Package Explorer**. We might need to fix some configuration issues in these projects. Our development environment can have different paths and different versions of the Android SDK, than the ones in the sample's default configuration. Any resulting errors are reported in the **Problems** tab as shown in the following screenshot:

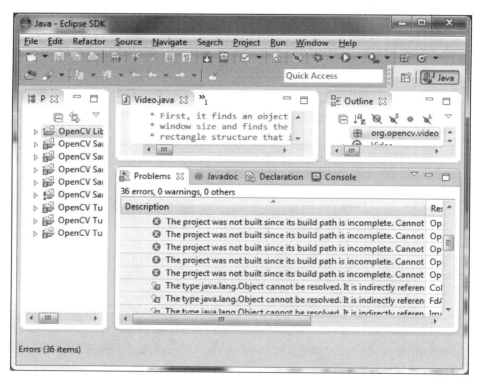

 We should start by resolving any errors in the **OpenCV Library** project as the samples and tutorials depend on the library.

The following are some of the common configuration problems and their symptoms and solutions:

- The target Android version might not be properly specified. The symptoms of these are that the imports from the `java` and `android` packages fail, and there are error messages such as **The project was not built since its build path is incomplete**. The solution is to right-click on the project in **Package Explorer**, select **Properties** from the context menu, select the **Android** section, and checkmark one of the available Android versions. These steps should be repeated for all projects. At compile time, OpenCV and its samples must target Android 3.0 (API level 11) or greater, though at runtime they also support Android 2.2 (API level 8) or greater.

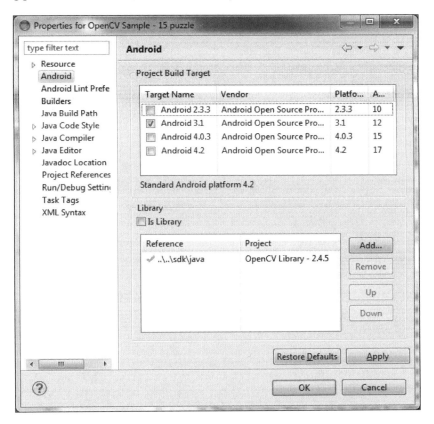

- If we are working on Mac or Linux, the C++ samples might be misconfigured to use the Windows build executable. The symptom of this problem is an error message such as **Program "{ndk}/ndk-build.cmd" not found in PATH**. The solution is to right-click on the project in **Package Explorer**, select **Properties** from the context menu, select the **C/C++ Build** section, and edit the **Build command:** field to remove the .cmd extension. These steps should be repeated for all the native (C++) projects, which include **OpenCV Sample - face-detection** and **OpenCV Tutorial 2 - Mixed Processing** as shown in the following screenshot:

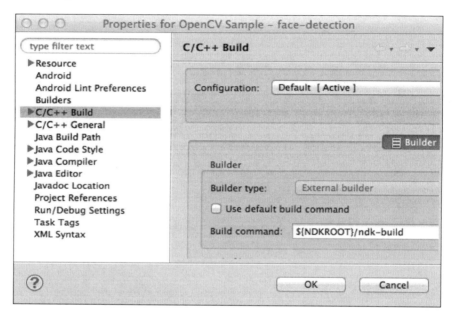

 We only need to troubleshoot the projects that have names starting with OpenCV. For this book's purposes, the other TADP samples are not relevant.

Once the OpenCV projects no longer show any errors, we can prepare to test them on an Android device. Remember that the device must have Android 2.2 (Froyo) or a later version, and a camera. For Eclipse to communicate with the device, we must enable the device's **USB debugging** option with the help of the following steps:

1. Open the **Settings** app.
2. On Android 4.2 or a later version, go to the **About phone** or **About tablet** section and tap **Build number** seven times. This step enables the **Developer options** section.

3. Go to the **Developer options** section (on Android 4.0 or a later version) or the **Applications | Development** section (on Android 3.2 or an earlier version). Enable the **USB debugging** option. Now, open the Play Store app and find and install the OpenCV Manager app. OpenCV Manager takes care of checking for any OpenCV library updates when we run any OpenCV applications.

 If you do not have the Play Store app on your device, then you need to install OpenCV Manager and certain OpenCV libraries via USB as per the instructions at `http://docs.opencv.org/android/ service/doc/UseCases.html`.

Now, we must prepare our main computer for communication with the Android device. The required steps vary depending on our operating system:

- On Windows, we need to install the proper USB drivers for the Android device. Different vendors and devices have different drivers. The official Android documentation provides links to the various vendors' driver download sites at `http://developer.android.com/tools/extras/oem- usb.html#Drivers`.

- On Linux, before connecting an Android device via USB, we must specify the device's vendor in a permissions file. Each vendor has a unique ID number, as listed in the official Android documentation at `http://developer. android.com/tools/device.html#VendorIds`. We will refer to this ID number as `<vendor_id>`. To create the permissions file, open a command prompt application (such as Terminal) and run the following commands:

```
$ cd /etc/udev/rules.d/
$ sudo touch 51-android.rules
$ sudo chmod a+r 51-android-rules
```

Note that the permissions file needs to have root ownership, so we will use `sudo` while creating or modifying it. Now, open the file in an editor such as `gedit`:

```
$ sudo gedit 51-android-rules
```

For each vendor, append a new line to the file. Each of these lines should have the following format:

```
SUBSYSTEM=="usb", ATTR{idVendor}=="<vendor_id>", MODE="0666",
GROUP="plugdev"
```

Save the permissions file and quit the editor.

- On Mac, no special drivers or permissions are required.

Plug the Android device into your computer's USB port. In Eclipse, select one of the OpenCV sample projects in **Package Explorer**. Then, from the menu system, navigate to **Run | Run As... | Android Application**:

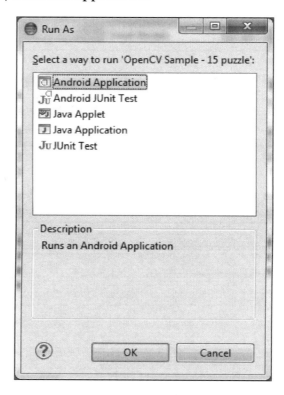

An **Android Device Chooser** window should appear. Your Android device should be listed under **Choose a running Android device**. (If the device is not listed, try unplugging it and plugging it back in. If that does not work, also try disabling and re-enabling the device's **USB debugging** option, as described earlier.)

Select the device and click on **OK**.

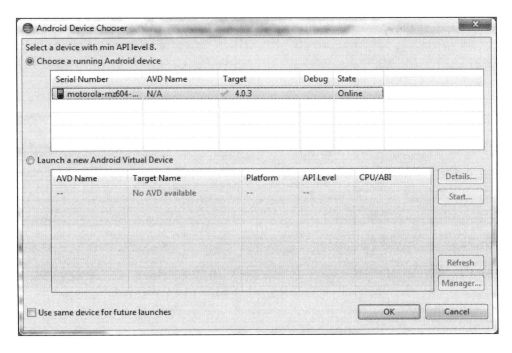

If the **Auto Monitor Logcat** window appears, select the **Yes** radio button and the **verbose** drop-down option and click on **OK**. This option ensures that all the log output from the application will be visible in Eclipse.

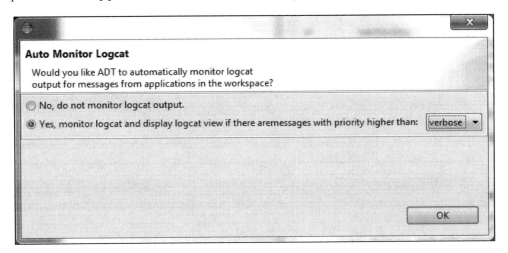

On the Android device, you might get a message, **OpenCV library package was not found! Try to install it?**. Make sure that the device is connected to the Internet and then click on the **Yes** button on your device. The **Play Store** will open to show an OpenCV package. Install the package and then press the physical back button to return to the sample application, which should be ready for use.

For OpenCV 2.4.8.2, the samples and tutorials have the following functionality:

- **Sample – 15 puzzle**: This splits up a camera feed to make a sliding block puzzle. The user can swipe blocks to move them.

- **Sample – camera-calibration**: This estimates the projection and distortion characteristics of the camera. The user prints a test pattern located at `https://raw.githubusercontent.com/Itseez/opencv/2.4/doc/acircles_pattern.png` and then takes pictures of it from various angles by tapping the screen. After taking several pictures, the user must press the **...** menu and the **Calibrate** button to run the calibration algorithm.

- **Sample – color-blob-detection**: This detects color regions in a camera feed. The user can touch anywhere to see the outline of a color region.

- **Sample – face-detection**: This draws green rectangles around faces in a camera feed.

- **Sample – image-manipulations**: This applies filters to a camera feed. The user can press the Android menu button to select from a list of filters.

- **Sample – native-activity**: This displays a camera feed using native (C++) code.

- **Tutorial 1 – Camera Preview**: This displays a camera feed. The user can press the **...** menu to select a different camera feed implementation (Java or native C++).

- **Tutorial 2 – Mixed Processing**: This applies filters to a camera feed using native (C++) code. The user can press the **...** menu to select from a list of filters. One of the filters draws red circles around interest points or features in a camera feed. Generally speaking, interest points or features lie along the high-contrast edges in an image. They are potentially useful in image recognition and tracking applications.

- **Tutorial 3 – Camera Control**: This applies filters to a camera feed, which has a customizable resolution. The user can press the **...** menu to select from a list of filters and a list of resolutions.

Try these applications on your Android device! While an application is running, its log output should appear in the **LogCat** tab in Eclipse as shown in the following screenshot:

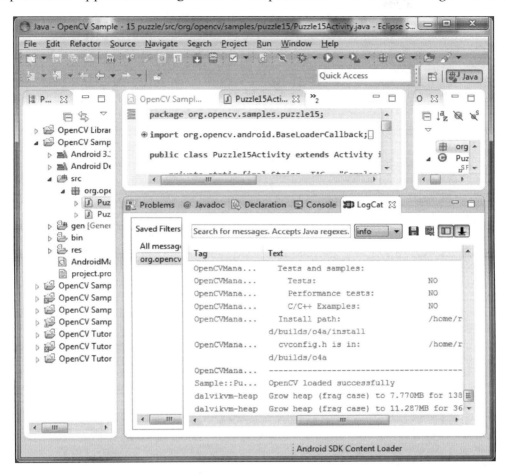

Feel free to browse the project's source code via **Package Explorer** to see how it was made. Alternatively, you might want to return to the official samples and tutorials later, after we have built our own projects over the course of this book.

Unity

Unity is a 3D game engine that supports development on Windows or Mac and deployment to many platforms, including Windows, Mac, Linux, iOS, Android, a web browser plugin, and several game consoles. For one of our projects, we will use an OpenCV plugin for Unity.

Unity comes in two editions, Standard and Pro, which both support the plugin that we want to use. The Standard edition is free. The Pro edition has a free 30-day trial; otherwise, its price starts from $75 a month or a one-time payment of $1,500. If you do not already have a Unity Pro license, wait until you are ready to start working on our Unity project (which comes late in the book) in case you want to try out some Pro-only functionality at the same time. Once you are ready, download and install the trial from `http://unity3d.com/unity/download`.

Even before installing Unity, we can get inspiration from the playable demos at `https://unity3d.com/gallery/demos/live-demos`. Most of these demos are web-based. You will be prompted to download and install the free Unity Web Player when you navigate to one of the web-based games.

After installing Unity, we can learn from other demo projects that include complete source code and art assets. They can be downloaded and opened from `https://unity3d.com/gallery/demos/demo-projects`. Also check out the tutorials, videos, and documentation at `https://unity3d.com/learn`.

As you can see, there are a lot of official resources for Unity beginners, so I will let you explore these on your own for now.

Setting up Raspberry Pi

Raspberry Pi is a **single-board computer (SBC)** with a low cost and low power consumption. It can be used as a desktop, a server, or an embedded system that controls other electronics. The Pi comes in two versions, Model A and Model B. We want Model B because it has more memory (an important consideration for image processing) and it has an Ethernet port, whereas Model A does not. Model B costs about $35.

Several operating systems are available for Raspberry Pi. We will use Raspbian, which is a port of Debian Wheezy (a major Linux distribution) to ARM.

Download the latest Raspbian disk image from `http://downloads.raspberrypi.org/raspbian_latest`. Unzip the downloaded file. At the time of writing, the ZIP file is called `2014-09-09-wheezy-raspbian.zip` and the unzipped file is called `2014-09-09-wheezy-raspbian.img`. Since your filenames can differ, we will refer to the unzipped file as `<raspbian_image>`.

We need to burn `<raspbian_image>` to an SD card of size 4 GB or larger. Any existing data on the card will be lost in the process. The steps to burn the disk image are platform-specific, as follows:

- On Windows, download Win32 Disk Imager from `http://sourceforge.net/projects/win32diskimager/` and unzip it to any destination. With the SD card inserted, run `Win32DiskImage.exe`, which should be inside the unzipped folder. Click the folder icon next to the **Image File** field and open `<raspbian_image>`. Select the SD card in the **Device** drop-down menu. Click the **Write** button.

- On Mac, first we must check which device path is assigned to the SD card. Before inserting the card, run the following command in Terminal:

  ```
  $ diskutil list
  ```

  You should see information on one or more devices such as `/dev/disk0`. Now, insert the SD card and rerun the same command. A new device, such as `/dev/disk1`, should be in the list this time. This device is the SD card and we will refer to it as `<sd_card_device>`.

  Run the following commands in Terminal to format the card and burn the image to it:

  ```
  $ sudo diskutil eraseDisk FAT32 UNTITLED <sd_card_device>
  $ diskutil unmountDisk <sd_card_device>
  $ sudo dd if=<raspbian_image> of=<sd_card_device> bs=1m
  $ diskutil eject <sd_card_device>
  ```

  The `dd` command might run for several minutes without producing any command-line output. Do not assume it is frozen.

- On Linux, first we must check which device path is assigned to the SD card. Before inserting the card, run the following command in Terminal:

  ```
  $ df -h
  ```

  You should see information on one or more devices such as `/dev/sda1`. Now, insert the SD card and rerun the same command. One or more new devices, such as `/dev/sdb1`, `/dev/mmcblk0p1`, or `/dev/ssd1`, should be in the list this time. These devices are partitions of the SD card. Their common suffix (before the last number or the last p and number), such as `/dev/sdb`, `/dev/mmcblk0`, or `/dev/sdd`, is the SD card itself and we will refer to it as `<sd_card_device>`.

Run the following commands in Terminal to format the card and burn the image to it:

```
$ sudo mkdosfs -F 32 <sd_card_device>
$ for n in <sd_card_device>* ; do umount $n ; done
$ sudo dd if=<raspbian_image> of=<sd_card_device> bs=1m
$ for n in <sd_card_device>* ; do umount $n ; done
```

Again, the dd command might run for several minutes without producing any command-line output. Do not assume it is frozen.

 On Unix systems such as Mac and Linux, the path of the SD card device can change between insertions. For instance, the path might depend on the number of other devices that are already inserted. If you go back later and burn the disk image again, recheck the device path.

Ensure that the Raspberry Pi's Micro USB power cable is disconnected. Connect an HDMI monitor or TV, USB keyboard, USB mouse, and Ethernet cable. Then, insert the SD card firmly into the slot on the bottom on the Pi. Connect the Pi's power cable. The Pi should start booting from the SD card as shown in the following screenshot:

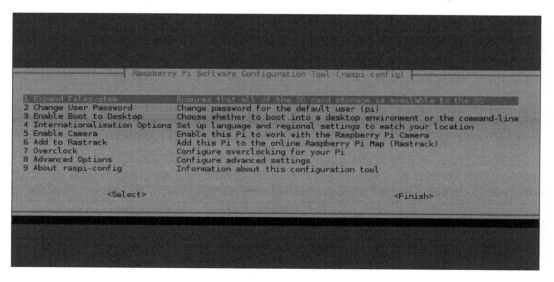

Soon, we should see a configuration menu like the one in the preceding screenshot. With option **1 Expand Filesystem** selected, hit *Enter*. This option ensures that the entire space on the SD card is available to Raspbian for storage.

Use the up and down arrow keys to select other options. For option **3 Enable Boot to Desktop**, hit *Enter*, select **Yes**, and hit *Enter* again. For option **4 Internationalisation Options**, select an appropriate locale, time zone, and keyboard. Raspbian defaults to a UK keyboard layout, which will cause problems if you have a US or other keyboard. If you are using the Raspberry Pi Camera Module or Pi NoIR (as described in the next section of this chapter), select option **5 Enable Camera**, hit *Enter*, Select **Enable**, and hit *Enter* again. Configure all other options as you wish. Once you are satisfied with the configuration, use the right arrow key to select **Finish**. Hit *Enter*.

 Later, from the LXTerminal application, we can return to the configuration menu by running the following command:

```
$ sudo raspi-config
```

A login screen should appear. Enter the username **pi** and the password **raspberry**. Prepare to witness the wonders of the Raspbian desktop!

The grand raspberry stands before us in all its flavorful glory!

At heart (or in its seeds), Raspbian is "just" Debian Linux with an LXDE desktop and some special developer tools. If you are familiar with Debian or derivatives such as Ubuntu, you should feel right at home. Otherwise, you might want to explore the tutorials for beginners that are posted on the Raspberry Pi site at `http://www.raspberrypi.org/archives/tag/tutorials`.

Now, as an exercise, let's share our Raspbian desktop via **Virtual Network Computing (VNC)** so that we can control it from a Windows, Mac, or Linux machine.

On the Pi, we first need to determine our local network address, which we will refer to as `<pi_ip_address>`. Open LXTerminal and run the following command:

```
$ ifconfig
```

The output should include a line beginning with something like `inet addr:192.168.1.93`, though the numbers will probably differ. In this example, `<pi_ip_address>` is `192.168.1.93`.

Now, we need to install a VNC server on the Pi by running the following command:

```
$ sudo apt-get install tightvncserver
```

To start the server, run this command:

```
$ tightvncserver
```

When prompted, enter a password that other users must enter while connecting to this VNC server. Later, if you want to change the password, run this command:

```
$ vncpasswd
```

> Unless the Pi (or the Ethernet socket to which it is connected) has a static IP address, the address can change whenever we reboot. Thus, on reboot, we would need to run `ifconfig` again to determine the new address. Also, after rebooting, we need to run `tightvncserver` to relaunch the VNC server. For instructions on making the Pi's IP address static and automatically running `tightvncserver` on boot, refer to Neil Black's online Raspberry Pi Beginner Guide: `http://www.neil-black.co.uk/raspberry-pi-beginners-guide#.UsuIVPYnXnY`.

Now, on another machine on the same local network, we can access the Pi's desktop via a VNC client. The steps are platform-dependent, as follows:

- On Windows, download VNC Viewer from `https://www.realvnc.com/download/`. Unzip it to any destination and run the executable file (such as `VNC-Viewer-5.1.0-Windows-64bit.exe`), which is inside the unzipped folder. Enter `vnc://<pi_ip_address>:5901` in the **VNC Server** field and click the **Connect** button. When prompted, enter the VNC password that you created earlier.

- On Mac, open Safari and enter `vnc://<pi_ip_address>:5901` in the address bar. A window, **Connect to Shared Computer**, should appear. Click the **Connect** button. When prompted, enter the VNC password that you created earlier.

- Ubuntu normally comes with a VNC client called Vinagre. However, if we do not already have Vinagre, we can install it on Ubuntu or any Debian-based system by running the following command in Terminal:

  ```
  $ sudo apt-get install vinagre
  ```

  Open Vinagre. (It might be listed as **Remote Desktop Viewer** in our **Applications** menu or launcher.) Click the **Connect** button in the toolbar. Enter `vnc://<pi_ip_address>:5901` in the **Host:** field. Click the **Connect** button in the lower-right corner.

Now you know how to prepare and serve Pi.

Setting up the Raspberry Pi Camera Module

Raspbian supports most USB webcams out of the box. Also, it supports the following **Camera Serial Interface (CSI)** cameras, which offer faster transfer speeds:

- Raspberry Pi Camera Module: A $25 RGB camera
- Pi NoIR: A $30 variant of the same camera, with the infrared (IR) block filter removed so that it is sensitive to not only the visible light, but also the adjacent part of the infrared spectrum (near infrared or NIR)

Refer to the official tutorial for details on setting up either the Camera Module or the NoIR at `http://www.raspberrypi.org/help/camera-module-setup/`.

Compared to a USB webcam, the Camera Module or NoIR improves our chances of achieving high enough frame rates for interactive computer vision on the Pi. For this reason, I recommend these Pi-specific CSI cameras. However, commensurate with the low price, they have poor color rendition, mediocre auto-exposure, and fixed focus.

If in doubt, choose the Camera Module over the NoIR because, depending on the subject and lighting, NIR may interfere with vision rather than aid it.

At the time of writing, the Camera Module and NoIR do not work out of the box with OpenCV. We need to load a kernel module that adds support for the cameras via the **Video for Linux 2 (V4L2)** drivers. To do this for a single session, run the following command in Terminal:

```
$ sudo modprobe bcm2835-v4l2
```

Alternatively, to always load the kernel module on boot up, run the following command that appends the module to the /etc/modules file:

```
$ echo "bcm2835-v4l2" | sudo tee -a /etc/modules
```

> Future versions of Raspbian (later than the 2014-09-09 version) might be preconfigured to use this kernel module. You can edit /etc/modules to check whether bcm2835-v4l2 is already listed there.

Now we can use the Camera Module or the NoIR with any camera software that supports V4L2 drivers, including OpenCV.

Finding OpenCV documentation, help, and updates

OpenCV's documentation is online at http://docs.opencv.org/. The documentation includes a combined API reference for OpenCV's current C++ API, its current Python API (which is based on the C++ API), its old C API, and its old Python API (which is based on the C API). When you look up a Python class or function, be sure to read the section about the current Python API (cv2 module), not the old Python API (cv module). The Java API documentation is online at http://docs.opencv.org/java/.

Much of the documentation is also available as downloadable PDF files:

- API reference: http://docs.opencv.org/opencv2refman.pdf.
- Tutorials: http://docs.opencv.org/opencv_tutorials.pdf. (These tutorials use C++ code. For a Python port of the tutorial's code, refer to Abid Rahman K's repository at http://goo.gl/EPsD1.)
- User guide (not a complete guide to all modules but it covers some common points of confusion): http://docs.opencv.org/opencv_user.pdf.

If the documentation seems to leave your question unanswered, try reaching out to the OpenCV community instead. The following sites are good venues for questions, answers, and shared experience:

- Official OpenCV forum: `http://www.answers.opencv.org/questions/`
- David Millán Escrivá's blog: `http://blog.damiles.com/`
- Jay Ramhbia's blog: `http://jayrambhia.wordpress.com/`
- *OpenCV-Python Tutorials* by Alexander Mordvintsev and Abid Rahman K: `http://opencv-python-tutroals.readthedocs.org/en/latest/`
- The support site for my OpenCV books: `http://nummist.com/opencv/`

Last, if you are an advanced user who wants to try new features, bug fixes, and sample scripts from the latest (unstable) OpenCV source code, have a look at the project's repository at `https://github.com/Itseez/opencv/`.

Alternatives to Raspberry Pi

Besides Raspberry Pi, many other low-cost SBCs are suitable for running a desktop Linux distribution and OpenCV applications. While the Pi uses a single-core ARMv6 CPU, some of the alternatives use dual-core or even quad-core ARMv7 CPUs that consume more power but can run more advanced computer vision applications in real time. Here are some examples:

- Odroid U3: A $65 quad-core SBC. One of the Linux distributions it can run is Lubuntu, a variant of Ubuntu. Its official website is `http://www.hardkernel.com/main/products/prdt_info.php?g_code=G138745696275`.
- Marsboard A20: A dual-core SBC that costs around $75 (or less if ordered directly from the factory). It has many connectors. It can run Lubuntu, among other Linux distributions. Its official page is `http://www.marsboard.com/new_marsboard_a20_feature.html`.
- Banana Pi: A dual-core SBC that costs around $60 (or less if ordered directly from the factory). It is compatible with many Raspberry Pi accessories and can run numerous Linux distributions, including Lubuntu, Raspbian, and its own optimized distribution called Bananian (based on Debian Wheezy). Its official page is `http://www.bananapi.org/p/product.html`.

Of these alternatives, I have tested Odroid U3 (running Lubuntu) and found it capable of using OpenCV for face detection and recognition in GUI applications in real time.

If you would like to share your experience with using SBCs in computer vision projects, please write to me at josephhowse@nummist.com. I will post the community's wisdom to http://nummist.com/opencv.

Summary

"This was all a setup!" I hear you gasp. Yes, but we did it for good reason. Now we have a diverse set of development tools that will enable us to explore OpenCV in many contexts. Besides, it never hurts to learn something about a lot of application frameworks and to have them all set up in case someone asks us to do a project in a hurry.

Remember, James Bond has encyclopedic knowledge. In a highly symbolic conversation about rare and deadly fish, he goes toe-to-toe with Karl Stromberg, the diabolical oceanographer in the movie *The Spy Who Loved Me* (1977). Though we never see Bond studying fish books, he must do it as bedtime reading after the camera cuts out.

The moral is, be prepared.

2
Searching for Luxury Accommodations Worldwide

Today the bridal suite, tomorrow a prison. A secret agent's sleeping arrangements are horribly unpredictable.

Each day someone in MI6 gets the job of booking a stellar hotel room and conversely, some evil henchman has to pick a warehouse or dilapidated apartment, plus a lamp, a chair, and implements of bondage. For mini missions or brief beatings, it is tolerable to leave the choice of venue to a fallible human being. However, for long-term rentals or acquisitions, would it not be wiser to develop a specialized search engine that takes the legwork and the guesswork out of the equation?

With this motivation, we are going to develop a desktop app called *Luxocator: The Luxury Locator*. This is a search engine that will find images on the web by keyword search and will classify each image as a "Luxury, interior" scene, "Luxury, exterior" scene, "Stalinist, interior" scene, or "Stalinist, exterior" scene, according to certain visual cues in the image.

Particularly, our classifier relies on comparing statistical distributions of color in different images or sets of images. This topic is called **color histogram analysis**. We will learn how to efficiently store and process our statistical model, and how to redistribute it along with our code in an application bundle.

 The completed project for this chapter can be downloaded from my website at http://nummist.com/opencv/7376_02.zip.

Planning the Luxocator app

This chapter uses Python. Being a high-level interpreted language with great third-party libraries for numeric and scientific computing, Python lets us focus on the functionality of the system rather than implementing subsystem details. For our first project, such a high-level perspective is precisely what we need.

Let's take an overview of Luxocator's functionality and our choice of Python libraries that support this functionality. Like many computer vision applications, Luxocator has 6 basic steps:

1. **Acquire a static set of reference images**: For Luxocator, we (the developers) will choose certain images that we will deem to be "Luxury, indoor" scenes, other images that we will consider as "Stalinist, indoor" scenes, and so on. We will load these images into memory.

2. **Train a model based on the reference images**: For Luxocator, our model will describe each image in terms of its normalized color histogram, that is, the distribution of colors across the image's pixels. We will use OpenCV and NumPy to perform the calculations.

3. **Store the results of the training**: For Luxocator, we will use SciPy to compress the reference histograms and write/read them to/from the disk.

4. **Acquire a dynamic set of query images**: For Luxocator, we will acquire query images using the Bing Search API via a Python wrapper. We will also use the Requests library to download the full resolution images.

5. **Compare the query images with the reference images**: For Luxocator, we will compare each query image and each reference image based on the intersection of their histograms. We will then make a classification based on the average results of these comparisons. We will use NumPy to perform the calculations.

6. **Present the results of the comparison**: For Luxocator, we will provide a GUI to initiate a search and navigate the results. This cross-platform GUI will be developed in wxPython. A classification label, such as "Stalinist, exterior", will be shown below each image. See the following screenshot:

Optionally, we will use PyInstaller to build Luxocator so that it can be deployed to users who do not have Python or the aforementioned libraries. However, remember that you might need to do extra troubleshooting of your own to make PyInstaller work in some environments, including Raspberry Pi or other ARM devices.

Creating, comparing, and storing histograms

A grey-green colour that often finds itself on the walls of public institutions – e.g., hospitals, schools, government buildings – and, where appropriated, on sundry supplies and equipment.

– "Institutional green", Segen's Medical Dictionary (2012)

I hesitate to make sweeping statements about the ideal color of paint on a wall. It depends. I have found solace in many walls of many colors. My mother is a painter and I like paint in general.

But not all color is paint. Some color is dirt. Some color is concrete or marble; plywood or mahogany. Some color is the sky through big windows, the ocean, the golf course, or the swimming pool or jacuzzi. Some color is discarded plastics and beer bottles, baked food on the stove, or perished vermin. Some color is unknown. Maybe the paint camouflages the dirt.

A typical camera can capture at least 16.7 million (256 * 256 * 256) distinct colors. For any given image, we can count the number of pixels of each color. This set of counts is called the **color histogram** of the image. Typically, most entries in the histogram will be 0 because most scenes are not polychromatic (many colored).

We can **normalize** the histogram by dividing the color counts by the total number of pixels. Since the number of pixels is factored out, normalized histograms are comparable even if the original images have different resolutions.

Given a pair of normalized histograms, we can measure the histograms' **similarity** on a scale of 0 to 1. One measure of similarity is called the **intersection** of the histograms. It is computed as follows:

$$d(H_1, H_2) = \Sigma_I min(H_1(I), H_2(I))$$

Here is the equivalent Python code (which we will optimize later):

```
def intersection(hist0, hist1):
  assert len(hist0) == len(hist1),
    'Histogram lengths are mismatched'
  result = 0
  for i in range(len(hist0)):
    result += min(hist0[i], hist1[i])
  return result
```

For example, suppose that in one image 50 percent of the pixels are black and 50 percent are white. In another image, 100 percent of the pixels are black. The similarity is:

```
min(50%, 100%) + min(50%, 0%) = 50% = 0.5.
```

Here, a similarity of 1 does not mean that the images are identical; it means that their normalized histograms are identical. Relative to the first image, the second image could be of a different size, could be flipped, or could even contain the same pixel values in a randomly different order.

Conversely, a similarity of 0 does not mean that the images look completely different to a layperson; it just means that they have no color values in common. For example, an image that is all black and another image that is all charcoal gray have histograms with a similarity of 0 by our definition.

For the purpose of classifying images, we want to find the **average similarity** between a query histogram and a set of multiple reference histograms. A single reference histogram (and a single reference image) would be much too specific for a broad classification such as "Luxury, indoor."

Although we will focus on one approach to compare histograms, there are many alternatives. For a discussion of several algorithms and their implementations in Python, see this blog post by Adrian Rosebrock: http://www.pyimagesearch.com/2014/07/14/3-ways-compare-histograms-using-opencv-python/.

Let's write a class called `HistogramClassifier`, which creates and stores sets of references histograms and finds the average similarity between a query histogram and each set of reference histograms. To support this functionality, we will use OpenCV, NumPy, and SciPy. Create a file called `HistogramClassifier.py` and add the following import statements at the top:

```
import numpy
import cv2
import scipy.io
import scipy.sparse
```

An instance of `HistogramClassifier` stores several variables. A public Boolean called `verbose` controls the level of logging. A public float called `minimumSimilarityForPositiveLabel` defines a similarity threshold; if all the average similarities fall below this value, then the query image is given an `"Unknown"` classification. Several variables store values related to the color space. We will assume that our images have 3 color channels with 8 bits (256 possible values) per channel. Finally, and most importantly, a dictionary called `_references` maps string keys such as `"Luxury, interior"` to lists of reference histograms. Let's declare the variables in the `__init__` method belonging to `HistogramClassifier`, as follows:

```
class HistogramClassifier(object):

    def __init__(self):

        self.verbose = False
        self.minimumSimilarityForPositiveLabel = 0.075

        self._channels = range(3)
        self._histSize = [256] * 3
        self._ranges = [0, 255] * 3
        self._references = {}
```

> By convention, in a Python class, a variable or method name is prefixed with an underscore if the variable or method is meant to be protected (accessed only within the class and its subclasses). However, this level of protection is not actually enforced. Most of our member variables and methods in this book are marked as protected, but a few are public. Python supports private variables and methods (denoted by a double underscore prefix) that are meant to be inaccessible even to subclasses. However, we will avoid private variables and methods in this book because Python classes should typically be highly extensible.

`HistogramClassifier` has a method, `_createNormalizedHist`, which takes two arguments: an image and a Boolean value indicating whether to store the resulting histogram in a **sparse** (compressed) format. The histogram is computed using an OpenCV function, `cv2.calcHist`. As arguments, it takes the image, the number of channels, the histogram size (that is, the dimensions of the color space), and the range of each color channel. We will flatten the resulting histogram into a one-dimensional format that uses memory more efficiently. Then, optionally, we will convert the histogram to a sparse format using a SciPy function called `scipy.sparse.csc_matrix`.

A sparse matrix uses a form of compression that relies on a default value, normally 0. That is to say, we won't bother to store all the zeroes individually, instead we will note the ranges that are full of zeroes. For histograms, this is an important optimization because in a typical image, most of the possible colors are absent. Thus, most of the histogram values are 0.

Compared to an uncompressed format, a sparse format offers better memory efficiency but worse computational efficiency. The same tradeoff applies to compressed formats in general.

Here is the implementation of _createNormalizedHist:

```
def _createNormalizedHist(self, image, sparse):
  # Create the histogram.
  hist = cv2.calcHist([image], self._channels, None,
    self._histSize, self._ranges)
  # Normalize the histogram.
  hist[:] = hist * (1.0 / numpy.sum(hist))
  # Convert the histogram to one column for efficient storage.
  hist = hist.reshape(16777216, 1)
  if sparse:
    # Convert the histogram to a sparse matrix.
    hist = scipy.sparse.csc_matrix(hist)
  return hist
```

A public method, addReference, accepts two arguments: an image and a label. (The label is a string that describes the classification.) We will pass the image to _createNormalizedHist in order to create a normalized histogram in a sparse format. For a reference histogram, the sparse format is more appropriate because we want to keep many reference histograms in memory for the entire duration of a classification session. After creating the histogram, we will add it to a list in _references using the label as the key. Here is the implementation of addReference:

```
def addReference(self, image, label):
  hist = self._createNormalizedHist(image, True)
  if label not in self._references:
    self._references[label] = [hist]
  else:
    self._references[label] += [hist]
```

For the purposes of Luxocator, reference images come from the files on disk. Let's give `HistogramClassifier` a public method, `addReferenceFromFile`, which accepts a file path instead of directly accepting an image. It also accepts a label. We will load the image from a file using an OpenCV method called `cv2.imread`, which accepts a path and a color format. Based on our earlier assumption about having 3 color channels, we always want to load images in color, not grayscale. This option is represented by the value `cv2.CV_LOAD_IMAGE_COLOR`. Having loaded the image, we will pass it and the label to `addReference`. The implementation of `addReferenceFromFile` is as follows:

```
def addReferenceFromFile(self, path, label):
    image = cv2.imread(path, cv2.CV_LOAD_IMAGE_COLOR)
    self.addReference(image, label)
```

Now, we have arrived at the crux of the matter: the `classify` public method, which accepts a query image as well as an optional string to identify the image in a log output. For each set of reference histograms, we will compute the average similarity to the query histogram. If all similarity values fall below `minimumSimilarityForPositiveLabel`, we will return the `'Unknown'` label. Otherwise, we will return the label of the most similar set of reference histograms. If `verbose` is `true`, we will also log all the labels and their respective average similarities. Here is the method's implementation:

```
def classify(self, queryImage, queryImageName=None):
    queryHist = self._createNormalizedHist(queryImage, False)
    bestLabel = 'Unknown'
    bestSimilarity = self.minimumSimilarityForPositiveLabel
    if self.verbose:
        print '============================================='
        if queryImageName is not None:
            print 'Query image:'
            print '    %s' % queryImageName
        print 'Mean similarity to reference images by label:'
    for label, referenceHists in self._references.iteritems():
        similarity = 0.0
        for referenceHist in referenceHists:
            similarity += numpy.sum(numpy.minimum(
                referenceHist.todense(), queryHist))
        similarity /= len(referenceHists)
        if self.verbose:
            print '    %8f  %s' % (similarity, label)
        if similarity > bestSimilarity:
            bestLabel = label
```

```
      bestSimilarity = similarity
  if self.verbose:
    print '==============================================='
  return bestLabel
```

OpenCV has a function, `cv2.compareHist`, to calculate the similarity between two histograms. However, at the time of writing, `cv2.compareHist` has a bug that causes it to crash when comparing color histograms. As a workaround, we will write our own comparison using the NumPy arithmetic.

Note the use of the `todense` method to decompress a sparse matrix.

We will also provide a public method, `classifyFromFile`, which accepts a filepath instead of directly accepting an image. The following code defines this method:

```
def classifyFromFile(self, path, queryImageName=None):
  if queryImageName is None:
    queryImageName = path
  queryImage = cv2.imread(path, cv2.CV_LOAD_IMAGE_COLOR)
  return self.classify(queryImage, queryImageName)
```

Computing all our reference histograms will take a bit of time. We do not want to recompute them every time we run Luxocator. Thus, we need to serialize and deserialize (save and load) the histograms to/from the disk. For this purpose, SciPy provides two functions, `scipy.io.savemat` and `scipy.io.loadmat`. They accept a file and various optional arguments.

We can implement a `serialize` method with optional compression, as follows:

```
def serialize(self, path, compressed=False):
  file = open(path, 'wb')
  scipy.io.savemat(
    file, self._references, do_compression=compressed)
```

While deserializing, we will get a dictionary from `scipy.io.loadmat`. However, this dictionary contains more than our original _references dictionary. It also contains some serialization metadata and some additional arrays that wrap the lists that were originally in _references. We will strip out these unwanted added contents and store the result back in _references. The implementation is as follows:

```
def deserialize(self, path):
  file = open(path, 'rb')
  self._references = scipy.io.loadmat(file)
  for key in self._references.keys():
    value = self._references[key]
```

```
if not isinstance(value, numpy.ndarray):
  # This entry is serialization metadata so delete it.
  del self._references[key]
  continue
# The serializer wraps the data in an extra array.
# Unwrap the data.
self._references[key] = value[0]
```

That is our classifier. Next, we will test our classifier by feeding it some reference images and a query image.

Training the classifier with reference images

> *Can you identify this coastline? Given time, yes.*
>
> — *Photo caption, Dante Stella*
> (http://www.dantestella.com/technical/hex352.html)

A small selection of reference images is included in this chapter's code bundle, which can be downloaded from my website, http://nummist.com/opencv/7376_02.zip. They are in a folder called images. Feel free to experiment with the classifier by adding more reference images, since a larger set might yield more reliable results. Bear in mind that our classifier relies on average similarity, so the more times you include a given color scheme in the reference images, the more heavily you are weighting the classifier in favor of that color scheme.

At the end of HistogramClassifier.py, let's add a main method to train and serialize a classifier using our reference images. We will also run the classifier on a couple of the images as a test. A partial implementation of the method is as follows:

```
def main():
  classifier = HistogramClassifier()
  classifier.verbose = True

  # 'Stalinist, interior' reference images
  classifier.addReferenceFromFile(
    'images/communal_apartments_01.jpg',
    'Stalinist, interior')
  # ...
  # Other reference images are omitted for brevity.
```

```
# See this chapter's code bundle for the full implementation.
# ...

classifier.serialize('classifier.mat')
classifier.deserialize('classifier.mat')
classifier.classifyFromFile('images/dubai_damac_heights.jpg')
classifier.classifyFromFile('images/communal_apartments_01.jpg')

if __name__ == '__main__':
    main()
```

Depending on the number of reference images, this method might take several minutes (or even longer) to run. Fortunately, since we are serializing the trained classifier, we will not have to run such a method every time we open our main application.

> For a large number of training images, you might wish to modify the `main` function of `HistogramClassifier.py` to use all images in a specified folder. (Refer to the file `describe.py` provided for *Chapter 3, Training a Smart Alarm to Recognize the Villain and his Cat*, for examples of iteration over all images in a folder.) However, for a small number of training images, I find it more convenient to specify a list of images in code so that we can comment and uncomment individual images in order to see the effect on the training.

Next, let's consider how our main application will acquire query images.

Acquiring images from the Web

Our query images will come from a web search. Before we start implementing the search functionality, let's write some helper functions, which let us fetch images via the Requests library and convert them to an OpenCV-compatible format. Because this functionality is highly reusable, we will put it in a module of static utility functions. Let's create a file called `RequestsUtils.py` and import OpenCV, NumPy, and Requests, as follows:

```
import numpy
import cv2
import requests
import sys
```

As a global variable, let's store HEADERS, a dictionary of headers that we will use while making web requests. Some servers reject requests that appear to come from a bot. To improve the chance of our requests being accepted, let's set the 'User-Agent' header to a value that mimics a web browser, as follows:

```
# Spoof a browser's User-Agent string.
# Otherwise, some sites will reject us as a bot.
HEADERS = {
  'User-Agent': 'Mozilla/5.0 (Macintosh; Intel Mac OS X 10.9; ' + \
    'rv:25.0) Gecko/20100101 Firefox/25.0'
}
```

Whenever we receive a response to a web request, we want to check whether the status code is 200 OK. This is only a cursory test of whether the response is valid, but it is a good enough test for our purposes. We will implement this test in the following method, validateResponse, which returns True if the response is deemed valid; otherwise it logs an error message and returns False:

```
def validateResponse(response):
  statusCode = response.status_code
  if statusCode == 200:
    return True
  url = response.request.url
  print >> sys.stderr, \
    'Received unexpected status code (%d) when requesting %s' % \
      (statusCode, url)
  return False
```

With the help of HEADERS and validateResponse, we can try to get an image from a URL and return that image in an OpenCV-compatible format (failing that, we will return None.) As an intermediate step, we will read raw data from a web response into a NumPy array using a function called numpy.fromstring. We will then interpret this data as an image using a function called cv2.imdecode. Here is our implementation of a function called cvImageFromUrl that accepts a URL as an argument:

```
def cvImageFromUrl(url):
  response = requests.get(url, headers=HEADERS)
  if not validateResponse(response):
    return None
  imageData = numpy.fromstring(response.content, numpy.uint8)
  image = cv2.imdecode(imageData, cv2.CV_LOAD_IMAGE_COLOR)
  if image is None:
    print >> sys.stderr, \
      'Failed to decode image from content of %s' % url
  return image
```

To test these two functions, let's give `RequestsUtils.py` a `main` function that downloads an image from the web, converts it to an OpenCV-compatible format, and writes it to the disk using an OpenCV function called `imwrite`. This is covered in the following implementation:

```
def main():
    image = \
        cvImageFromUrl('http://nummist.com/images/ceiling.gaze.jpg')
    if image is not None:
        cv2.imwrite('image.png', image)

if __name__ == '__main__':
    main()
```

To confirm that everything worked, open `image.png` (which should be in the same directory as `RequestsUtils.py`) and compare it to the online image, which you can view in a web browser at `http://nummist.com/images/ceiling.gaze.jpg`.

 Although we are putting a simple test of our `RequestUtils` module in a `main` function, a more sophisticated and maintainable approach to write tests in Python is to use the classes in the `unittest` module of the standard library. Refer to the official tutorial here for more information: `https://docs.python.org/2/library/unittest.html`.

Acquiring images from Bing image search

Microsoft's search engine, Bing, has an API that enables us to send queries and receive results in our own application. For a certain number of queries (currently, 5,000 per month), Bing Search API is free to use. However, we must register for it by taking the following steps:

1. Go to `http://datamarket.azure.com/` and log in. You will need to create a Microsoft account if you do not already have one.

2. Enter `Bing Search API` in the **Search the Marketplace** field. A list of results should appear. Click on the link for **Bing Search API** (not any variant such as **Bing Search API – Web Results Only**).

3. Next to the **$0.00 per month** option, click on the **SIGN UP** button.
   Alternatively, if you plan to use Luxocator obsessively, to the exclusion of
   normal activities, sign up for one of the paid options that allows more than
   5,000 queries per month.

4. Click on the **My Account** tab. You should see a list of **Account Information**,
   including a **Primary Account Key**, which is a 43-character string. Copy this
   string to the clipboard. We will need to use it in our code to associate our
   Bing session with our Microsoft account.

Bing Search API has a third-party Python wrapper called pyBingSearchAPI.
Download a ZIP archive of this wrapper from https://github.com/xthepoet/
pyBingSearchAPI/archive/master.zip. Unzip it to our project folder. A script,
bing_search_api.py, should now be located alongside our other scripts.

To build atop pyBingSearchAPI, we want a high-level interface to submit a query
string and navigate through a resulting list of images, which should be in an
OpenCV-compatible format. We will make a class, ImageSearchSession, offering
such an interface. First, let's create a file, ImageSearchSession.py, and add the
following import statements at the start of the file:

```
import bing_search_api
import numpy
import cv2
import pprint

import RequestsUtils
```

Note that we are using OpenCV, as well as pyBingSearchAPI, pretty-print (to log
JSON results from the search), and our networking utility functions.

ImageSearchSession has member variables that store our Bing session (initialized
using the Primary Account Key that we had copied from Azure Marketplace), the
current query, metadata about the current image results, and metadata that helps us
navigate to the previous and next results. We can initialize these variables as seen in
the following code:

```
class ImageSearchSession(object):

    def __init__(self):
        # Replace the x's with the Primary Account Key of your
        # Microsoft Account.
        bingKey = 'xxxxxxxxxxxxxxxxxxxxxxxxxxxxxxxxxxxxxxxxxxx'

        self.verbose = False

        self._bing = bing_search_api.BingSearchAPI(bingKey)
```

```
self._query = ''
self._results = []
self._offset = 0
self._numResultsRequested = 0
self._numResultsReceived = 0
self._numResultsAvailable = 0
```

 As an alternative to being hardcoded in the script, our Primary Account Key can be loaded from a custom environment variable. For example, if we defined an environment variable called `BING_KEY`, we will get its value in Python as `os.environ['BING_KEY']`. (We would need to import the `os` module of the Python standard library.) This change would make it easier to securely share our script because we would not need to blank out our Primary Account Key.

We will provide getters for many of the member variables, as follows:

```
@property
def query(self):
    return self._query

@property
def offset(self):
    return self._offset

@property
def numResultsRequested(self):
    return self._numResultsRequested

@property
def numResultsReceived(self):
    return self._numResultsReceived

@property
def numResultsAvailable(self):
    return self._numResultsAvailable
```

Given these variables, we can navigate through a large set of results by fetching only a few results at a time, that is, by looking at a **window** into the results. We can move our window to earlier or later results, as needed, by simply adjusting the offset by the number of requested results and clamping the offset to the valid range. Here are the implementations of `searchPrev` and `searchNext` methods, which rely on a more general search method that we will implement afterwards:

```
def searchPrev(self):
    if self._offset == 0:
```

```
      return
    offset = max(0, self._offset - self._numResultsRequested)
    self.search(self._query, self._numResultsRequested,
      offset)

  def searchNext(self):
    if self._offset + self._numResultsRequested >= \
      self._numResultsAvailable:
      return
    offset = self._offset + self._numResultsRequested
    self.search(self._query, self._numResultsRequested,
      offset)
```

The more general-purpose `search` method accepts a query string, a maximum number of results, and an offset relative to the first available result. We will store these arguments in member variables for reuse in the `searchPrev` and `searchNext` methods. Here is the first part of this method's implementation:

```
def search(self, query, numResultsRequested=20, offset=0):

  self._query = query
  self._numResultsRequested = numResultsRequested
  self._offset = offset
```

Then, we set up our search parameters, specifying that the results should be in the JSON format and should include color photos only:

```
params = {
  'ImageFilters': '"color:color+style:photo"',
  '$format': 'json',
  '$top': numResultsRequested,
  '$skip': offset
}
```

We will request the results and parse the response to get the portion of the JSON related to image metadata, which we will store for use in other methods:

```
response = self._bing.search('image', query, params)
if not RequestsUtils.validateResponse(response):
  self._offset = 0
  self._numResultsReceived = 0
  return
```

```
# In some versions, requests.Response.json is a dict.
# In other versions, it is a method returning a dict.
# Get the dict in either case.
json = response.json
if (hasattr(json, '__call__')):
  json = json()

metaResults = json[u'd'][u'results'][0]
if self.verbose:
  print \
    'Got results of Bing image search for "%s":' % \
    query
  pprint.pprint(metaResults)

self._results = metaResults[u'Image']
```

We will also parse and store metadata of the actual offset, actual number of results received, and number of results available:

```
self._offset = int(metaResults[u'ImageOffset'])
self._numResultsReceived = len(self._results)
self._numResultsAvailable = \
int(metaResults[u'ImageTotal'])
```

Although the search method fetches a textual description of results, including image URLs, it does not actually fetch any full-sized images. This is good because the full-sized images might be large and we do not need them all at once. Instead, we will provide another method, getCvImageAndUrl, to retrieve the image and image URL that have a specified index in the current results. The index is given as an argument. As an optional second argument, this method accepts a Boolean value that indicates whether a thumbnail should be used instead of the full-sized image. Thumbnails are included directly in the query results, so retrieval is very quick in this case. Full-sized images must be downloaded, so we use cvImageFromUrl to fetch and convert them. This implementation is done in the following code:

```
def getCvImageAndUrl(self, index, useThumbnail = False):
  if index >= self._numResultsReceived:
    return None, None
  result = self._results[index]
  url = result[u'MediaUrl']
  if useThumbnail:
    result = result[u'Thumbnail'], url
  return RequestsUtils.cvImageFromUrl(url), url
```

The caller of `getCvImageAndUrl` is responsible for dealing gracefully with the image downloads that are slow or that fail. Remember that our `cvImageFromUrl` function just logs an error and returns `None` if the download fails.

To test `ImageSearchSession`, let's write a main function that instantiates the class, sets verbose to `True`, searches for `'luxury condo sales'`, and writes the first resulting image to disk as shown in the following implementation:

```
def main():
  session = ImageSearchSession()
  session.verbose = True
  session.search('luxury condo sales')
  image, url = session.getCvImageAndUrl(0)
  cv2.imwrite('image.png', image)


if __name__ == '__main__':
  main()
```

Now that we have a classifier and a search session, we are almost ready to proceed to the frontend of the Luxocator. We just need a few more utility functions to help us prepare data and images to bundle and display them.

Preparing images and resources for the app

Alongside `RequestsUtils.py` and `ImageSearchSession.py`, let's create another file called `ResizeUtils.py` with the following import statements:

```
import numpy
import cv2
```

For display in a GUI, images often must be resized. One popular mode of resizing is called **aspect fill**. This means that we want to preserve the image's aspect ratio while changing its larger dimension (width for a landscape image or height for a portrait image) to a certain value. OpenCV does not directly provide this resizing mode but it does provide a function, `cv2.resize`, which accepts an image, target dimensions, and optional arguments including an interpolation method. We can write our own function, `cvResizeAspectFill`, which accepts an image, maximum size, and preferred interpolation methods for upsizing and downsizing the images. It determines the appropriate arguments for `cv2.resize` and passes them along. Here is the implementation:

```
def cvResizeAspectFill(src, maxSize,
  upInterpolation=cv2.INTER_LANCZOS4,
```

```
downInterpolation=cv2.INTER_AREA):
h, w = src.shape[:2]
if w > h:
  if w > maxSize:
    interpolation=downInterpolation
  else:
    interpolation=upInterpolation
  h = int(maxSize * h / float(w))
  w = maxSize
else:
  if h > maxSize:
    interpolation=downInterpolation
  else:
    interpolation=upInterpolation
  w = int(maxSize * w / float(h))
  h = maxSize
dst = cv2.resize(src, (w, h), interpolation=interpolation)
return dst
```

For a description of the interpolation methods that OpenCV supports, refer to the official documentation at http://docs.opencv. org/modules/imgproc/doc/geometric_transformations. html#resize. For upsizing, we default to cv2.INTER_LANCZOS4, which produces sharp results. For downsizing, we default on cv2. INTER_AREA, which produces moiré free results. (**Moiré** is an artifact that makes parallel lines or concentric curves look like crosshatching when they are sharpened at certain magnifications.)

Now, let's create another file called WxUtils.py with the following import statements:

```
import numpy
import cv2
import wx
```

OpenCV and wxPython use different image formats, so we will implement a conversion function, wxBitmapFromCvImage. OpenCV stores color channels in a BGR order, whereas wxPython expects an RGB order. We can use an OpenCV function, cv2.cvtColor, to reformat the image data accordingly. Then, we can use a wxPython function, wx.BitmapFromBuffer, to read the reformatted data into a wxPython bitmap, which we return. Here is the implementation:

```
def wxBitmapFromCvImage(image):
    image = cv2.cvtColor(image, cv2.cv.CV_BGR2RGB)
    h, w = image.shape[:2]
    bitmap = wx.BitmapFromBuffer(w, h, image)
    return bitmap
```

At the time of writing, `wx.BitmapFromBuffer` suffers from a platform-specific bug such that it fails on Raspberry Pi (specifically, Raspbian). As a workaround, we can do a less efficient, two-step conversion using the functions `wx.ImageFromBuffer` and `wx.BitmapFromImage`. Here is some code to check whether we are running on Raspbian Pi (based on the CPU model) and to implement our wxBitmapFromCVImage function appropriately:

```
# Try to determine whether we are on Raspberry Pi.
IS_RASPBERRY_PI = False
try:
  with open('/proc/cpuinfo') as f:
    for line in f:
      line = line.strip()
      if line.startswith('Hardware') and \
        line.endswith('BCM2708'):
        IS_RASPBERRY_PI = True
        break
except:
  pass


if IS_RASPBERRY_PI:
  def wxBitmapFromCvImage(image):
    image = cv2.cvtColor(image, cv2.COLOR_BGR2RGB)
    h, w = image.shape[:2]
    wxImage = wx.ImageFromBuffer(w, h, image)
    bitmap = wx.BitmapFromImage(wxImage)
    return bitmap
else:
  def wxBitmapFromCvImage(image):
    image = cv2.cvtColor(image, cv2.COLOR_BGR2RGB)
    h, w = image.shape[:2]
    # The following conversion fails on Pi.
    bitmap = wx.BitmapFromBuffer(w, h, image)
    return bitmap
```

We have one more utility module to make. Let's create a file, `PyInstallerUtils.py`, with import statements for the `os` and `sys` modules from Python's standard library:

```
import os
import sys
```

When we bundle our application using PyInstaller, the paths to the resources will change. Thus, we need a function that correctly resolves paths regardless of whether our application has been bundled or not. Let's add a function, pyInstallerResourcePath, which resolves a given path relative to the app directory (the '_MEIPASS' attribute) or, failing that, the current working directory ('.'). This is implemented as follows:

```
def pyInstallerResourcePath(relativePath):
    basePath = getattr(sys, '_MEIPASS', os.path.abspath('.'))
    return os.path.join(basePath, relativePath)
```

Our utilities modules are done now and we can move on to implement the frontend of the Luxocator.

Integrating everything into the GUI

For Luxocator's frontend, let's create a file called Luxocator.py. This module depends on OpenCV, wxPython, and some of Python's standard OS and threading functionality. It also depends on all the other modules that we have written in this chapter. Add the following import statements at the top of the file:

```
import numpy
import cv2
import os
import threading
import wx

from HistogramClassifier import HistogramClassifier
from ImageSearchSession import ImageSearchSession
import PyInstallerUtils
import ResizeUtils
import WxUtils
```

Now, let's implement the Luxocator class as a subclass of wx.Frame, which represents a GUI frame such as the contents of a window. Most of our GUI code is in the Luxocator class's __init__ method, which is therefore a big method but is not very complicated. Our GUI elements include a search control, previous and next buttons, a bitmap, and a label to show the classification result. All of these GUI elements are stored in the member variables. The bitmap is confined to a certain maximum size (by default, 768 pixels in the larger dimension) and the other elements are laid out below it.

Several methods are registered as callbacks to handle events such as the window closing, a search string being entered, or the next or previous button being clicked. Besides the GUI elements, other member variables include instances of our `HistogramClassifier` and `ImageSearchSession` classes. Here is the implementation of the initializer, interspersed with some remarks on the GUI elements that we are using:

 For more information about using bitmaps, controls, and layouts in wxPython, refer to the official wiki at `http://wiki.wxpython.org/`.

```python
class Luxocator(wx.Frame):

    def __init__(self, classifierPath, maxImageSize=768,
        verboseSearchSession=False,
        verboseClassifier=False):

        style = wx.CLOSE_BOX | wx.MINIMIZE_BOX | wx.CAPTION | \
            wx.SYSTEM_MENU | wx.CLIP_CHILDREN
        wx.Frame.__init__(self, None, title='Luxocator', \
            style=style)
        self.SetBackgroundColour(wx.Colour(232, 232, 232))

        self._maxImageSize = maxImageSize
        border = 12
        defaultQuery = 'luxury condo sales'

        self._index = 0
        self._session = ImageSearchSession()
        self._session.verbose = verboseSearchSession
        self._session.search(defaultQuery)

        self._classifier = HistogramClassifier()
        self._classifier.verbose = verboseClassifier
        self._classifier.deserialize(classifierPath)

        self.Bind(wx.EVT_CLOSE, self._onCloseWindow)
```

The search control (coming up next) deserves special attention because it contains multiple controls within it and its behavior differs slightly across operating systems. It can have up to three sub-controls: a text field, a search button, and a cancel button. There can be a callback for the *Enter* key being pressed while the text field is active. If the search and cancel buttons are present, they have callbacks on being clicked. We can set up the search control and its callbacks as follows:

```
self._searchCtrl = wx.SearchCtrl(
    self, size=(self._maxImageSize / 3, -1),
    style=wx.TE_PROCESS_ENTER)
self._searchCtrl.SetValue(defaultQuery)
self._searchCtrl.Bind(wx.EVT_TEXT_ENTER,
    self._onSearchEntered)
self._searchCtrl.Bind(wx.EVT_SEARCHCTRL_SEARCH_BTN,
    self._onSearchEntered)
self._searchCtrl.Bind(wx.EVT_SEARCHCTRL_CANCEL_BTN,
    self._onSearchCanceled)
```

By contrast, the label, previous and next buttons, and bitmap do not have any sub-controls that need to concern us. We can set them up as follows:

```
self._labelStaticText = wx.StaticText(self)

self._prevButton = wx.Button(self, label='Prev')
self._prevButton.Bind(wx.EVT_BUTTON,
    self._onPrevButtonClicked)

self._nextButton = wx.Button(self, label='Next')
self._nextButton.Bind(wx.EVT_BUTTON,
    self._onNextButtonClicked)

self._staticBitmap = wx.StaticBitmap(self)
```

Our controls are lined up horizontally, with the search control on the left edge of the window, the previous and next buttons on the right edge, and a label halfway in between the search control and previous button. We will use an instance of wx.BoxSizer to define this horizontal layout:

```
controlsSizer = wx.BoxSizer(wx.HORIZONTAL)
controlsSizer.Add(self._searchCtrl, 0,
    wx.ALIGN_CENTER_VERTICAL | wx.RIGHT, border)
controlsSizer.Add((0, 0), 1) # Spacer
controlsSizer.Add(
    self._labelStaticText, 0,
    wx.ALIGN_CENTER_VERTICAL)
```

```
controlsSizer.Add((0, 0), 1) # Spacer
controlsSizer.Add(
  self._prevButton, 0,
  wx.ALIGN_CENTER_VERTICAL | wx.LEFT | wx.RIGHT,
  border)
controlsSizer.Add(
  self._nextButton, 0, wx.ALIGN_CENTER_VERTICAL)
```

The best thing about layouts (and Russian dolls) is that they can be nested, one inside another. Our horizontal layout of controls needs to appear below the bitmap. This relationship is a vertical layout, which we will define using another `wx.BoxSizer` instance:

```
self._rootSizer = wx.BoxSizer(wx.VERTICAL)
self._rootSizer.Add(self._staticBitmap, 0,
  wx.TOP | wx.LEFT | wx.RIGHT, border)
self._rootSizer.Add(controlsSizer, 0, wx.EXPAND | wx.ALL,
  border)

self.SetSizerAndFit(self._rootSizer)

self._updateImageAndControls()
```

This is the end of the __init__ method.

As seen in the following code, we provide getters and setters for the `verbose` property of our `ImageSearchSession` instance and our `HistogramClassifier` instance:

```
@property
def verboseSearchSession(self):
  return self._session.verbose

@verboseSearchSession.setter
def verboseSearchSession(self, value):
  self._session.verbose = value

@property
def verboseClassifier(self):
  return self._classifier.verbose

@verboseClassifier.setter
def verboseClassifier(self, value):
  self._classifier.verbose = value
```

Our `_onCloseWindow` callback just cleans up the application by calling the `Destroy` method of the superclass. Here is the implementation:

```
def _onCloseWindow(self, event):
  self.Destroy()
```

Our `_onSearchEntered` callback submits the query string via the search method `ImageSearchSession`. Then, it calls a helper method, `_updateImageAndControls`, which asynchronously fetches images and updates the GUI, as we will see later. Here is the implementation of `_onSearchEntered`:

```
def _onSearchEntered(self, event):
  query = event.GetString()
  if len(query) < 1:
    return
  self._session.search(query)
  self._index = 0
  self._updateImageAndControls()
```

Our `_onSearchCanceled` callback simply clears the search control's text field, as seen in the following code:

```
def _onSearchCanceled(self, event):
  self._searchCtrl.Clear()
```

Our remaining GUI event callbacks `_onNextButtonClicked` and `_onPrevButtonClicked` check whether more results are available and if so, use the `searchNext` or `searchPrev` method of `ImageSearchSession`. Then, using the `_updateImageAndControls` helper method, images are fetched asynchronously and the GUI is updated. Here are the implementations of the callbacks:

```
def _onNextButtonClicked(self, event):
  self._index += 1
  if self._index >= self._session.offset + \
    self._session.numResultsReceived - 1:
    self._session.searchNext()
  self._updateImageAndControls()

def _onPrevButtonClicked(self, event):
  self._index -= 1
  if self._index < self._session.offset:
    self._session.searchPrev()
  self._updateImageAndControls()
```

The `_disableControls` method disables the search control and the previous and next buttons, as follows:

```
def _disableControls(self):
    self._searchCtrl.Disable()
    self._prevButton.Disable()
    self._nextButton.Disable()
```

Conversely, the `_enableControls` method enables the search control, the previous button (if we are not already at the first available search result), and the next button (if we are not already at the last available search result). Here is the implementation:

```
def _enableControls(self):
    self._searchCtrl.Enable()
    if self._index > 0:
        self._prevButton.Enable()
    if self._index < self._session.numResultsAvailable - 1:
        self._nextButton.Enable()
```

The `_updateImageAndControls` method first disables the controls because we do not want to handle any new queries until the current query is handled. Then, a busy cursor is shown and another helper method, `_updateImageAndControlsAsync`, is started on a background thread. Here is the implementation:

```
def _updateImageAndControls(self):
    # Disable the controls.
    self._disableControls()
    # Show the busy cursor.
    wx.BeginBusyCursor()
    # Get the image in a background thread.
    threading.Thread(
        target=self._updateImageAndControlsAsync).start()
```

The background method, `_updateImageAndControlsAsync`, starts by fetching an image and converting it to the OpenCV format. If the image cannot be fetched and converted, an error message is used as the label. Otherwise, the image is classified and resized to an appropriate size for display. Then, the resized image and the classification label are passed to a third and final helper method, `_updateImageAndControlsResync`, which updates the GUI on the main thread. Here is the implementation of `_updateImageAndControlsAsync`:

```
def _updateImageAndControlsAsync(self):
    # Get the current image.
    image, url = self._session.getCvImageAndUrl(
        self._index % self._session.numResultsRequested)
```

```
if image is None:
  # Provide an error message.
  label = 'Failed to decode image'
else:
  # Classify the image.
  label = self._classifier.classify(image, url)
  # Resize the image while maintaining its aspect ratio.
  image = ResizeUtils.cvResizeAspectFill(
    image, self._maxImageSize)
# Update the GUI on the main thread.
wx.CallAfter(self._updateImageAndControlsResync, image,
  label)
```

The synchronous callback, _updateImageAndControlsResync, hides the busy
cursor, creates a wxPython bitmap from the fetched image (or just a black bitmap
if no image was successfully fetched and converted), shows the image and its
classification label, resizes GUI elements, re-enables controls, and refreshes the
window. Here is its implementation:

```
def _updateImageAndControlsResync(self, image, label):
  # Hide the busy cursor.
  wx.EndBusyCursor()
  if image is None:
    # Provide a black bitmap.
    bitmap = wx.EmptyBitmap(self._maxImageSize,
      self._maxImageSize / 2)
  else:
    # Convert the image to bitmap format.
    bitmap = WxUtils.wxBitmapFromCvImage(image)
  # Show the bitmap.
  self._staticBitmap.SetBitmap(bitmap)
  # Show the label.
  self._labelStaticText.SetLabel(label)
  # Resize the sizer and frame.
  self._rootSizer.Fit(self)
  # Re-enable the controls.
  self._enableControls()
  # Refresh.
  self.Refresh()
```

When the image cannot be successfully fetched and converted, the user sees something like the following screenshot:

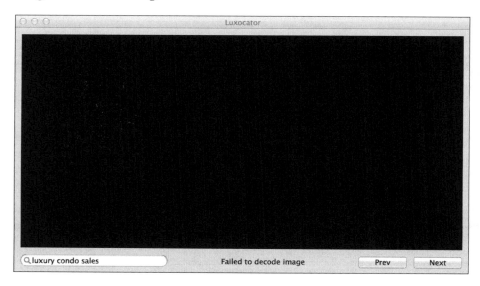

Conversely, when an image is successfully fetched and converted, the user sees the classification result, as shown in the following screenshot:

That completes the implementation of the `Luxocator` class. Now, let's write a main method to set resource paths and launch an instance of `Luxocator`:

```
def main():
  os.environ['REQUESTS_CA_BUNDLE'] = \
    PyInstallerUtils.resourcePath('cacert.pem')
  app = wx.App()
  luxocator = Luxocator(
    PyInstallerUtils.resourcePath('classifier.mat'),
    verboseSearchSession=False, verboseClassifier=False)
  luxocator.Show()
  app.MainLoop()

if __name__ == '__main__':
  main()
```

Note that one of the resources is a certificate bundle called `cacert.pem`. It is required by Requests in order to make an SSL connection, which is in turn required by Bing. You can find a copy of it inside this chapter's code bundle, which is downloadable from my website at `http://nummist.com/opencv/7376_02.zip`. Place `cacert.pem` in the same folder as `Luxocator.py`. Note that our code sets an environment variable, `REQUESTS_CA_BUNDLE`, which is used by Requests to locate the certificate bundle.

> Depending on how it is installed or how it is bundled with an app, Requests might or might not have an internal version of the certificate bundle. For predictability, it is better to provide this external version.

Building Luxocator for distribution

To instruct PyInstaller how to build Luxocator, we must create a **specification file**, which we will call `Luxocator.spec`. Actually, the specification file is a Python script that uses a PyInstaller class called `Analysis` and PyInstaller functions called `PYZ`, `EXE`, and `BUNDLE`. The `Analysis` class is responsible for analyzing one or more Python scripts (in our case, just `Luxocator.py`) and tracing all the dependencies that must be bundled with these scripts in order to make a redistributable application. Sometimes, `Analysis` makes mistakes or omissions, so we will modify the list of dependencies after it is initialized. Then, we will zip the scripts, make an executable, and make an app bundle using `PYZ`, `EXE`, and `BUNDLE`, respectively. Here is the implementation:

```
import os

a = Analysis(['Luxocator.py'],
```

```
    pathex=['.'],
    hiddenimports=[],
    hookspath=None,
    runtime_hooks=None)

# Determine the platform.
platform = os.name

if platform == 'nt':
    # We are on Windows.
    # A bug causes the 'pyconfig' module to be included twice.
    # Remove the duplicate.
    for data in a.datas:
        if 'pyconfig' in data[0]:
            a.datas.remove(data)
            break

# Include SSL certificates for the sake of the 'requests' module.
a.datas.append(('cacert.pem', 'cacert.pem', 'DATA'))

# Include our app's classifier data.
a.datas.append(('classifier.mat', 'classifier.mat', 'DATA'))

pyz = PYZ(a.pure)

exe = EXE(pyz,
    a.scripts,
    a.binaries,
    a.zipfiles,
    a.datas,
    name='Luxocator',
    icon='win\icon-windowed.ico',
    debug=False,
    strip=None,
    upx=True,
    console=False )

app = BUNDLE(exe,
    name='Luxocator.app',
    icon=None)
```

Note that this script specifies three resource files that must be bundled with the app: `cacert.pem`, `classifier.mat`, and `win\icon-windowed.ico`. We have already discussed `cacert.pem` in the previous section and `classifier.mat` is the output of our main function in `HistogramClassifier.py`. The Windows icon file, `win\icon-windowed.ico`, is included in this chapter's code bundle, which is downloadable from my website at `http://nummist.com/opencv/7376_02.zip`. Alternatively, you can provide your own icon file if you prefer.

 For more information about PyInstaller's Analysis class, specification files, and other functionality, see the official documentation at `http://pythonhosted.org/PyInstaller/`.

Now, let's write a platform-specific shell script to clean any old builds, train our classifier, and then bundle the app using PyInstaller. On Windows, create a script called `build.bat`, which contains the following commands:

```
set PYINSTALLER=C:\PyInstaller\pyinstaller.py

REM Remove any previous build of the app.
rmdir build /s /q
rmdir dist /s /q

REM Train the classifier.
python HistogramClassifier.py

REM Build the app.
python "%PYINSTALLER%" Luxocator.spec

REM Make the app an executable.
rename dist\Luxocator Luxocator.exe
```

Similarly, on Mac or Linux, create a script called `build.sh`. Make it executable (for example, by running $ `chmod +x build.sh` in Terminal). The file should contain the following commands:

```
#!/bin/sh

PYINSTALLER=~/PyInstaller/pyinstaller.py

# Remove any previous build of the app.
rm -rf build
rm -rf dist

# Train the classifier.
```

```
python HistogramClassifier.py

# Build the app.
python "$PYINSTALLER" Luxocator.spec

# Determine the platform.
platform=`uname -s`

if [ "$platform" = 'Darwin' ]; then
  # We are on Mac.
  # Copy custom metadata and resources into the app bundle.
  cp -r mac/Contents dist/Luxocator.app
fi
```

Note that on Mac (the 'Darwin' platform), we are manually modifying the app
bundle's contents as a post-build step. We do this in order to overwrite the default
app icon and default properties file that PyInstaller puts in all Mac apps. (Notably,
the default properties do not include support for the Retina mode, so they make the
app look pixelated on recent Mac hardware. Our customizations fix this issue.) This
chapter's code bundle, which is downloadable from my website at http://nummist.
com/opencv/7376_02.zip, includes the custom Mac app contents in a folder called
mac/Contents. You can modify its files to provide any icon and properties you want.

After running the platform-specific build script, we should have a redistributable
build of Luxocator at dist/Luxocator.exe (in Windows), dist/Luxocator.app
(in Mac), or dist/Luxocator (in Linux). If we are using 64-bit Python libraries on
our development machine, this build will only work on 64-bit systems. Otherwise,
it should work on both 32-bit and 64-bit systems. The best test of the build is to
run it on another machine that does not have any of the relevant libraries (such as
OpenCV) installed.

Summary

So much can happen in a single mission! We trained an OpenCV/NumPy/SciPy
histogram classifier, performed Bing image searches, built a wxPython app, and used
PyInstaller to bundle it all for redistribution to Russia with love (or, indeed, to any
destination with any sentiment). At this point, you are well primed to create other
Python applications that combine computer vision, web requests, and a GUI.

For our next mission, we will dig our claws deeper into OpenCV and computer
vision by building a fully functional cat recognizer!

3
Training a Smart Alarm to Recognize the Villain and His Cat

The naming of cats is a difficult matter.

— T. S. Eliot, Old Possum's Book of Practical Cats (1939)

Blofeld: I've taught you to love chickens, to love their flesh, their voice.

— On Her Majesty's Secret Service (1969)

If you saw Ernst Stavro Blofeld, would you recognize him?

Let me remind you that Blofeld, as the Number 1 man in **SPECTRE (SPecial Executive for Counterintelligence, Terrorism, Revenge, and Extortion)**, is a supervillain who eludes James Bond countless times before being written out of the movies due to an intellectual property dispute. Blofeld last appears as an anonymous character in the introductory sequence of the movie *For Your Eyes Only* (1981), where we see him fall from a helicopter and down a factory's smokestack as he shouts, "Mr. Booooooooond!"

Despite this dramatic exit, the evidence of Blofeld's death is unclear. After all, Blofeld is a notoriously difficult man to recognize. His face is seldom caught on camera. As early as the 1960s, he was using plastic surgery to change his identity and to turn his henchmen into look-alikes of himself. A half-century later we must ask, is Blofeld a dead man or is he just made over, perhaps as a beautiful actress in a Colombian telenovela?

One thing is certain. If Blofeld is alive, he is accompanied by a blue-eyed, white Angora cat (preserved by a veterinary miracle or taxidermy). Patting this cat is Blofeld's telltale habit in every movie. His face might be different but his lap cat is the same. We last see the cat jumping out of Blofeld's lap just before the fateful helicopter ride in the movie.

Some commentators have noted a resemblance between Blofeld and Dr. Evil, the nemesis of Austin Powers. However, by comparing the respective lap cats, we can prove that these two villains are not the same.

The moral is that two approaches to identification are better than one. Though we cannot see the man's face, we should not lose sight of his cat.

To automate the search for villains and their cats, we are going to develop a desktop or a Raspberry Pi application called *Angora Blue* (an innocent sounding codename that alludes to the blue eyes of Blofeld's cat). Angora Blue will send us an e-mail alert when it recognizes a specified villain or a specified cat with a certain level of confidence. We will also develop a GUI app called *Interactive Recognizer*, which will train Angora Blue's recognition model based on camera images and names that we will provide interactively. To distinguish faces from the background, Interactive Recognizer depends on a human face detection model that comes with OpenCV and a cat face detection model that we are going to train using an original script and third-party image databases.

This is a big chapter, but it is rewarding because you will learn a process that can be applied to detecting and recognizing any kind of animal face and even objects!

The completed project for this chapter can be downloaded from my website at http://nummist.com/opencv/7376_03.zip. It excludes the datasets of annotated training images, which are large downloads and should be obtained separately from the sources described in this chapter.

Understanding machine learning in general

Our work throughout this chapter builds on the techniques of **machine learning**, meaning that the software makes predictions or decisions based on statistical models. Our approach is one of **supervised learning**, meaning that we (programmers and users) will provide the software with examples of data and correct responses. The software creates the statistical model to extrapolate from these examples. The human-provided examples are referred to as **reference data** or **training data** (or **reference images** or **training images** in the context of computer vision). Conversely, the software's extrapolations pertain to **test data** (or **test images** or **scenes** in the context of computer vision).

Supervised learning is much like the "flashcard" pedagogy used in early childhood education. The teacher shows the child a series of pictures (**training images**) and says, "This is a cow. Moo! This is a horse. Neigh!"

Then, on a field trip to a farm (a **scene**), the child can hopefully distinguish between a horse and a cow. However, I must confess that I once mistook a horse for a cow and I was teased about this misclassification for many years thereafter.

 Apart from supervised learning, which is widely used in problems of vision and semantics, there are two other broad approaches to machine learning: **unsupervised learning** and **reinforcement learning**. Unsupervised learning requires the software to find some structure, such as clusters, in data where no meaning or correct examples are assigned by a human. Analyzing biological structures, such as genomes, is a common problem for unsupervised learning. On the other hand, reinforcement learning requires the software to experimentally optimize a solution on a sequence of problems, where a human assigns the final goal, but the software must set the intermediate goals. Piloting a vehicle and playing a game are common problems for reinforcement learning.

Besides being a computer vision library, OpenCV offers a general-purpose machine learning module that can process any kind of data, not necessarily images. For more information on this module and the underlying machine learning concepts, refer to the *Machine Learning* section of the *OpenCV-Python Tutorials* by Alexander Mordvintsev and Abid Rahman K at `http://opencv-python-tutroals.readthedocs.org/en/latest/py_tutorials/py_ml/py_table_of_contents_ml/py_table_of_contents_ml.html`. Meanwhile, our chapter proceeds with more specialized machine learning functionality and concepts that OpenCV users often apply to face detection and recognition.

Planning the Interactive Recognizer app

Let's begin this project with the middle layer, the Interactive Recognizer app, in order to see how all layers connect. Like Luxocator (the previous chapter's project), Interactive Recognizer is a GUI app built with wxPython. Refer to the following screenshot, which features one of my colleagues, Chief Science Officer Sanibel "San" Delphinium Andromeda, Oracle of the Numm:

The app uses a face detection model, which is loaded from a disk, and it maintains a face recognition model that is saved or loaded to/from a disk. The user might specify the identity of any detected face and this input is added to the face recognition model. A detection result is shown by outlining the face in the video feed, while a recognition result is shown by displaying the name of the face in the text below. To elaborate, we can say that the app has the following flow of execution:

1. The app loads a face detection model from a file. The role of the **detection** model is to distinguish faces from the background.

2. It loads a face recognition model from a file, if any such model was saved during a previous run of Interactive Recognizer. Otherwise (if there is no such model to load), it creates a new one. The role of the **recognition** model is to distinguish faces of different individuals from each other.

3. It captures and displays a live video from a camera.

4. For each frame of video, it detects the largest face, if any. If a face is detected:

    1. It draws a rectangle around the face.

    2. It permits the user to enter the face's identity as a short string (up to four characters), such as Joe or Puss. When the user hits the **Add to Model** button, the model becomes trained to recognize the face as whomever the user specified (Joe, Puss, or another identity).

    3. If the recognition model is trained for at least one face, the GUI displays the recognizer's **prediction** for the current face, that is, it displays the most probable identity of the current face according to the recognizer. Also, it displays a measure of **distance** (non-confidence) for this prediction.

5. If the recognition model is trained for at least one face, the GUI permits the user to hit the **Clear Model** button to delete the model (including any version saved to the file) and create a new one.

6. After exiting, if the recognition model is trained for at least one face, the app saves the model to a file so that it can be loaded in subsequent runs of Interactive Recognizer and Angora Blue.

We could generalize by using the term **object** instead of **face**. Depending on the models that it loads, Interactive Recognizer can detect and recognize any kind of object, not necessarily faces.

We will use a type of detection model called a **Haar cascade** and a type of recognition model called **Local Binary Patterns (LBP)** or **Local Binary Pattern Histograms (LBPH)**. Alternatively, we can use LBPH for both detection and recognition. As detection models, LBP cascades are faster but generally less reliable, compared to Haar cascades. OpenCV comes with some Haar cascade and LBP cascade files including several face detection models. Command-line tools are also included with OpenCV along with these files. The APIs offer high-level classes for loading and using Haar or LBP cascades and for loading, saving, training, and using LBPH recognition models. Let's look at the basic concepts of these models.

Understanding Haar cascades and LBPH

Cookie Monster: Hey, you know what? A round cookie with one bite out of it looks like a "C". A round donut with one bite out of it also looks like a "C" but it is not as good as a cookie. Oh, and the moon sometimes looks like a "C" but you can't eat that.

— *"C is for Cookie", Sesame Street*

Think about cloud watching. If you lie on the ground and look up at the clouds, maybe you imagine that one cloud is shaped like a mound of mashed potatoes on a plate. If you board an airplane and fly to this cloud, you will still see some resemblance between the cloud's surface and the fluffy, lumpy texture of hearty mashed potatoes. However, if you could slice off a piece of cloud and examine it under a microscope, you might see ice crystals that do not resemble the microscopic structure of mashed potatoes at all.

Similarly, in an image made up of pixels, a person or a computer vision algorithm can see many distinctive shapes or patterns, partly depending on the level of magnification. During the creation of a Haar cascade, various parts of the image are cropped and/or scaled so that we consider only a few pixels at a time (though these pixels might represent any level of magnification). This sample of the image is called a **window**. We will subtract some of the grayscale pixel values from others in order to measure the window's similarity to certain common shapes where a dark region meets a light region. Examples include an edge, a corner, or a thin line, as seen in the following diagram. If a window is very similar to one of these archetypes, it can be selected as a **feature**. We expect to find similar features, at similar positions and magnifications relative to each other, across all images of the same subject.

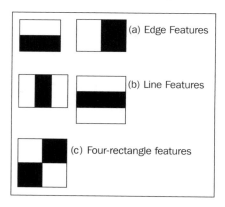

Not all features are equally significant. Across a set of images, we can notice whether a feature is truly typical of images that include our subject (the **positive training set**) and atypical of images that exclude our subject (the **negative training set**). We will give the features a different rank or **stage** depending on how well they distinguish subjects from non-subjects. Together, a set of stages forms a **cascade** or a series of comparison criteria. Every stage must be passed in order to reach a positive detection result. Conversely, a negative detection result can be reached in fewer stages, perhaps only a single stage (an important optimization). Like the training images, scenes are examined through various windows and we might end up detecting multiple subjects in one scene.

For more information about Haar and LBP cascades in OpenCV, refer to the official documentation at `http://docs.opencv.org/trunk/doc/py_tutorials/py_objdetect/py_face_detection/py_face_detection.html`.

An LBPH model, as the name suggests, is based on a kind of histogram. The histogram has three dimensions: height and localized x and y coordinates. For each pixel in a window, we will note whether each neighboring pixel in a certain radius is brighter or darker. Our histogram's height at a given position is a count of the darker pixels in each neighbor position. For example, suppose a window contains the following two neighborhoods of 1 pixel radius:

Black	White	Black
White	White	White
Black	White	Black

Black	Black	Black
White	White	White
White	White	White

Counting these two neighborhoods (and not yet counting other neighborhoods in the window), our histogram has the following height values:

2	1	2
0	0	0
1	0	1

If we compute the LBPH of multiple sets of reference images for multiple subjects, we can determine which set of LBPH references is the least distant from the LBPH of a piece of a scene, such as a detected face. Based on the least distant set of references, we can predict the identity of the face (or other object) in the scene.

An LBPH model is good at capturing fine texture detail in any subject, not just faces. Moreover, it is good for applications where the model needs to be updated, such as the Interactive Recognizer. The histograms for any two images are computed independently, so a new reference image can be added without recomputing the rest of the model.

> OpenCV also implements other models that are popular for face recognition, namely Eigenfaces and Fisherfaces. We wil use LBPH because it supports updates in real time, whereas Eigenfaces and Fisherfaces do not. For more information on these three recognition models, refer to the official documentation at `http://docs.opencv.org/modules/contrib/doc/facerec/facerec_tutorial.html`.

Alternatively, for detection rather than recognition, we can organize LBPH models into a cascade of multiple tests, much like a Haar cascade. Unlike an LBPH recognition model, an LBP cascade cannot be updated in real time.

Haar cascades, LBP cascades, and LBPH recognition models are not robust with respect to rotation or flipping. For example, if we look at a face upside down, it will not be detected by a Haar cascade that was trained only for upright faces. Similarly, if we had an LBPH recognition model trained for a cat whose face is black on the cat's left-paw side and orange on the cat's right-paw side, the model might not recognize the same cat in a mirror. The exception is that we could include mirror images in the training set, but then we might get a false positive recognition for a different cat whose face is orange on the cat's left-paw side and black on the cat's right-paw side.

> Unless otherwise noted, we can assume that a Haar cascade or LBPH model is trained for an **upright** subject. That is, the subject is not tilted or upside down in the image's coordinate space. If a man is standing on his head, we can take an upright photo of his face by turning the camera upside down or, equivalently, by applying a 180-degree rotation in software.

Some other directional terms are worth noting. A **frontal**, **rear**, or **profile** subject has its front, rear, or profile visible in the image. Most computer vision people, including the authors of OpenCV, express **left** and **right** in the image's coordinate space. For example, if we say "left eye", for an upright, frontal, nonmirrored face, we mean the subject's right eye, since left and right in image space are opposite from an upright, frontal, nonmirrored subject's left-hand and right-hand directions. Refer to the following image. It shows how we would label the "left eye" and "right eye" in a nonmirrored image (shown on the left-hand side) and mirrored image (as seen on the right-hand side).

Our human and feline detectors deal with upright, frontal faces.

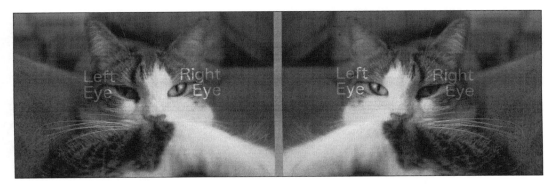

Of course, in a real-world photo, we cannot expect a face to be perfectly upright. The person's head or the camera might have been slightly tilted. Moreover, we cannot expect boundary regions, where a face meets the background, to be similar across images. We must take great care to preprocess the training images so that the face is rotated to a nearly perfect upright pose and the boundary regions are cropped off. While cropping, we should place the major features of the face, such as eyes, in a consistent position. These considerations are addressed further in the *Planning the cat detection model* section later in this chapter.

If we must detect faces in various rotations, one option is to rotate the scene before sending it to the detector. For example, we can try to detect faces in the original scene, then in a version of the scene that has been rotated 15 degrees, then a version rotated -15 degrees (345 degrees), then a version rotated 30 degrees, and so on. Similarly, we can send mirrored versions of the scene to the detector. Depending on how many variations of the scene are tested, such an approach might be too slow for real-time use and thus, we do not use it in this chapter.

Implementing the Interactive Recognizer app

Let's create a new folder, where we will store this chapter's project, including the following subfolders and files that are relevant to the Interactive Recognizer app:

- `cascades/haarcascade_frontalface_alt.xml`: This is a detection model for a frontal, human face. It should be included with OpenCV at a path such as `<opencv_unzip_destination>/data/haarcascades/haarcascade_frontalface_alt.xml`, or for a MacPorts installation at `/opt/local/share/OpenCV/haarcascades/haarcascade_frontalface_alt.xml`. Create a copy of it or a link to it. (Alternatively, you can get it from this chapter's code bundle.)

- `cascades/lbpcascade_frontalface.xml`: This is an alternative (faster but less reliable) detection model for a frontal, human face. It should be included with OpenCV at a path such as `<opencv_unzip_destination>/data/lbpcascades/lbpcascade_frontalface.xml`, or for a MacPorts installation at `/opt/local/share/OpenCV/lbpcascades/lbpcascade_frontalface.xml`. Create a copy of it or a link to it. (Alternatively, you can get it from this chapter's code bundle.)

- `cascades/haarcascade_frontalcatface.xml`: This is a detection model for a frontal, feline face. We will build it later in this chapter. (Alternatively, you can get a prebuilt version from this chapter's code bundle.)

- `cascades/haarcascade_frontalcatface_extended.xml`: This is an alternative detection model for a frontal, feline face. This version is sensitive to diagonal patterns, which could include whiskers and ears. We will build it later in this chapter. (Alternatively, you can get a prebuilt version from this chapter's code bundle.)

- `cascades/lbpcascade_frontalcatface.xml`: This is another alternative (faster but less reliable) detection model for a frontal, feline face. We will build it later in this chapter. (Alternatively, you can get a prebuilt version from this chapter's code bundle.)

- `recognizers/lbph_human_faces.xml`: This is a recognition model for the faces of certain human individuals. It is generated by `InteractiveHumanFaceRecognizer.py`.

- `recognizers/lbph_cat_faces.xml`: This is a recognition model for the faces of certain feline individuals. It is generated by `InteractiveCatFaceRecognizer.py`.

- ResizeUtils.py: This contains the utility functions to resize images. Copy or link to the previous chapter's version of ResizeUtils.py. We will add a function to resize the camera capture dimensions.

- WxUtils.py: This contains the utility functions for wxPython GUI applications. Copy or link to the previous chapter's version of WxUtils.py.

- BinasciiUtils.py: This contains the utility functions to convert human-readable identifiers to numbers and back.

- InteractiveRecognizer.py: This is a class that encapsulates the Interactive Recognizer app and exposes certain variables for configuration. We will implement it in this section.

- InteractiveHumanFaceRecognizer.py: This is a script to launch a version of Interactive Recognizer that is configured for frontal, human faces. We will implement it in this section.

- InteractiveCatFaceRecognizer.py: This is a script to launch a version of Interactive Recognizer that is configured for frontal, feline faces. We will implement it in this section.

Let's start with an addition to our existing ResizeUtils module. We want to be able to specify the resolution at which a camera captures images. Camera input is represented by an OpenCV class called VideoCapture, with get and set methods that pertain to various camera parameters including resolution. (Incidentally, VideoCapture can also represent a video file.) There is no guarantee that a given capture resolution is supported by a given camera. We need to check the success or failure of any attempt to set the capture resolution. Accordingly, let's add the following utility function to ResizeUtils.py to attempt to set a capture resolution and to return the actual capture resolution:

```
def cvResizeCapture(capture, preferredSize):
    # Try to set the requested dimensions.
    w, h = preferredSize
    successW = capture.set(cv2.cv.CV_CAP_PROP_FRAME_WIDTH, w)
    successH = capture.set(cv2.cv.CV_CAP_PROP_FRAME_HEIGHT, h)
    if successW and successH:
        # The requested dimensions were successfully set.
        # Return the requested dimensions.
        return preferredSize
    # The requested dimensions might not have been set.
    # Return the actual dimensions.
    w = capture.get(cv2.cv.CV_CAP_PROP_FRAME_WIDTH)
    h = capture.get(cv2.cv.CV_CAP_PROP_FRAME_HEIGHT)
    return (w, h)
```

Now, let's consider the requirements for our new `BinasciiUtils` module. OpenCV's recognizers use 32-bit integers as identifiers. For a GUI, asking the user to give a face a number instead of a name is not very friendly. We could keep a dictionary that maps numbers to names, and we could save this dictionary to the disk alongside the recognition model, but here is my lazier solution. Four or fewer ASCII characters can be cast to a 32-bit integer (and vice versa). We will let the user name each face by entering up to four characters and, behind the scenes, we will convert the names to and from the 32-bit integers that the model stores. Let's create `BinasciiUtils.py` and put the following imports and conversion functions in it:

```
import binascii

def fourCharsToInt(s):
    return int(binascii.hexlify(s), 16)

def intToFourChars(i):
    return binascii.unhexlify(format(i, 'x'))
```

Now, let's proceed to write `InteractiveRecognizer.py`. It should start with the following import statements:

```
import numpy
import cv2
import os
import sys
import threading
import wx

import BinasciiUtils
import ResizeUtils
import WxUtils
```

Our application's class, `InteractiveRecognizer`, accepts several arguments that allow us to create variants of the app with different titles, highlight colors, recognition models, detection models, and tweaks to the detection behavior. Let's look at the initializer's declaration:

```
class InteractiveRecognizer(wx.Frame):

    def __init__(self, recognizerPath, cascadePath,
        scaleFactor=1.3, minNeighbors=4,
        minSizeProportional=(0.25, 0.25),
        flags=cv2.cv.CV_HAAR_SCALE_IMAGE,
        rectColor=(0, 255, 0),
        cameraDeviceID=0, imageSize=(1280, 720),
        title='Interactive Recognizer'):
```

The initializer's arguments are defined as follows:

- `recognizerPath`: This file contains the recognition model. It does not need to exist when the app starts. Rather, the recognition model (if any) is saved here when the app exits.

- `cascadePath`: This file contains the detection model. It does need to exist when the app starts.

- `scaleFactor`: Remember that, the detector searches for faces at several different scales. This argument specifies the ratio of each scale to the next smaller scale. A bigger ratio implies a faster search but fewer detections.

- `minNeighbors`: If the detector encounters two overlapping regions that both might pass detection as faces, they are called neighbors. The `minNeighbors` argument specifies the minimum number of neighbors that a face must have in order to pass detection. Where `minNeighbors>0`, the rationale is that a true face could be cropped at several alternative places and still look like a face. A greater number of required neighbors implies fewer detections and a lower proportion of false positives.

- `minSizeProportional`: This is used to define a face's minimum width and height. They are expressed as a proportion of the camera's vertical resolution or horizontal resolution, whichever is less. For example, if the camera resolution is 640 x 480 and `minSizeProportional=(0.25, 0.25)`, a face must measure at least 120 x 120 (in pixels) in order to pass detection. A bigger minimum size implies a faster search but fewer detections. The default value, `(0.25, 0.25)`, is appropriate for a face that is close to a webcam.

- `flags`: This is one of the techniques used to narrow the detector's search. When the detector is using a cascade file trained in a recent version of OpenCV, these flags do nothing. However, they might do some good when using an old cascade file. Not all combinations are valid. The valid standalone flags and valid combinations include the following:

    ○ `cv2.cv.CV_HAAR_SCALE_IMAGE`: This is used to apply certain optimizations when changing the scale of the search. This flag must not be combined with others.

    ○ `cv2.cv.CV_HAAR_DO_CANNY_PRUNING`: This is used to eagerly reject regions that contain too many or too few edges to pass detection. This flag should not be combined with `cv2.cv.CV_HAAR_FIND_BIGGEST_OBJECT`.

    ○ `cv2.cv.CV_HAAR_FIND_BIGGEST_OBJECT`: This is used to detect, at most, one face (the biggest).

- ° `cv2.cv.CV_HAAR_FIND_BIGGEST_OBJECT | cv2.cv.HAAR_DO_ROUGH_SEARCH`: This detects, at most, one face (the biggest) and skips some steps that would refine (shrink) the region of this face. This flag requires `minNeighbors>0`.

- `rectColor`: This is the color of the rectangle that outlines a detected face. Like most color tuples in OpenCV, it is specified in the BGR order (not RGB).

- `cameraDeviceID`: This argument shows the device ID of the camera that should be used for input. Typically, webcams are numbered starting from `0`, and any connected external webcams come before any internal webcams. Some camera drivers reserve fixed device IDs. For example, OpenNI reserves `900` for Kinect and `910` for Asus Xtion.

- `imageSize`: This shows the preferred resolution for captured images. If the camera does not support this resolution, another resolution is used.

- `title`: This shows the app's title, as seen in the window's title bar.

We will also provide a public Boolean variable for configuration to check whether or not the camera feed is mirrored. By default, it is mirrored because users find a mirrored image of themselves to be more intuitive:

```
self.mirrored = True
```

Another Boolean variable tracks whether the app should still be running or whether it is closing. This information is relevant to cleaning up a background thread:

```
self._running = True
```

Using an OpenCV class called `cv2.VideoCapture`, we can open a camera feed and get its resolution, as follows:

```
self._capture = cv2.VideoCapture(cameraDeviceID)
size = ResizeUtils.cvResizeCapture(
  self._capture, imageSize)
self._imageWidth, self._imageHeight = size
```

Next, we will set up variables related to detection and recognition. Many of these variables just store initialization arguments for later use. Also, we will keep a reference to the currently detected face, which is initially `None`. We will initialize an LBPH recognizer and load any recognition model that we might have saved on a previous run on the app. Likewise, we will initialize a detector by loading a Haar cascade or LBP cascade from a file, as shown in the following code:

```
self._currDetectedObject = None

self._recognizerPath = recognizerPath
```

```
self._recognizer = cv2.createLBPHFaceRecognizer()
if os.path.isfile(recognizerPath):
  self._recognizer.load(recognizerPath)
  self._recognizerTrained = True
else:
  self._recognizerTrained = False

self._detector = cv2.CascadeClassifier(cascadePath)
self._scaleFactor = scaleFactor
self._minNeighbors = minNeighbors
minImageSize = min(self._imageWidth, self._imageHeight)
self._minSize = (int(minImageSize * minSizeProportional[0]),
  int(minImageSize * minSizeProportional[1]))
self._flags = flags
self._rectColor = rectColor
```

Having set up the variables that are relevant to computer vision, we will proceed to the GUI implementation, which is mostly boilerplate code. First, in the following code snippet, we will set up the window with a certain style, size, title, and background color and we will bind a handler for its close event:

```
style = wx.CLOSE_BOX | wx.MINIMIZE_BOX | wx.CAPTION | \
  wx.SYSTEM_MENU | wx.CLIP_CHILDREN
wx.Frame.__init__(self, None, title=title,
  style=style, size=size)
self.SetBackgroundColour(wx.Colour(232, 232, 232))

self.Bind(wx.EVT_CLOSE, self._onCloseWindow)
```

Next, we will set a callback for the *Esc* key. Since a key is not a GUI widget, there is no Bind method directly associated with a key, and we need to set up the callback a bit differently than we have previously seen with wxWidgets. We will bind a new menu event and callback to the InteractiveRecognizer instance and we will map a keyboard shortcut to the menu event using a class called wx.AcceleratorTable, as shown in the following code. Note, however, that our app actually has no menu, nor is an actual menu item required for the keyboard shortcut to work:

```
quitCommandID = wx.NewId()
self.Bind(wx.EVT_MENU, self._onQuitCommand,
  id=quitCommandID)
acceleratorTable = wx.AcceleratorTable([
  (wx.ACCEL_NORMAL, wx.WXK_ESCAPE, quitCommandID)
])
self.SetAcceleratorTable(acceleratorTable)
```

The following code initializes the GUI widgets (including an image holder, text field, buttons, and label) and sets their event callbacks:

```
self._staticBitmap = wx.StaticBitmap(self, size=size)
self._showImage(None)

self._referenceTextCtrl = wx.TextCtrl(
  self, style=wx.TE_PROCESS_ENTER)
self._referenceTextCtrl.SetMaxLength(4)
self._referenceTextCtrl.Bind(
  wx.EVT_KEY_UP, self._onReferenceTextCtrlKeyUp)

self._predictionStaticText = wx.StaticText(self)
# Insert an endline for consistent spacing.
self._predictionStaticText.SetLabel('\n')

self._updateModelButton = wx.Button(
  self, label='Add to Model')
self._updateModelButton.Bind(
  wx.EVT_BUTTON, self._updateModel)
self._updateModelButton.Disable()

self._clearModelButton = wx.Button(
  self, label='Clear Model')
self._clearModelButton.Bind(
  wx.EVT_BUTTON, self._clearModel)
if not self._recognizerTrained:
  self._clearModelButton.Disable()
```

Similar to Luxocator (the previous chapter's project), Interactive Recognizer lays out the image in the top part of the window and a row of controls in the bottom part of the window. The following code performs the layout:

```
border = 12

controlsSizer = wx.BoxSizer(wx.HORIZONTAL)
controlsSizer.Add(self._referenceTextCtrl, 0,
  wx.ALIGN_CENTER_VERTICAL | wx.RIGHT,
  border)
controlsSizer.Add(
  self._updateModelButton, 0,
  wx.ALIGN_CENTER_VERTICAL | wx.RIGHT, border)
controlsSizer.Add(self._predictionStaticText, 0,
  wx.ALIGN_CENTER_VERTICAL)
controlsSizer.Add((0, 0), 1) # Spacer
```

```
controlsSizer.Add(self._clearModelButton, 0,
  wx.ALIGN_CENTER_VERTICAL)

rootSizer = wx.BoxSizer(wx.VERTICAL)
rootSizer.Add(self._staticBitmap)
rootSizer.Add(controlsSizer, 0, wx.EXPAND | wx.ALL, border)
self.SetSizerAndFit(rootSizer)
```

Finally, the initializer starts a background thread that performs image capture and image processing, including detection and recognition. It is important to perform the intensive computer vision work on a background thread so it does not stall the handling of GUI events. Here is the code that starts the thread:

```
self._captureThread = threading.Thread(
  target=self._runCaptureLoop)
self._captureThread.start()
```

With a variety of input events and background work, InteractiveRecognizer has many methods that run in an indeterminate order. We will look at input event handlers first before proceeding to the image pipeline (capture, processing, and display), which partly runs on the background thread.

When the window is closed, we will ensure that the background thread stops. Then, if the recognition model is trained, we will save it to a file. Here is the implementation of the relevant callback:

```
def _onCloseWindow(self, event):
  self._running = False
  self._captureThread.join()
  if self._recognizerTrained:
    modelDir = os.path.dirname(self._recognizerPath)
    if not os.path.isdir(modelDir):
      os.makedirs(modelDir)
    self._recognizer.save(self._recognizerPath)
  self.Destroy()
```

Besides closing the window when its standard **X** button is clicked, we will also close it in the _onQuitCommand callback, which we had linked to the *Esc* button. Here is this callback's implementation:

```
def _onQuitCommand(self, event):
  self.Close()
```

When the user adds or deletes text in the text field, our `_onReferenceTextCtrlKeyUp` callback, which is as follows, calls a helper method to check whether the **Add to Model** button should be enabled or disabled:

```
def _onReferenceTextCtrlKeyUp(self, event):
    self._enableOrDisableUpdateModelButton()
```

When the **Add to Model** button is clicked, its callback provides new training data to the recognition model. If the LBPH model has no prior training data, we must use the recognizer's `train` method; otherwise, we must use its `update` method. Both methods accept two arguments: a list of images (the faces) and a NumPy array of integers (the faces' identifiers). We will train or update the model with just one image at a time so that the user can interactively test the effect of each incremental change to the model. The image is the most recently detected face and the identifier is converted from the text in the text field using our `BinasciiUtils.fourCharsToInt` function. Here is the code for the implementation of the **Add to Model** button's callback:

```
def _updateModel(self, event):
    labelAsStr = self._referenceTextCtrl.GetValue()
    labelAsInt = BinasciiUtils.fourCharsToInt(labelAsStr)
    src = [self._currDetectedObject]
    labels = numpy.array([labelAsInt])
    if self._recognizerTrained:
        self._recognizer.update(src, labels)
    else:
        self._recognizer.train(src, labels)
        self._recognizerTrained = True
        self._clearModelButton.Enable()
```

When the **Clear Model** button is clicked, its callback deletes the recognition model (including any version that has been saved to the disk) and creates a new one. Also, we will record that the model is untrained and will disable the **Clear Model** button until the model is retrained, as shown in the following code:

```
def _clearModel(self, event=None):
    self._recognizerTrained = False
    self._clearModelButton.Disable()
    if os.path.isfile(self._recognizerPath):
        os.remove(self._recognizerPath)
    self._recognizer = cv2.createLBPHFaceRecognizer()
```

Our background thread runs a loop. On each iteration, we will capture an image using the `VideoCapture` object's `read` method. Along with the image, the `read` method returns a `success` flag, which we do not need because instead, we will just check whether the image is `None`. If the image is not `None`, we will pass it to a helper method called `_detectAndRecognize` and then we can mirror the image for display. We will finish the iteration by passing the image (potentially `None`) to a `_showImage` method, which runs on the main thread (because we invoke the method using `wx.CallAfter`). Here is the implementation of the loop:

```
def _runCaptureLoop(self):
  while self._running:
    success, image = self._capture.read()
    if image is not None:
      self._detectAndRecognize(image)
    if (self.mirrored):
      image[:] = numpy.fliplr(image)
    wx.CallAfter(self._showImage, image)
```

Recall that the loop ends after our `_onCloseWindow` callback sets `_running` to `False`.

The helper method, `_detectAndRecognize`, is also running on the background thread. It begins the process by creating an equalized grayscale version of the image. An **equalized** image has a uniform histogram; every value of gray is equally common. It is a kind of contrast adjustment that makes a subject's appearance more predictable despite different lighting conditions in different images; thus, it aids detection or recognition. We will pass the equalized image to the classifier's `detectMultiScale` method with the `scaleFactor`, `minNeighbors`, `minSize`, and `flags` arguments that were specified during the initialization of `InteractiveRecognizer`. As the return value from `detectMultiScale`, we get a list of rectangle measurements that describe the bounds of the detected faces. For display, we will draw green outlines around these faces. If at least one face is detected, we will store an equalized, grayscale version of the first face in a member variable, `_currDetectedObject`. Here is the implementation of this first portion of the `_detectAndRecognize` method:

```
def _detectAndRecognize(self, image):
  grayImage = cv2.cvtColor(image, cv2.COLOR_BGR2GRAY)
  equalizedGrayImage = cv2.equalizeHist(grayImage)
  rects = self._detector.detectMultiScale(
    equalizedGrayImage, scaleFactor=self._scaleFactor,
    minNeighbors=self._minNeighbors,
    minSize=self._minSize, flags=self._flags)
  for x, y, w, h in rects:
    cv2.rectangle(image, (x, y), (x+w, y+h),
      self._rectColor, 1)
```

```
    if len(rects) > 0:
      x, y, w, h = rects[0]
      self._currDetectedObject = cv2.equalizeHist(
        grayImage[y:y+h, x:x+w])
```

If a face is currently detected and the recognition model is trained for at least one individual, we can proceed to predict the identity of the face. We will pass the equalized face to the `predict` method of the recognizer and get two return values: an integer identifier and a measure of distance (non-confidence). Using our `BinasciiUtils.intToFourChars` function, we will convert the integer to a string (of at most four characters), which will be one of the face names that the user previously entered. We will show the name and distance so that the user can read the recognition result. If an error occurs (for example, if an invalid model was loaded from a file), we will delete and recreate the model. If the model is not yet trained, we will show the instructions about training the model. Here is the implementation of the middle portion of the `_detectAndRecognize` method:

```
    if self._recognizerTrained:
      try:
        labelAsInt, distance = self._recognizer.predict(
          self._currDetectedObject)
        labelAsStr = BinasciiUtils.intToFourChars(
          labelAsInt)
        self._showMessage(
          'This looks most like %s.\n'
          'The distance is %.0f.' % \
          (labelAsStr, distance))
      except cv2.error:
        print >> sys.stderr, \
          'Recreating model due to error.'
        self._clearModel()
    else:
      self._showInstructions()
```

If no face was detected, we will set `_currDetectedObject` to `None` and show either the instructions (if the model is not yet trained) or no descriptive text (otherwise). Under all conditions, we will end the `_detectAndRecognize` method by ensuring that the **Add to Model** button is enabled or disabled, as appropriate. Here is the final portion of the method's implementation:

```
    else:
      self._currDetectedObject = None
      if self._recognizerTrained:
        self._clearMessage()
      else:
```

```
        self._showInstructions()

    self._enableOrDisableUpdateModelButton()
```

The **Add to Model** button should be enabled only when a face is detected and the
text field is non-empty. We can implement this logic in the following manner:

```
def _enableOrDisableUpdateModelButton(self):
    labelAsStr = self._referenceTextCtrl.GetValue()
    if len(labelAsStr) < 1 or \
        self._currDetectedObject is None:
        self._updateModelButton.Disable()
    else:
        self._updateModelButton.Enable()
```

Like in Luxocator (the previous chapter's project), we will show a black image if the
image is None; otherwise, we will convert the image from the OpenCV format and
show it, as follows:

```
def _showImage(self, image):
    if image is None:
        # Provide a black bitmap.
        bitmap = wx.EmptyBitmap(self._imageWidth,
            self._imageHeight)
    else:
        # Convert the image to bitmap format.
        bitmap = WxUtils.wxBitmapFromCvImage(image)
    # Show the bitmap.
    self._staticBitmap.SetBitmap(bitmap)
```

Since we will set the label's text under several different conditions, we will use the
following helper functions to reduce the repetition of code:

```
def _showInstructions(self):
    self._showMessage(
        'When an object is highlighted, type its name\n'
        '(max 4 chars) and click "Add to Model".')

def _clearMessage(self):
    # Insert an endline for consistent spacing.
    self._showMessage('\n')

def _showMessage(self, message):
    wx.CallAfter(self._predictionStaticText.SetLabel, message)
```

Note the use of the `wx.CallAfter` function to ensure that the label is updated on the main thread.

That is all the functionality of Interactive Recognizer. Now, we just need to write the main functions for the two variants of the app, starting with Interactive Human Face Recognizer. Just as we passed arguments to the initializer of `InteractiveRecognizer`, we will provide the app's title and PyInstaller-compatible paths to the relevant detection model and recognition model. We will run the app. Here is the implementation, which we can put in `InteractiveHumanFaceRecognizer.py`:

```python
import wx

from InteractiveRecognizer import InteractiveRecognizer
import PyInstallerUtils


def main():
    app = wx.App()
    recognizerPath = PyInstallerUtils.resourcePath(
        'recognizers/lbph_human_faces.xml')
    cascadePath = PyInstallerUtils.resourcePath(
        # Uncomment the next argument for LBP.
        #'cascades/lbpcascade_frontalface.xml')
        # Uncomment the next argument for Haar.
        'cascades/haarcascade_frontalface_alt.xml')
    interactiveDetector = InteractiveRecognizer(
        recognizerPath, cascadePath,
        title='Interactive Human Face Recognizer')
    interactiveDetector.Show()
    app.MainLoop()


if __name__ == '__main__':
    main()
```

Remember that `cascades/haarcascade_frontalface_alt.xml` or `cascades/lpbcascade_frontalface.xml` needs to be obtained from OpenCV's samples or from this chapter's code bundle. Feel free to test Interactive Human Face Recognizer now!

Our second variant of the app, Interactive Cat Face Recognizer, uses very similar code. We will change the app's title and the paths of the detection and recognition models. Also, we will raise the `minNeighbors` value to 8 to make the detector a little more conservative. (Our cat face detection model turns out to be more prone to false positives than our human face detection model.) Here is the implementation, which we can put in `InteractiveCatFaceRecognizer.py`:

```
import wx

from InteractiveRecognizer import InteractiveRecognizer
import PyInstallerUtils


def main():
    app = wx.App()
    recognizerPath = PyInstallerUtils.resourcePath(
        'recognizers/lbph_cat_faces.xml')
    cascadePath = PyInstallerUtils.resourcePath(
        # Uncomment the next argument for LBP.
        #'cascades/lbpcascade_frontalcatface.xml')
        # Uncomment the next argument for Haar with basic
        # features.
        'cascades/haarcascade_frontalcatface.xml')
        # Uncomment the next argument for Haar with extended
        # features.
        #'cascades/haarcascade_frontalcatface_extended.xml')
    interactiveDetector = InteractiveRecognizer(
        recognizerPath, cascadePath,
        minNeighbors=8,
        title='Interactive Cat Face Recognizer')
    interactiveDetector.Show()
    app.MainLoop()

if __name__ == '__main__':
    main()
```

At this stage, Interactive Cat Face Recognizer will not run properly because `cascades/haarcascade_frontalcatface.xml`, `cascades/haarcascade_frontalcatface_extended.xml`, or `cascades/lpbcascade_frontalcatface.xml` does not exist (unless you copied the prebuilt version from this chapter's code bundle). OpenCV 2.x does not come with any cat detection model, but we will soon create our own! (OpenCV 3.0 and later versions will contain this book's cat detection models!).

Planning the cat detection model

When I said *soon*, I meant in a day or two. Training a Haar cascade takes a lot of processing time. Training an LBP cascade is relatively quick. However, in either case, we need to download some big collections of images before we even start. Settle down with a reliable Internet connection, a power outlet, at least 4 GB of free disk space, and the fastest CPU and biggest RAM you can find. Do not attempt this segment of the project on Raspberry Pi. Keep the computer away from external heat sources or things that might block its fans. My processing time for Haar cascade training was 24 hours (or more for the whisker-friendly version that is sensitive to diagonal patterns), with 100 percent usage on four cores, on a MacBook Pro with a 2.6 GHz Intel Core i7 CPU, and 16 GB RAM.

We will use the following sets of images, which are freely available for research purposes:

- The **PASCAL Visual Object Classes Challenge 2007 (VOC2007)** dataset. VOC2007 contains 10,000 images of diverse subjects against diverse backgrounds and diverse lighting conditions, so it is suitable as the basis of our negative training set. The images come with annotation data, including a count of cats for each image (most often 0). Thus, while building our negative training set, we can easily omit images that contain cats.

- The frontal face dataset from the **California Institute of Technology (Caltech Faces 1999)**. This set contains 450 images of frontal human faces under diverse lighting conditions and against diverse backgrounds. These images make a useful addition to our negative training set because our frontal cat face detector might be deployed in places where frontal human faces are also likely to be present. None of these images contain cats.

- The cat head dataset from Microsoft Research (**Microsoft Cat Dataset 2008**), has 10,000 images of cats against diverse backgrounds and under diverse lighting conditions. The rotation of the cat's head varies but in all cases the nose, mouth, both eyes, and both ears are clearly visible. Thus, we can say that all the images include frontal faces and are suitable for use as our positive training set. Each image comes with annotation data, that indicates coordinates of the center of the mouth, centers of the eyes, and corners of the hollow of the ear (three corners per ear; refer to the following image for a better understanding.) Based on the annotation data, we can straighten and crop the cat's face in order to make the positive training images more similar to each other.

The annotated datasets are generously provided by the following authors, as part of the following websites, events, and publications:

- Frontal face dataset. collected by Markus Weber at California Institute of Technology, 1999. For more details refer to `http://www.vision.caltech.edu/html-files/archive.html`.

- Mark Everingham, Luc Van Gool, Christopher K. I Williams, John Winn, and Andrew Zisserman, VOC2007 Results. For more details refer to `http://www.pascal-network.org/challenges/VOC/voc2007/workshop/index.html`. (Also refer to `http://pascallin.ecs.soton.ac.uk/challenges/VOC/voc2007/`.)

- Weiwei Zhang, Jian Sun, and Xiaoou Tang, "Cat Head Detection - How to Effectively Exploit Shape and Texture Features", *Proc. of European Conf.. Computer Vision*, volume 4, pp. 802-816, 2008. (Also refer to `http://137.189.35.203/WebUI/CatDatabase/catData.html` for more details.)

We will preprocess the images and generate files describing the positive and negative training sets. After preprocessing, all the training images are in the equalized, grayscale format and the positive training images are upright and cropped. The description files conform to certain formats expected by OpenCV's training tools. With the training sets prepared, we will run OpenCV's training tools with appropriate parameters. The output will be a Haar cascade file to detect upright frontal cat faces.

Implementing the training script for the cat detection model

Praline: I've never seen so many aerials in me life. The man told me, their equipment could pinpoint a purr at 400 yards and Eric, being such a happy cat, was a piece of cake.

— The Fish License sketch, Monty Python's Flying Circus, Episode 23 (1970)

This segment of the project uses tens of thousands of files including images, annotation files, scripts, and intermediate and final output of the training process. Let's organize all of this new material by giving our project a subfolder, cascade_training, which will ultimately have the following contents:

- cascade_training/CAT_DATASET_01: The first half of the Microsoft Cat Dataset 2008. Download it from http://137.189.35.203/WebUI/CatDatabase/Data/CAT_DATASET_01.zip and unzip it.

- cascade_training/CAT_DATASET_02: The second half of the Microsoft Cat Dataset 2008. Download it from http://137.189.35.203/WebUI/CatDatabase/Data/CAT_DATASET_02.zip and unzip it.

- cascade_training/faces: The Caltech Faces 1999 dataset. Download it from http://www.vision.caltech.edu/Image_Datasets/faces/faces.tar and decompress it.

- cascade_training/VOC2007: The VOC2007 dataset. Download it from http://pascallin.ecs.soton.ac.uk/challenges/VOC/voc2007/VOCtest_06-Nov-2007.tar and decompress it. Move the VOC2007 folder from the VOCdevkit folder.

- cascade_training/describe.py: A script to preprocess and describe the positive and negative training sets. As output, it creates new images in the dataset directories (as explained in the preceding bullet points) and the text description files (as given in the following bullet points).

- `cascade_training/negative_description.txt`: A generated text file that describes the negative training set.

- `cascade_training/positive_description.txt`: A generated text file that describes the positive training set.

- `cascade_training/train.bat` (in Windows) or `cascade_training/train.sh` (in Mac or Linux): A script to run OpenCV's cascade training tools with appropriate parameters. As input, it uses the text description files (as shown in the preceding bullet points). As output, it generates a binary description file and cascade files (as shown in the following bullet points).

- `cascade_training/binary_description`: A generated binary file that describes the positive training set.

- `cascade_training/lbpcascade_frontalcatface/*.xml`: Intermediate and final results of the LBP cascade training.

- `cascades/lbpcascade_frontalcatface.xml`: A copy of the final result of the LBP cascade training in a location where our apps expect it.

- `cascade_training/haarcascade_frontalcatface/*.xml`: Intermediate and final results of the Haar cascade training.

- `cascades/haarcascade_frontalcatface.xml`: A copy of the final result of the Haar cascade training in a location where our apps expect it.

> Some of the datasets are compressed as TAR files. On Windows, we need to install a tool such as 7-Zip (`http://www.7-zip.org/`) to decompress this format.
>
> For Mac and Linux, this chapter's code bundle contains a script, `cascade_training/download_datasets.sh`, to automate the downloading and decompression of the image datasets. The script depends on `wget`, which comes preinstalled with most Linux distributions. On Mac, `wget` can be installed via MacPorts using the following Terminal command:
>
> `$ sudo port install wget`
>
> To change the script's permissions and execute it, run the following Terminal commands from the `cascade_training` folder:
>
> `$ chmod +x download_datasets.sh`
>
> `$ ./download_datasets.sh`

Once the datasets are downloaded and decompressed to the proper locations, let's write `describe.py`. It needs to start with the following imports:

```
import cv2
import glob
import math
import sys
```

All our source images need some preprocessing to optimize them as training images. We need to save the preprocessed versions, so let's globally define an extension that we will use for these files:

```
outputImageExtension = '.out.jpg'
```

We need to create equalized grayscale images at several points in this script, so let's write the following helper function for this purpose:

```
def equalizedGray(image):
    return cv2.equalizeHist(cv2.cvtColor(
        image, cv2.cv.CV_BGR2GRAY))
```

Similarly, we need to append to the negative description file at more than one point in the script. Each line in the negative description is just an image's path. Let's add the following helper method, which accepts an image path and a file object for the negative description, loads the image and saves an equalized version, and appends the equalized version's path to the description file:

```
def describeNegativeHelper(imagePath, output):
    outputImagePath = '%s%s' % (imagePath, outputImageExtension)
    image = cv2.imread(imagePath)
    # Save an equalized version of the image.
    cv2.imwrite(outputImagePath, equalizedGray(image))
    # Append the equalized image to the negative description.
    print >> output, outputImagePath
```

Now, let's write the `describeNegative` function that calls `describeNegativeHelper`. The process begins by opening a file in write mode so that we can write the negative description. Then, we iterate over all the image paths in the Caltech Faces 1999 set, which contains no cats. We will skip any paths to output images that were written on a previous call of this function. We will pass the remaining image paths, along with the newly opened negative description file to `describeNegativeHelper`, as follows:

```
def describeNegative():
    output = open('negative_description.txt', 'w')
    # Append all images from Caltech Faces 1999, since all are
    # non-cats.
```

```
for imagePath in glob.glob('faces/*.jpg'):
  if imagePath.endswith(outputImageExtension):
    # This file is equalized, saved on a previous run.
    # Skip it.
    continue
  describeNegativeHelper(imagePath, output)
```

The remainder of the `describeNegative` function is responsible for passing relevant file paths from the VOC2007 image set to `describeNegativeHelper`. Some images in VOC2007 do contain cats. An annotation file, `VOC2007/ImageSets/Main/cat_test.txt`, lists image IDs and a flag that indicates whether or not any cats are present in the image. The flag can be -1 (no cats), 0 (one or more cats as background or secondary subjects of the image), or 1 (one or more cats as foreground or foreground subjects of the image). We will parse this annotation data and, if an image contains no cats, we will pass its path and the description file to `describeNegativeHelper`, as follows:

```
# Append non-cat images from VOC2007.
input = open('VOC2007/ImageSets/Main/cat_test.txt', 'r')
while True:
  line = input.readline().rstrip()
  if not line:
    break
  imageNumber, flag = line.split()
  if int(flag) < 0:
    # There is no cat in this image.
    imagePath = 'VOC2007/JPEGImages/%s.jpg' % imageNumber
    describeNegativeHelper(imagePath, output)
```

Now, let's move on to helper functions in order to generate the positive description. When rotating a face to straighten it, we also need to rotate a list of coordinate pairs that represent features of the face. The following helper function accepts such a list along with a center of rotation and angle of rotation, and returns a new list of the rotated coordinate pairs:

```
def rotateCoords(coords, center, angleRadians):
  # Positive y is down so reverse the angle, too.
  angleRadians = -angleRadians
  xs, ys = coords[::2], coords[1::2]
  newCoords = []
  n = min(len(xs), len(ys))
  i = 0
  centerX = center[0]
  centerY = center[1]
  cosAngle = math.cos(angleRadians)
```

```
    sinAngle = math.sin(angleRadians)
    while i < n:
      xOffset = xs[i] - centerX
      yOffset = ys[i] - centerY
      newX = xOffset * cosAngle - yOffset * sinAngle + centerX
      newY = xOffset * sinAngle + yOffset * cosAngle + centerY
      newCoords += [newX, newY]
      i += 1
    return newCoords
```

Next, let's write a long helper function to preprocess a single positive training image. This function accepts two arguments: a list of coordinate pairs (which is named `coords`) and an OpenCV image. Refer back to the image of feature points on a cat face. The numbering of the points signifies their order in a line of annotation data and in `coords`. To begin the function, we will get the coordinates for the eyes and mouth. If the face is upside down (not an uncommon pose in playful or sleepy cats), we will swap our definitions of left and right eyes to be consistent with an upright pose. (In determining whether the face is upside down, we will rely in part on the position of the mouth relative to the eyes.) Then, we will find the angle between the eyes and we will rotate the image such that the face becomes upright. An OpenCV function called `cv2.getRotationMatrix2D` is used to define the rotation and another function called `cv2.warpAffine` is used to apply it. As a result of rotating border regions, some blank regions are introduced into the image. We can specify a fill color for these regions as an argument to `cv2.warpAffine`. We will use 50 percent gray, since it has the least tendency to bias the equalization of the image. Here is the implementation of this first part of the `preprocessCatFace` function:

```
def preprocessCatFace(coords, image):

  leftEyeX, leftEyeY = coords[0], coords[1]
  rightEyeX, rightEyeY = coords[2], coords[3]
  mouthX = coords[4]
  if leftEyeX > rightEyeX and leftEyeY < rightEyeY and \
    mouthX > rightEyeX:
    # The "right eye" is in the second quadrant of the face,
    # while the "left eye" is in the fourth quadrant (from the
    # viewer's perspective.) Swap the eyes' labels in order to
    # simplify the rotation logic.
    leftEyeX, rightEyeX = rightEyeX, leftEyeX
    leftEyeY, rightEyeY = rightEyeY, leftEyeY

  eyesCenter = (0.5 * (leftEyeX + rightEyeX),
```

```
    0.5 * (leftEyeY + rightEyeY))

eyesDeltaX = rightEyeX - leftEyeX
eyesDeltaY = rightEyeY - leftEyeY
eyesAngleRadians = math.atan2(eyesDeltaY, eyesDeltaX)
eyesAngleDegrees = eyesAngleRadians * 180.0 / cv2.cv.CV_PI

# Straighten the image and fill in gray for blank borders.
rotation = cv2.getRotationMatrix2D(
  eyesCenter, eyesAngleDegrees, 1.0)
imageSize = image.shape[1::-1]
straight = cv2.warpAffine(image, rotation, imageSize,
  borderValue=(128, 128, 128))
```

To straighten the image, we will call `rotateCoords` to make the feature coordinates that match the straightened image. Here is the code for this function call:

```
# Straighten the coordinates of the features.
newCoords = rotateCoords(
  coords, eyesCenter, eyesAngleRadians)
```

At this stage, the image and feature coordinates are transformed such that the cat's eyes are level and upright. Next, let's crop the image to eliminate most of the background and to standardize the eyes' position relative to the bounds. Arbitrarily, we will define the cropped face to be a square region, as wide as the distance between the outer base points of the cat's ears. This square is positioned such that half its area lies to the left of the midpoint between the cat's eyes and half lies to the right, 40 percent lies above, and 60 percent lies below. For an ideal frontal cat face, this crop excludes all background regions but includes the eyes, chin, and several fleshy regions: the nose, mouth, and part of the inside of the ears. We will equalize and return the cropped image. Accordingly, the implementation of `preprocessCatFace` proceeds as follows:

```
# Make the face as wide as the space between the ear bases.
# (The ear base positions are specified in the reference
# coordinates.)
w = abs(newCoords[16] - newCoords[6])
# Make the face square.
h = w
# Put the center point between the eyes at (0.5, 0.4) in
# proportion to the entire face.
minX = eyesCenter[0] - w/2
if minX < 0:
  w += minX
  minX = 0
```

```
minY = eyesCenter[1] - h*2/5
if minY < 0:
  h += minY
  minY = 0

# Crop the face.
crop = straight[minY:minY+h, minX:minX+w]
# Convert the crop to equalized grayscale.
crop = equalizedGray(crop)
# Return the crop.
return crop
```

 During cropping, we usually eliminate the blank border region that was introduced during rotation. However, if the cat's face was close to the border of the original image, some of the rotated gray border region might still remain.

The pair of following images is an example of input and output for the `processCatFace` function. First, let's look at the input:

The output is displayed as follows:

To generate the positive description file, we will iterate over all the images in the Microsoft Cat Dataset 2008. For each image, we will parse the cat feature coordinates from the corresponding .cat file and will generate the straightened, cropped, and equalized image by passing the coordinates and original image to our processCatFace function. We will append each processed image's path and measurements to the positive description file. Here is the implementation:

```
def describePositive():
  output = open('positive_description.txt', 'w')
  dirs = ['CAT_DATASET_01/CAT_00',
    'CAT_DATASET_01/CAT_01',
    'CAT_DATASET_01/CAT_02',
    'CAT_DATASET_02/CAT_03',
    'CAT_DATASET_02/CAT_04',
    'CAT_DATASET_02/CAT_05',
    'CAT_DATASET_02/CAT_06']
  for dir in dirs:
    for imagePath in glob.glob('%s/*.jpg' % dir):
      if imagePath.endswith(outputImageExtension):
        # This file is a crop, saved on a previous run.
        # Skip it.
        continue
```

```
# Open the '.cat' annotation file associated with this
# image.
input = open('%s.cat' % imagePath, 'r')
# Read the coordinates of the cat features from the
# file. Discard the first number, which is the number
# of features.
coords = [int(i) for i in input.readline().split()[1:]]
# Read the image.
image = cv2.imread(imagePath)
# Straighten and crop the cat face.
crop = preprocessCatFace(coords, image)
if crop is None:
  print >> sys.stderr, \
    'Failed to preprocess image at %s.' % \
    imagePath
  continue
# Save the crop.
cropPath = '%s%s' % (imagePath, outputImageExtension)
cv2.imwrite(cropPath, crop)
# Append the cropped face and its bounds to the
# positive description.
h, w = crop.shape[:2]
print >> output, cropPath, 1, 0, 0, w, h
```

Here, let's take note of the format of a positive description file. Each line contains a path to a training image followed by a series of numbers that indicate the count of positive objects in the image and the measurements (x, y, width, and height) of rectangles that contains those objects. In our case, there is always one cat face filling the entire cropped image, so we get lines such as the following, which is for a 64 x 64 image:

```
CAT_DATASET_02/CAT_06/00001493_005.jpg.out.jpg 1 0 0 64 64
```

Hypothetically, if the image had two 8 x 8 pixel cat faces in opposite corners, its line in the description file would look like this:

```
CAT_DATASET_02/CAT_06/00001493_005.jpg.out.jpg 2 0 0 8 8 56 56 8 8
```

The main function of `describe.py` simply calls our `describeNegative` and `describePositive` functions, as follows:

```
def main():
  describeNegative()
  describePositive()


if __name__ == '__main__':
  main()
```

Run `describe.py` and then feel free to have a look at the generated files, including `negative_description.txt`, `positive_description.txt`, and the cropped cat faces whose filenames follow the pattern `CAT_DATASET_*/CAT_*/*.out.jpg`.

Next, we will use two command-line tools that come with OpenCV. We will refer to them as `<opencv_createsamples>` and `<opencv_traincascade>` respectively. They are responsible for converting the positive description to a binary format and generating the Haar cascade in an XML format. On Windows, these executables are named `opencv_createsamples.exe` and `opencv_traincascade.exe`. They are located in the following directories, one of which we should add to the system's `Path` variable:

- `<opencv_unzip_destination>\build\x64\vc10\bin` (64-bit, requires Visual C++ 2010 Runtime Redistributable)
- `<opencv_unzip_destination>\build\x64\vc11\bin` (64-bit, requires Visual C++ 2011 Runtime Redistributable)
- `<opencv_unzip_destination>\build\x86\vc10\bin` (32-bit, requires Visual C++ 2010 Runtime Redistributable)
- `<opencv_unzip_destination>\build\x86\vc11\bin` (32-bit, requires Visual C++ 2011 Runtime Redistributable)

On Mac or Linux, the executables are named `opencv_createsamples` and `opencv_traincascade`. They are located in one of the following directories, which should already be in the system's `PATH` variable:

- Mac with MacPorts: `/opt/local/bin`
- Mac with Homebrew: `/opt/local/bin` or `opt/local/sbin`
- Debian Wheezy and its derivatives with my custom installation script: `/usr/local/bin`
- Other Linux setups: `/usr/bin` or `/usr/local/bin`

Many flags can be used to provide arguments to `<opencv_createsamples>` and `<opencv_traincascade>`, as described in the official documentation at `http://docs.opencv.org/doc/user_guide/ug_traincascade.html`. We will use the following flags and values:

- `vec`: This consists of the path to a binary description of the positive training images. This file is generated by `<opencv_createsamples>`.
- `info`: The path to a text description of the positive training images. We generated this file using `describe.py`.
- `bg`: The path to a text description of the negative training images. We generated this file using `describe.py`.

- `num`: The number of positive training images in `info`.

- `numStages`: The number of stages in the cascade. As we discussed earlier that conceptualizing Haar cascades and LBPH, each stage is a test that is applied to a region in an image. If the region passes all tests, it is classified as a frontal cat face (or whatever class of object the positive training set represents). We will use `15` for our project.

- `numPos`: The number of positive training images used in each stage. It should be significantly smaller than `num`. (Otherwise, the trainer will fail, complaining that it has run out of new images to use in new stages.) We will use 90 percent of `num`.

- `numNeg`: The number of negative training images used in each stage. We will use 90 percent of the number of negative training images in `bg`.

- `minHitRate`: The minimum proportion of training images that each stage must classify correctly. A higher proportion implies a longer training time but a better fit between the model and the training data. (A better fit is normally a good thing, though it is possible to **overfit** such that the model does not make correct extrapolations beyond the training data.) We will use `0.999`.

- `featureType`: The type of features used are either `HAAR` (the default) or `LBP`. As discussed in the preceding points, Haar cascades tend to be more reliable but are much slower to train and somewhat slower at runtime.

- mode: The subset of Haar features used. (For LBP, this flag has no effect.) The valid options are BASIC (the default), CORE, and ALL. The CORE option makes the model slower to train and run, but the benefit to this is to make the model sensitive to little dots and thick lines. The ALL option goes further, making the model even slower to train and run but adds sensitivity to the diagonal patterns (whereas BASIC and CORE are only sensitive to horizontal and vertical patterns). The ALL option has nothing to do with detecting nonupright subjects; rather, it relates to detecting subjects that contain diagonal patterns. For example, a cat's whiskers and ears might qualify as diagonal patterns.

Let's write a shell script to run `<opencv_createsamples>` and `<opencv_traincascade>` with the appropriate flags and to copy the resulting Haar cascade to the path where Interactive Cat Face Recognizer expects it. On Windows, let's call our `train.bat` script and implement it as follows:

```
set vec=binary_description
set info=positive_description.txt
set bg=negative_description.txt

REM Uncomment the next 4 variables for LBP training.
REM set featureType=LBP
```

```
REM set data=lbpcascade_frontalcatface\
REM set dst=..\cascades\lbpcascade_frontalcatface.xml
REM set mode=BASIC

REM Uncomment the next 4 variables for Haar training with basic
REM features.
set featureType=HAAR
set data=haarcascade_frontalcatface\
set dst=..\cascades\haarcascade_frontalcatface.xml
set mode=BASIC

REM Uncomment the next 4 variables for Haar training with
REM extended features.
REM set featureType=HAAR
REM set data=haarcascade_frontalcatface_extended\
REM set dst=..\cascades\haarcascade_frontalcatface_extended.xml
REM set mode=ALL

REM Set numPosTotal to be the line count of info.
for /f %c in ('find /c /v "" ^< "%info%"') do set numPosTotal=%c

REM Set numNegTotal to be the line count of bg.
for /f %c in ('find /c /v "" ^< "%bg%"') do set numNegTotal=%c

set /a numPosPerStage=%numPosTotal%*9/10
set /a numNegPerStage=%numNegTotal%*9/10
set numStages=15
set minHitRate=0.999

REM Ensure that the data directory exists and is empty.
if not exist "%data%" (mkdir "%data%") else del /f /q "%data%\*.xml"

opencv_createsamples -vec "%vec%" -info "%info%" -bg "%bg%" ^
  -num "%numPosTotal%"
opencv_traincascade -data "%data%" -vec "%vec%" -bg "%bg%" ^
  -numPos "%numPosPerStage%" -numNeg "%numNegPerStage%" ^
  -numStages "%numStages%" -minHitRate "%minHitRate%" ^
  -featureType "%featureType%" -mode "%mode%"

cp "%data%\cascade.xml" "%dst%"
```

On Mac or Linux, let's call our `train.sh` script instead and implement it as follows:

```sh
#!/bin/sh

vec=binary_description
info=positive_description.txt
bg=negative_description.txt

# Uncomment the next 4 variables for LBP training.
#featureType=LBP
#data=lbpcascade_frontalcatface/
#dst=../cascades/lbpcascade_frontalcatface.xml
#mode=BASIC

# Uncomment the next 4 variables for Haar training with basic
# features.
featureType=HAAR
data=haarcascade_frontalcatface/
dst=../cascades/haarcascade_frontalcatface.xml
mode=BASIC

# Uncomment the next 4 variables for Haar training with
# extended features.
#featureType=HAAR
#data=haarcascade_frontalcatface_extended/
#dst=../cascades/haarcascade_frontalcatface_extended.xml
#mode=ALL

# Set numPosTotal to be the line count of info.
numPosTotal=`wc -l < $info`

# Set numNegTotal to be the line count of bg.
numNegTotal=`wc -l < $bg`

numPosPerStage=$(($numPosTotal*9/10))
numNegPerStage=$(($numNegTotal*9/10))
numStages=15
minHitRate=0.999

# Ensure that the data directory exists and is empty.
```

```
if [ ! -d "$data" ]; then
  mkdir "$data"
else
  rm "$data/*.xml"
fi

opencv_createsamples -vec "$vec" -info "$info" -bg "$bg" \
  -num "$numPosTotal"
opencv_traincascade -data "$data" -vec "$vec" -bg "$bg" \
  -numPos "$numPosPerStage" -numNeg "$numNegPerStage" \
  -numStages "$numStages" -minHitRate "$minHitRate" \
  -featureType "$featureType" -mode "$mode"

cp "$data/cascade.xml" "$dst"
```

The preceding versions of the training script are configured to use basic Haar features and will take a long, long time to run, perhaps more than a day. By commenting out the variables related to a basic Haar configuration and uncommenting the variables related to an LBP configuration, we can cut the training time down to several minutes. As a third alternative, variables for an extended Haar configuration (sensitive to diagonal patterns) are also present but are currently commented out.

When the training is done, feel free to have a look at the generated files, including the following:

- For basic Haar features, `cascades/haarcascade_frontalcatface.xml` and `cascade_training/haarcascade_frontalcatface/*`

- For extended Haar features, `cascades/haarcascade_frontalcatface_extended.xml` and `cascade_training/haarcascade_frontalcatface_extended/*`

- For LBP, `cascades/lbpcascade_frontalcatface.xml` and `cascade_training/lbpcascade_frontalcatface/*`

Finally, let's run `InteractiveCatFaceRecognizer.py` to test our cascade!

Remember that our detector is designed for frontal upright cat faces. The cat should be facing the camera and might need some incentive to hold that pose. For example, you could ask the cat to settle on a blanket or in your lap, and you could pat or comb the cat. Refer to the following screenshot of my colleague, Chancellor Josephine "Little Jo" Antoinette Puddingcat, GRL (Grand Rock of Lambda), sitting for a test.

If you do not have a cat (or even a person) who is willing to participate, then you can simply print a few images of a given cat (or person) from the Web. Use heavy matte paper and hold the print so that it faces the camera. Use prints of some images to train the recognizer and prints of other images to test it.

Our detector is pretty good at finding frontal cat faces. However, I encourage you to experiment further, make it better, and share your results! The current version sometimes mistakes the center of a frontal human face for a frontal cat face. Perhaps we should have used more databases of human faces as negative training images. Alternatively, if we had used faces of several mammal species as positive training images, could we have created a more general mammal face detector? Let me know what you discover!

Planning the Angora Blue app

Angora Blue reuses the same detection and recognition models that we created earlier. It is a relatively linear and simple app because it has no GUI and does not modify any models. It just loads the detection and recognition models from file and then silently runs a camera until a face is recognized with a certain level of confidence. After recognizing a face, the app sends an e-mail alert and exits. To elaborate, we can say the app has the following flow of execution:

1. Load face detection and face recognition models from file for both human and feline subjects.

2. Capture a live video from a camera for each frame of video:

    1. Detect all human faces in the frame. Perform recognition on each human face. If a face is recognized with a certain level of confidence, send an e-mail alert and exit the app.

    2. Detect all cat faces in the frame. Discard any cat faces that intersect with human faces. (We assume that such cat faces are false positives, since our cat detector sometimes mistakes human faces for cat faces.) For each remaining cat face, perform recognition. If a face is recognized with a certain level of confidence, send an e-mail alert and exit the app.

Angora Blue is capable of running on the Raspberry Pi. The Pi's small size makes it a nice platform for a hidden alarm system. Make sure that the Pi or other machine is connected to the Internet in order to send e-mail messages.

Implementing the Angora Blue app

The Angora Blue app uses three new files: `GeomUtils.py`, `MailUtils.py`, and `AngoraBlue.py`, which should all be in our project's top folder. Given the app's dependencies on our previous work, the following files are relevant to Angora Blue:

- `cascades/haarcascade_frontalface_alt.xml`
- `cascades/haarcascade_frontalcatface.xml`
- `recognizers/lbph_human_faces.xml`
- `recognizers/lbph_cat_faces.xml`
- `ResizeUtils.py`: This contains the utility functions to resize images, including camera capture dimensions
- `GeomUtils.py`: This consists of the utility functions used to perform geometric operations
- `MailUtils.py`: This provides the utility functions used to send e-mails
- `AngoraBlue.py`: This is the application that sends an e-mail alert when a person or cat is recognized

First, let's create `GeomUtils.py`. This does not need any import statements. Let's add the following `intersects` function, which accepts two rectangles as arguments and returns either `True` (if they intersect) or `False` (otherwise):

```
def intersects(rect0, rect1):
    x0, y0, w0, h0 = rect0
    x1, y1, w1, h1 = rect1
    if x0 > x1 + w1: # rect0 is wholly to right of rect1
```

```
    return False
  if x1 > x0 + w0: # rect1 is wholly to right of rect0
    return False
  if y0 > y1 + h1: # rect0 is wholly below rect1
    return False
  if y1 > y0 + h0: # rect1 is wholly below rect0
    return False
  return True
```

Using the `intersects` function let's write the following `difference` function, which accepts two lists of rectangles, `rects0` and `rects1`, and returns a new list that contains the rectangles in `rects0` that do not intersect with any rectangle in `rects1`:

```
def difference(rects0, rects1):
  result = []
  for rect0 in rects0:
    anyIntersects = False
    for rect1 in rects1:
      if intersects(rect0, rect1):
        anyIntersects = True
        break
    if not anyIntersects:
      result += [rect0]
  return result
```

Later, we will use the `difference` function to filter out cat faces that intersect with human faces.

Now, let's create `MailUtils.py`. This needs the following import statement:

```
import smtplib
```

For the task of sending an e-mail, let's copy the following function from Rosetta Code, a free wiki that offers utility functions in many programming languages:

```
def sendEmail(fromAddr, toAddrList, ccAddrList, subject, message,
  login, password, smtpServer='smtp.gmail.com:587'):

  # Taken from http://rosettacode.org/wiki/Send_an_email#Python

  header = 'From: %s\n' % fromAddr
  header += 'To: %s\n' % ','.join(toAddrList)
  header += 'Cc: %s\n' % ','.join(ccAddrList)
  header += 'Subject: %s\n\n' % subject
```

```
message = header + message

server = smtplib.SMTP(smtpServer)
server.starttls()
server.login(login,password)
problems = server.sendmail(fromAddr, toAddrList, message)
server.quit()
return problems
```

By default, the `sendEmail` function uses Gmail. By specifying the optional `smtpServer` argument, we can use a different service.

Since July 2014, the default security settings on Google accounts require apps to use not only SMTP authentication, but also OAuth authentication in order to send an e-mail via Gmail. Our `sendEmail` function uses a secure TLS connection, but handles SMTP authentication only (as this is sufficient for most e-mail services other than Gmail). To reconfigure your Google account for compatibility with our function, log in to your account, go to `https://www.google.com/settings/security/lesssecureapps`, select the **Enable** option, and click **Done**. For the best security, you might wish to create a dummy Google account for this project and apply the custom security setting to this dummy account only. Alternatively, most e-mail services besides Gmail should not require special configuration.

Now, we are ready to implement `AngoraBlue.py`. This starts with the following imports:

```
import cv2
import numpy # Hint to PyInstaller
import os
import socket
import sys

import BinasciiUtils
import GeomUtils
import MailUtils
import PyInstallerUtils
import ResizeUtils
```

Angora Blue simply uses a `main` function and one helper function, `recognizeAndReport`. This helper function begins as follows, by iterating over a given list of face rectangles and using a given recognizer (be it a human recognizer or a cat recognizer) to get a label and distance (non-confidence) for each face:

```
def recognizeAndReport(recognizer, grayImage, rects, maxDistance,
    noun='human'):
  for x, y, w, h in rects:
    crop = cv2.equalizeHist(grayImage[y:y+h, x:x+w])
    labelAsInt, distance = recognizer.predict(crop)
    labelAsStr = BinasciiUtils.intToFourChars(labelAsInt)
```

For testing, it is useful to log the recognition results here. However, we will comment out the logging in the final version, as follows:

```
#print noun, labelAsStr, distance
```

If any of the faces is recognized with a certain level of confidence (based on a `maxDistance` argument), we will attempt to send an e-mail alert. If the alert is sent successfully, the function returns `True`, meaning it did recognize and report a face. Otherwise, it returns `False`. Here is the remainder of the implementation:

```
    if distance <= maxDistance:
      fromAddr = 'username@gmail.com' # TODO: Replace
      toAddrList = ['username@gmail.com'] # TODO: Replace
      ccAddrList = []
      subject = 'Angora Blue'
      message = 'We have sighted the %s known as %s.' % \
        (noun, labelAsStr)
      login = 'username' # TODO: Replace
      password = 'password' # TODO: Replace
      # TODO: Replace if not using Gmail.
      smtpServer='smtp.gmail.com:587'
    try:
      problems = MailUtils.sendEmail(
        fromAddr, toAddrList, ccAddrList, subject,
        message, login, password, smtpServer)
      if problems:
        print >> sys.stderr, 'Email problems:', problems
      else:
        return True
    except socket.gaierror:
    print >> sys.stderr, 'Unable to reach email server'
  return False
```

The main function starts by defining paths to the detection and recognition models. If either recognition model does not exist (because it has not been trained), we will print an error and exit, as follows:

```
def main():

    humanCascadePath = PyInstallerUtils.resourcePath(
        # Uncomment the next argument for LBP.
        #'cascades/lbpcascade_frontalface.xml')
        # Uncomment the next argument for Haar.
        'cascades/haarcascade_frontalface_alt.xml')
    humanRecognizerPath = PyInstallerUtils.resourcePath(
        'recognizers/lbph_human_faces.xml')
    if not os.path.isfile(humanRecognizerPath):
        print >> sys.stderr, \
        'Human face recognizer not trained. Exiting.'
        return
    catCascadePath = PyInstallerUtils.resourcePath(
        # Uncomment the next argument for LBP.
        #'cascades/lbpcascade_frontalcatface.xml')
        # Uncomment the next argument for Haar with basic
        # features.
        'cascades/haarcascade_frontalcatface.xml')
        # Uncomment the next argument for Haar with extended
        # features.
        #'cascades/haarcascade_frontalcatface_extended.xml')
    catRecognizerPath = PyInstallerUtils.resourcePath(
        'recognizers/lbph_cat_faces.xml')
    if not os.path.isfile(catRecognizerPath):
        print >> sys.stderr, \
            'Cat face recognizer not trained. Exiting.'
        return
```

As in Interactive Recognizer, we will start capturing video from a camera and we will store the video's resolution in order to calculate the relative, minimum size of a face. Here is the relevant code:

```
capture = cv2.VideoCapture(0)
imageWidth, imageHeight = \
    ResizeUtils.cvResizeCapture(capture, (1280, 720))
minImageSize = min(imageWidth, imageHeight)
```

We will load detectors and recognizers from the file and set a minimum face size for detection and maximum distance (non-confidence) for recognition. We will specify the values separately for human and feline subjects. You might need to tweak the values based on your particular camera setup and models. The code proceeds as follows:

```
humanDetector = cv2.CascadeClassifier(humanCascadePath)
humanRecognizer = cv2.createLBPHFaceRecognizer()
humanRecognizer.load(humanRecognizerPath)
humanMinSize = (int(minImageSize * 0.25),
   int(minImageSize * 0.25))
humanMaxDistance = 10

catDetector = cv2.CascadeClassifier(catCascadePath)
catRecognizer = cv2.createLBPHFaceRecognizer()
catRecognizer.load(catRecognizerPath)
catMinSize = humanMinSize
catMaxDistance = 10
```

We will read frames from the camera continuously, until an e-mail alert is sent as a result of face recognition. Each frame is converted to grayscale and is equalized. Next, we will detect and recognize human faces and possibly send an alert, as follows:

```
while True:
  success, image = capture.read()
  if image is not None:
    grayImage = cv2.cvtColor(image, cv2.COLOR_BGR2GRAY)
    equalizedGrayImage = cv2.equalizeHist(grayImage)

    humanRects = humanDetector.detectMultiScale(
      equalizedGrayImage, scaleFactor=1.3,
      minNeighbors=4, minSize=humanMinSize,
      flags=cv2.cv.CV_HAAR_SCALE_IMAGE)
    if recognizeAndReport(
      humanRecognizer, grayImage, humanRects,
      humanMaxDistance, 'human'):
      break
```

If no alert has been sent, we will continue to perform cat detection and recognition. For cat detection, we will make extra efforts to eliminate false positives by specifying a higher minNeighbors value and by filtering out any cat faces that intersect human faces. Here is this final part of Angora Blue's implementation:

```
catRects = catDetector.detectMultiScale(
  equalizedGrayImage, scaleFactor=1.3,
```

```
          minNeighbors=8, minSize=catMinSize,
          flags=cv2.cv.CV_HAAR_SCALE_IMAGE)
     # Reject any cat faces that overlap with human faces.
        catRects = GeomUtils.difference(catRects, humanRects)
     if recognizeAndReport(
        catRecognizer, grayImage, catRects,
        catMaxDistance, 'cat'):
     break

if __name__ == '__main__':
  main()
```

Before testing Angora Blue, ensure that the two recognition models are trained using Interactive Human Face Recognizer and Interactive Cat Face Recognizer. Preferably, each model should contain two or more individuals. Then, set up a computer and webcam in a place where frontal human faces and frontal cat faces will be encountered. Try to get your friends and pets to participate in the following test cases:

- A human, who is unknown to the model looks into the camera. Nothing should happen. If you get an e-mail alert, increase `humanMaxDistance` and try again.

- A cat, who is unknown to the model looks into the camera. Nothing should happen. If you get an e-mail alert, increase `catMaxDistance` and try again.

- A human, who is known to the model looks into the camera. You should get an e-mail alert. If not, decrease `humanMaxDistance` or rerun Interactive Human Face Recognizer to add more samples of the given human face. Try Angora Blue again.

- A cat, who is known to the model looks into the camera. You should get an e-mail alert. If not, decrease `catMaxDistance` or rerun Interactive Cat Face Recognizer to add more samples of the given cat face. Try Angora Blue again.

 Again, if you do not have enough human or feline volunteers, just get some heavy, matte paper and print faces from the Web. Hold a print so that it is visible (and upright) from the camera's perspective but ensure that you stay out of the view so that the recognizer runs only on the print, and not on you.

Once the recognition model and Angora Blue are tweaked, we are ready to deploy our alarm system to a vast network of webcam-enabled computers! Let the search for the blue-eyed Angora begin!

Building Angora Blue for distribution

We can use PyInstaller to bundle Angora Blue along with the detection and recognition models for distribution. Since the build scripts should be quite similar to the ones we used for Luxocator (the previous chapter's project), we will not discuss their implementation here. However, they are included in this chapter's code bundle.

Further fun with finding felines

Kittydar (short for "kitty radar"), by Heather Arthur, is an open source, JavaScript library used to detect upright frontal cat faces. You can find its demo application at `http://harthur.github.io/kittydar/` and its source code at `https://github.com/harthur/kittydar`.

Another detector for upright frontal cat faces was developed by Microsoft Research using the Microsoft Cat Dataset 2008. The detector is described in the following research paper but no demo application or source code has been released:

- Weiwei Zhang, Jian Sun, and Xiaoou Tang. "Cat Head Detection - How to Effectively Exploit Shape and Texture Features", *Proc. of European Conference Computer Vision*, vol. 4, pp. 802-816, 2008.

If you know of other works on cat detectors, recognizers, or datasets, please write to me to tell me about them!

Summary

Like the previous chapter, this chapter has dealt with classification tasks, as well as interfaces among OpenCV, a source of images, and a GUI. This time, our classification labels have more objective meanings (a species or an individual's identity), so the classifier's success or failure is more obvious. To meet the challenge, we used much bigger sets of training images, we preprocessed the training images for greater consistency, and we applied two tried-and-true classification techniques in the sequence (either Haar cascades or LBP cascades for detection and then LBPH for recognition).

The methodology presented in this chapter, as well as in the entire Interactive Recognizer app and some of the other code, generalizes well with other original works in detection and recognition. With the right training images, you can detect and recognize many more animals in many poses. You can even detect an object such as a car and recognize the Batmobile!

For our next project, we turn our attention to a moving target, literally. We will try to detect a person who is in motion and then recognize particular gestures.

4

Controlling a Phone App with Your Suave Gestures

You've got all the moves.

— Lani Hall, Never Say Never Again (1983)

He raises an eyebrow; he lowers his chin; he twists the corners of his mouth; he folds one arm into the crook of the other as he points his pistol at the ceiling. It all looks very impressive, but is he simply dithering while trying to remember people's names?

Agent 007 has a few old friends with normal names, such as Bill Tanner and Felix Leiter. Almost every other name is a number, a single letter, a mash-up of multiple languages, or a blindingly obvious double entendre. After a few vodka martinis and tranquilizer darts, any man would start to wonder whether his memory for names was playing tricks on him.

To put such doubts to rest, we will develop an Android app that determines a person's name based on a series of yes/no questions. To allow a secret agent to use it discretely, the app will rely on gesture controls and audio output, which can go to a Bluetooth headset so that others cannot hear.

The app's logic is like the parlor game, Twenty Questions. First, the app asks a question by playing an audio clip. Then, the user responds with a nod or a shake of the head. Each question is more specific than the last, until the app is ready to guess a name or give up. Recognizing the two possible head gestures—a nod or a shake—is our computer vision task for this chapter.

The app's codename is *Goldgesture*.

 The completed project for this chapter can be downloaded from my website at http://nummist.com/opencv/7376_04.zip.

Planning the Goldgesture app

Goldgesture is a GUI app built with the Android SDK and OpenCV's Java bindings for Android. It has just a single view, as shown in the screenshot on the next page. The app has the following flow of execution:

1. The app constantly displays a live video feed from the front-facing (self-portrait) camera.

2. It performs human face detection using OpenCV's CascadeClassifier class.

3. When a human face is detected:

    1. It draws a blue rectangle around the face.

    2. It detects features of the face (points that should be easy to track in subsequent frames despite movement) using OpenCV's goodFeaturesToTrack function. It then draws green circles around these features.

4. As the face moves, the app tracks the features in every frame using OpenCV's calcOpticalFlowPyrLK function. This function can continuously track the features even though CascadeClassifier is unlikely to continuously detect a face.

5. When the features' center point moves up and down by a certain amount and a certain number of times, the app deems that a nod has occurred.

6. When the features' center point moves left and right by a certain amount and a certain number of times, the app deems that a shake of the head has occurred.

7. The app plays a sequence of audio clips. At each juncture, it chooses the next clip depending (in part) on whether a nod or shake of the head has occurred.

8. The app resets the tracking when its reliability deteriorates to a certain extent or when the user's head appears to be nodding and shaking at the same time.

The face detection functionality in Goldgesture should already be familiar to you from last chapter's project, *Angora Blue*. However, feature tracking, and specifically **optical flow**, is a new topic for us. Let's talk about the concepts a little before proceeding to set up our project.

Understanding optical flow

Optical flow is the pattern of apparent motion between two consecutive frames of video. We will select feature points in the first frame and try to determine where those features have gone in the second frame. This search is subject to a few caveats:

- We will make no attempt to distinguish between camera motion and subject motion.
- We assume that a feature's color or brightness remains similar between frames.
- We assume that neighboring pixels have a similar motion.

OpenCV's `calcOpticalFlowPyrLK` function implements the Lucas-Kanade method of computing optical flow. Lucas-Kanade relies on a 3 x 3 neighborhood (that is, 9 pixels) around each feature. Taking each feature's neighborhood from the first frame, we will try to find the best matching neighborhood in the second frame, based on the least squared error. OpenCV's implementation of Lucas-Kanade uses an image pyramid, meaning it performs the search at various scales. Thus, it supports large or small motions alike. `PyrLk` in the function name stands for *pyramidal Lucas-Kanade*. The following figure is a visualization of an image pyramid—a progression from low-resolution (or low-magnification) images to high-resolution (or high-magnification) images:

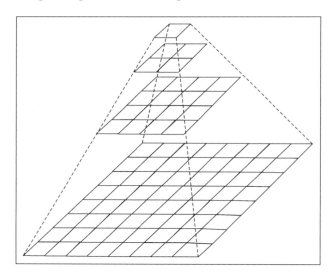

For more details on optical flow and the Lucas-Kanade method, see the official OpenCV documentation at http://docs.opencv.org/trunk/ doc/py_tutorials/py_video/py_lucas_kanade/py_lucas_ kanade.html.

OpenCV offers implementations of other optical flow algorithms as well. For example, the calcOpticalFlowSF function implements the SimpleFlow algorithm, which makes optimizations for high-resolution video by assuming that pixels in a smooth (uniform) image region move in unison. The calcOpticalFlowFarneback function implements Gunnar Farneback's algorithm, which posits that a neighborhood remains identifiable, even during motion, by the coefficients of a polynomial relationship among its pixel values. Both of these algorithms are forms of **dense** optical flow, meaning that they analyze every pixel in the image instead of just the selected (**sparse**) features. All of OpenCV's optical flow functions are documented at http://docs.opencv.org/modules/ video/doc/motion_analysis_and_object_tracking.html.

Of the several options, why choose calcOpticalFlowPyrLK? "You see, it is a pyramid," as Imhotep said to the Pharaoh Djoser, "and it has open spaces inside it." Hence, a pyramidal, sparse technique is a good way for us to cheaply and robustly track a few features in a face, which can change scale as it moves nearer or farther.

For our purposes, it is useful to select features inside a detected object, specifically a detected face. We will choose an inner portion of the face (to avoid background regions) and then use an OpenCV function called goodFeaturesToTrack, which selects features based on the algorithm described in the following paper:

Jianbo Shi and Carlo Tomasi, "Good Features to Track", *Proc. of IEEE Conf. on Computer Vision and Pattern Recognition*, pp. 593-600, June 1994.

As the name suggests, the Good Features to Track algorithm (also known as the Shi-Tomasi algorithm) attempts to select features that work well with the algorithms of tracking and the use cases of tracking. As described in detail in the paper, Good Features to Track must have a stable appearance with respect to small changes in the camera's perspective. Examples of poor features to track are reflections (such as sunlight on a car's hood) and lines crossing at different depths (such as a tree's branches), since these features move quickly as the viewer or camera moves. The effects of a change in perspective can be simulated (albeit imperfectly) by warping a given image and moving its contents linearly. Based on such a simulation, the most stable features can be selected.

OpenCV offers implementations of several more feature detection algorithms, besides Good Features to Track. Two of the other algorithms, called minimum eigenvalue corners and Harris corners, are precursors to Good Features to Track, which improves upon them. An official tutorial illustrates the relationship among them in a code sample at `http://docs.opencv.org/doc/tutorials/features2d/ trackingmotion/generic_corner_detector/generic_corner_ detector.html`.

Some of the more advanced feature detection algorithms in OpenCV are named FAST, ORB, SIFT, SURF, and FREAK. Compared to Good Features to Track, these more advanced alternatives evaluate a much larger set of potential features, at a much greater computational cost. They are overkill for a basic optical flow task such as ours. Once we have detected a face, we do not need many features in this region in order to distinguish between vertical motion (nodding) and horizontal motion (shaking). For our gesture recognition task, running at a fast frame rate is far more important than running with a large number of features. On the other hand, some computer vision tasks require a large number of features. Image recognition is a good example. If we put red lipstick on a poster of the *Mona Lisa*, the resulting image is not the *Mona Lisa* (or at least not Leonardo's version of her). An image's details can be considered fundamental to its identity. However, a change in lighting or perspective does not change an image's identity, so the feature detection and matching system still needs to be robust with respect to some changes.

For a project in image recognition and tracking, refer to *Chapter 4, Recognizing and Tracking Images,* and *Chapter 5, Combining Image Tracking with 3D Rendering,* of my book, *Android Application Programming with OpenCV,* by Packt Publishing.

For benchmarks of several feature detectors and matchers in OpenCV, refer to the series of articles on Ievgen Khvedchenia's blog, including `http://computer-vision-talks.com/articles/2011-07-13- comparison-of-the-opencv-feature-detection-algorithms/`.

For tutorials on several algorithms and their OpenCV implementations, refer to the *Feature Detection and Description* section of the OpenCV-Python Tutorials by Alexander Mordvintsev and Abid Rahman K at `http:// opencv-python-tutroals.readthedocs.org/en/latest/py_ tutorials/py_feature2d/py_table_of_contents_feature2d/ py_table_of_contents_feature2d.html`.

Setting up the Eclipse Workspace

 For a refresher on installing Eclipse and OpenCV as part of TADP, refer to the section *Tegra Android Development Pack* in *Chapter 1*, *Preparing for the Mission*. The same section also contains instructions for building and running OpenCV's Android demos.

To keep things organized, we should create a new Eclipse Workspace for our Android project. Start Eclipse. Eclipse might automatically open a **Workspace Launcher** window, where you can select a directory for a new workspace. Alternatively, you can open a **Workspace Launcher** window, as shown in the following screenshot, by going to **File | Switch Workspace | Other...**:

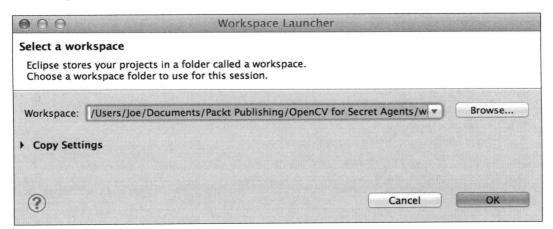

Click on the **Browse...** button and select a root folder for our projects, as shown in the preceding screenshot. We will use Eclipse to create individual project folders under this root folder.

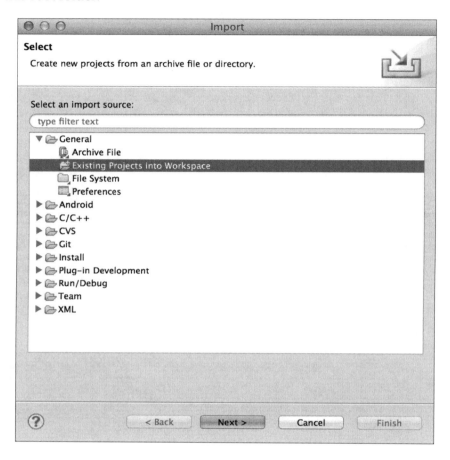

Since our apps will depend on OpenCV, we need to import the OpenCV library project that we obtained with TADP in *Chapter 1, Preparing for the Mission*. Go to **File | Import...**. From the **Import** window shown in the preceding screenshot, select **General | Existing Projects into Workspace** and click on the **Next >** button.

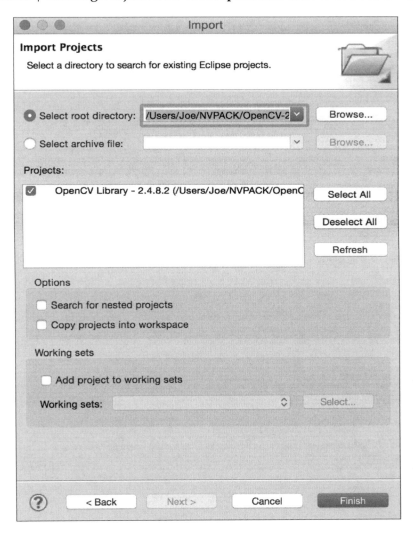

Next to the **Select root directory** field, click on the **Browse...** button and select the root folder of the OpenCV library project. Remember TADP's installation path, which we refer to as `<tadp>`. By default, `<tadp>` is `C:\NVPACK` (in Windows) or `~/NVPACK` (in Mac and Linux). The path to the OpenCV library project is `<tadp>/OpenCV-2.4.8.2-Tegra-sdk/sdk/java`, assuming the version is 2.4.8.2 (the latest at the time of writing). After selecting the path, ensure that the checkbox next to the **OpenCV Library – 2.8.4.2** project is checked and click on the **Finish** button, as shown in the preceding screenshot.

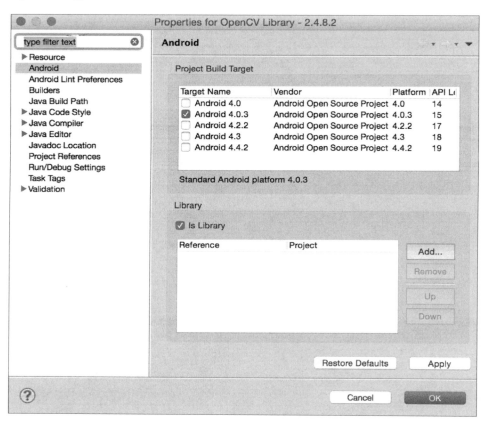

Right-click on the **OpenCV Library – 2.4.8.2** folder in the **Package Explorer** pane and select **Properties** from the context menu. Select the **Android** section and ensure that the **Is Library** checkbox is checked, as shown in the preceding screenshot. For the build target, ensure that a recent Android version is checkmarked. Generally, the latest stable Android version should be a safe choice, and particularly for OpenCV 2.4.x, Android 4.0+ should work. Regardless of the selected build target, OpenCV 2.4.x is built for backward compatibility with Android 2.2+. After reviewing the settings and making changes if needed, click on the **OK** button.

Now, we are ready to create the Eclipse project for Goldgesture. Go to **File | New | Android Application Project**. This opens the **New Android Application** window as shown in the following screenshot:

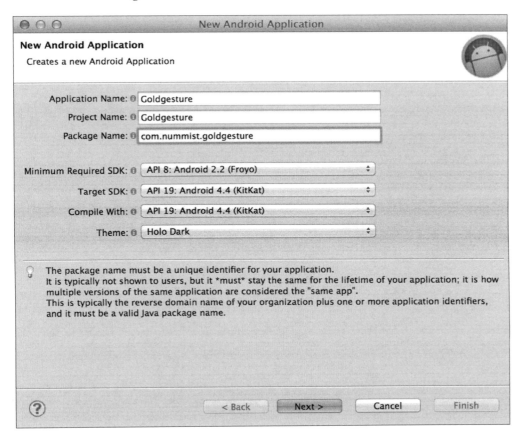

Our app name is `Goldgesture`, its package name is `com.nummist.goldgesture`, and its minimum Android SDK version is API level 8, which is Android 2.2 (as required by OpenCV 2.4.x). The app should target and be compiled with the latest stable Android SDK version. Configure the first form in the **New Android Application** window as shown in the preceding screenshot. Click the first form's **Next >** button. A new form appears, as shown in the following screenshot:

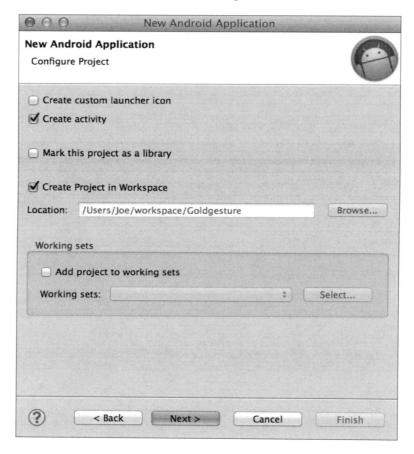

Uncheck the **Create custom launcher item** checkbox and click on the **Next >** button, as shown in the preceding screenshot. Now, select **Blank Activity** and click on the **Next >** button, as shown in the following screenshot:

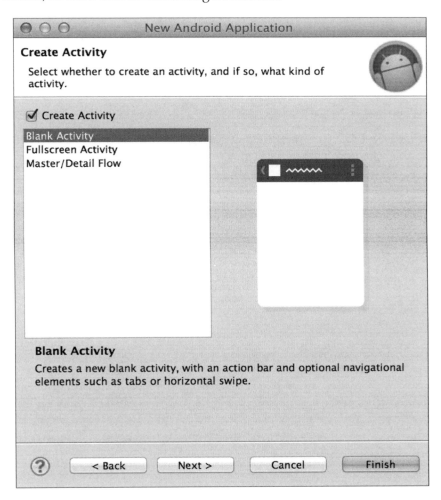

For the final form, enter `CameraActivity` in the **Activity Name** field. Click on the **Finish** button as shown in the following screenshot:

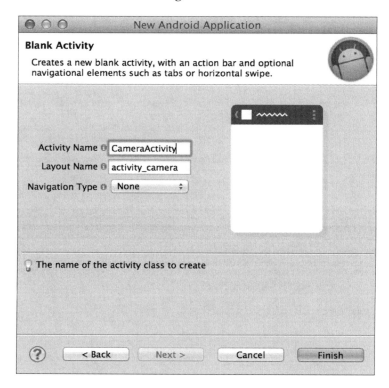

The Goldgesture project is created, but we still need to specify its dependency on the OpenCV library project. Right-click on the `Goldgesture` folder in the **Package Explorer** pane and select **Properties** from the context menu. Now, select the **Android** section and click on the **Add...** button next to the **Library** list, as shown in the following screenshot:

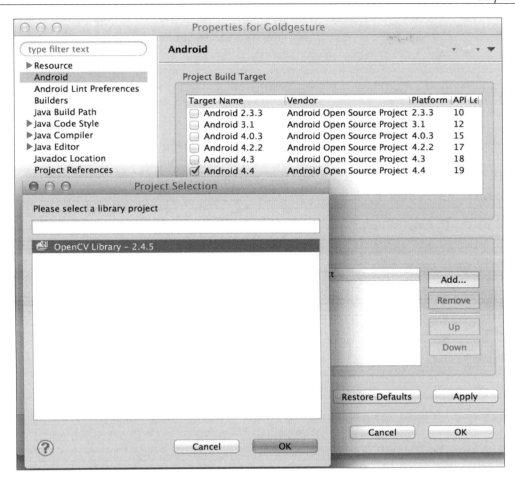

Then, select **OpenCV Library – 2.4.5**. Click on the **OK** buttons. The OpenCV library is now linked with Goldgesture.

Getting a cascade file and audio files

Like parts of the last chapter's project, Goldgesture performs human face detection and requires one of the cascade files that comes with OpenCV. Also, Goldgesture uses audio clips. Download the cascade file and audio clips from `http://nummist.com/opencv/7376_04_res.zip` and extract them to the project's `res/raw` folder. This folder is a location for files that we want bundled with the Android app in their raw (unmodified) form.

The audio clips are generated using the "Vicki" voice of the standard text-to-speech synthesizer on Mac. For example, one of the clips is created by running the following command in Terminal:

```
$ say -v Vicki -o win_007.mp4 'You are 007! I win!'
```

Speech synthesis is hours of fun for the whole family.

> The Mac speech synthesizer pronounces "007" as "double-O seven". This is an anomaly. For example, "008" is pronounced as "zero, zero, eight".

Specifying the app's requirements

The `AndroidManifest.xml` file (the **Android Manifest**) is the place where an app announces information that the system, Google Play, and other apps might need to know. For example, Goldgesture requires a front-facing camera and permission to use it (a license to shoot, one might say). Goldgesture also expects to run in landscape mode regardless of the physical orientation of the phone, because OpenCV's camera preview always uses the camera's landscape dimensions. (OpenCV's Android documentation does not indicate whether this behavior is intended. Perhaps future versions will provide better support for portrait orientation.) To specify these requirements, edit `AndroidManifest.xml` to match the following sample:

> When you open `AndroidManifest.xml` in Eclipse, you might see a form titled **Android Manifest**. To edit the source code directly instead of using the form, click on the **AndroidManifest.xml** tab below the form.

```
<?xml version="1.0" encoding="utf-8"?>
<manifest xmlns:android="http://schemas.android.com/apk/res/android"
  package="com.nummist.goldgesture"
  android:versionCode="1"
```

```
android:versionName="1.0" >

<uses-sdk
  android:minSdkVersion="8"
android:targetSdkVersion="19" />
<uses-permission android:name="android.permission.CAMERA" />

<uses-feature android:name="android.hardware.camera.front" />

<application
  android:allowBackup="true"
  android:icon="@drawable/ic_launcher"
  android:label="@string/app_name"
  android:theme="@style/AppTheme">
  <activity
    android:name="com.nummist.goldgesture.CameraActivity"
    android:label="@string/app_name"
    android:screenOrientation="landscape"
    android:theme="@android:style/Theme.NoTitleBar.Fullscreen">
    <intent-filter>
      <action android:name="android.intent.action.MAIN" />
      <category android:name=
        "android.intent.category.LAUNCHER" />
    </intent-filter>
  </activity>
</application>

</manifest>
```

Now, our app can use a camera and will remain in landscape mode. Also, if we publish it on Google Play, it will only be available to devices with a front-facing camera.

Laying out a camera preview as the main view

Android, like many systems, enables the programmer to specify GUI layouts in XML files. Our Java code can load an entire view or pieces of it from these XML files.

Goldgesture has a simple layout that contains only a camera preview on which we will draw some additional graphics using OpenCV. The camera preview is represented by an OpenCV class called `JavaCameraView`. Let's edit `res/layout/activity_camera.xml` to fill the layout with `JavaCameraView`, using the front-facing camera, as follows:

```xml
<?xml version="1.0" encoding="utf-8"?>
<LinearLayout
    xmlns:android="http://schemas.android.com/apk/res/android"
    xmlns:opencv="http://schemas.android.com/apk/res-auto"
    android:layout_width="match_parent"
    android:layout_height="match_parent" >

    <org.opencv.android.JavaCameraView
    android:layout_width="fill_parent"
    android:layout_height="fill_parent"
    android:id="@+id/camera_view"
    opencv:camera_id="front" />

</LinearLayout>
```

Alternatively, OpenCV also provides a class called `NativeCameraView`. Both `JavaCameraView` and `NativeCameraView` are implementations of an interface called `CameraBridgeViewBase`. The difference is that `NativeCameraView` accesses the camera via a lower-level API, which yields a higher frame rate but is often broken/not working on new devices and/or new versions of Android.

Tracking back and forth gestures

Several common gestures consist of a repetitive, back and forth movement. Consider the following examples of this type of gesture:

- Nodding (yes or I'm listening)
- Shaking one's head (no or dismay)
- Waving (a greeting)
- Shaking hands (a greeting)
- Shaking one's fist (a threat or a protest)
- Wagging a finger (scolding)
- Wiggling a finger or fingers (beckoning)
- Tapping one's foot against the ground (impatience)
- Tapping four fingers against a table (impatience)

- Tapping two fingers against a table ("Thanks for the green tea")
- Pacing (anxiety)
- Jumping up and down (excitement, joy)

To help us recognize such gestures, let's write a class, `BackAndForthGesture`, which keeps track of the number of times that a value (such as an x coordinate or a y coordinate) has oscillated between a low threshold and a high threshold. A certain number of oscillations can be considered as a complete gesture.

Create a file, `src/BackAndForthGesture.java`. As a member variable, `BackAndForthGesture` will store the minimum distance or threshold that defines a back or forth motion, an initial position, the latest delta from this position, and counts of the number of back movements and forth movements. Here is the first part of the class's code:

```
package com.nummist.goldgesture;

public final class BackAndForthGesture {

    private double mMinDistance;

    private double mStartPosition;
    private double mDelta;

    private int mBackCount;
    private int mForthCount;
```

The back and forth count (or number of oscillations) is the lesser of the back count and the forth count. Let's implement this rule in the following getter method:

```
public int getBackAndForthCount() {
    return Math.min(mBackCount, mForthCount);
}
```

The constructor takes one argument, the minimum distance or the threshold of movement:

```
public BackAndForthGesture(final double minDistance) {
    mMinDistance = minDistance;
}
```

To begin tracking movement, we will call a `start` method with an initial position as an argument. This method records the initial position and resets the delta and counts:

```
public void start(final double position) {
    mStartPosition = position;
    mDelta = 0.0;
    mBackCount = 0;
    mForthCount = 0;
}
```

 Note that we are considering position as a one-dimensional value because a head nodding (up and down) or shaking (left and right) is a linear gesture. For an upright head, only one of the image's two dimensions is relevant to a nod or shake gesture.

To continue tracking movement, we will call an `update` method with the new position as an argument. This method recalculates the delta and, if a threshold has just been passed, the back count or the forth count is incremented:

```
public void update(final double position) {
    double lastDelta = mDelta;
    mDelta = position - mStartPosition;
    if (lastDelta < mMinDistance &&
        mDelta >= mMinDistance) {
      mForthCount++;
    } else if (lastDelta > -mMinDistance &&
        mDelta < -mMinDistance) {
      mBackCount++;
    }
}
```

If we consider the gesture complete, or for some other reason we believe the counts to be invalid, we will call a `resetCounts` method:

```
public void resetCounts() {
    mBackCount = 0;
    mForthCount = 0;
  }
}
```

Note that `BackAndForthGesture` contains no computer vision functionality of its own, but the position values we pass to it will be derived from computer vision.

Playing audio clips as questions and answers

The logic of the question and answer sequence is another component that has no computer vision functionality. We will encapsulate it in a class called YesNoAudioTree, which is responsible for playing the next audio clip whenever the app's computer vision component notifies it of a "Yes" or "No" answer.

 Remember to download the audio clips and other resources from http://nummist.com/opencv/7376_04_res.zip and extract them to the project's res/raw folder. However, note that the audio clips in this download are by no means an exhaustive set of questions and guesses about characters in the Bond franchise. Feel free to add your own clips and your own logic for playing them.

Create a file, src/YesNoAudioTree.java. Our YesNoAudioTree class needs member variables to store a media player and a related context, an ID for the most recently played audio clip, and information gathered from the answers to the previous questions. Specifically, the next question depends on whether the unknown person is already identified as a member of MI6, the CIA, the KGB, or a criminal organization. This information, along with the answer to the most recent question, will be enough for us to build a simple tree of questions in order to identify several characters from the Bond franchise. The class's implementation begins as follows:

```
package com.nummist.goldgesture;

import android.content.Context;
import android.media.MediaPlayer;
import android.media.MediaPlayer.OnCompletionListener;

public final class YesNoAudioTree {

    private enum Affiliation { UNKNOWN, MI6, CIA, KGB, CRIMINAL }

    private int mLastAudioResource;
    private Affiliation mAffiliation;

    private Context mContext;
    private MediaPlayer mMediaPlayer;
```

The class is instantiated with `Context`, which is a standard abstraction of the app's Android environment:

```
public YesNoAudioTree(final Context context) {
  mContext = context;
}
```

The `context` object is needed later to create a media player.

 For more information about the Android SDK's `MediaPlayer` class, refer to the official documentation at `http://developer.android.com/reference/android/media/MediaPlayer.html`.

To (re)start from the first question, we will call a `start` method. It resets the data about the person and plays the first audio clip using a private helper method, `play`:

```
public void start() {
  mAffiliation = Affiliation.UNKNOWN;
  play(R.raw.intro);
}
```

To stop any current clip and clean up the audio player (for example, when the app pauses or finishes), we will call a `stop` method:

```
public void stop() {
  if (mMediaPlayer != null) {
    mMediaPlayer.release();
  }
}
```

When the user has answered "Yes" to a question, we will call the `takeYesBranch` method. It uses nested `switch` statements to pick the next audio clip based on the previous answers and the most recent question:

```
public void takeYesBranch() {

  if (mMediaPlayer != null && mMediaPlayer.isPlaying()) {
    // Do not interrupt the audio that is already playing.
    return;
  }

  switch (mAffiliation) {
  case UNKNOWN:
    switch (mLastAudioResource) {
    case R.raw.q_mi6:
```

```
      mAffiliation = Affiliation.MI6;

      play(R.raw.q_martinis);
      break;
    case R.raw.q_cia:
      mAffiliation = Affiliation.CIA;
      play(R.raw.q_bond_friend);
      break;
    case R.raw.q_kgb:
      mAffiliation = Affiliation.KGB;
      play(R.raw.q_chief);
      break;
    case R.raw.q_criminal:
      mAffiliation = Affiliation.CRIMINAL;
      play(R.raw.q_chief);
      break;
    }
    break;
  case MI5:
    // The person works for MI5.
    switch (mLastAudioResource) {
    case R.raw.q_martinis:
      // The person drinks shaken martinis (007).
      play(R.raw.win_007);
      break;
    // ...
    // See the code bundle for more cases.
    // ...
    default:
      // The person remains unknown.
      play(R.raw.lose);
      break;
    }
    break;
  // ...
  // See the code bundle for more cases.
  // ...
}
```

Similarly, when the user has answered "No" to a question, we will call the
`takeNoBranch` method, which also contains big, nested `switch` statements:

```
public void takeNoBranch() {

    if (mMediaPlayer != null && mMediaPlayer.isPlaying()) {
```

```
    // Do not interrupt the audio that is already playing.
    return;

  }

  switch (mAffiliation) {
  case UNKNOWN:
    switch (mLastAudioResource) {
    case R.raw.q_mi6:
      // The person does not work for MI6.
      // Ask whether the person works for a criminal
      // organization.
      play(R.raw.q_criminal);
      break;
    // ...
    // See the code bundle for more cases.
    // ...
    default:
      // The person remains unknown.
      play(R.raw.lose);
      break;
    }
    break;
  // ...
  // See the code bundle for more cases.
  // ...
  }
```

When certain clips finish playing, we want to automatically advance to another clip without requiring a Yes or No from the user. A private helper method, takeAutoBranch, implements the relevant logic in a switch statement:

```
    private void takeAutoBranch() {
      switch (mLastAudioResource) {
      case R.raw.intro:
        play(R.raw.q_mi6);
        break;
      case R.raw.win_007:
      case R.raw.win_blofeld:
      case R.raw.win_gogol:
      case R.raw.win_jaws:
      case R.raw.win_leiter:
      case R.raw.win_m:
      case R.raw.win_moneypenny:
      case R.raw.win_q:
```

```
case R.raw.win_rublevitch:
case R.raw.win_tanner:
case R.raw.lose:
  start();
  break;
}
}
```

Whenever we need to play an audio clip, the `play` private helper method is called. It creates an instance of `MediaPlayer` using the context and an audio clip's ID, which is given to `play` as an argument. The audio is played and a callback is set so that the media player will be cleaned up and `takeAutoBranch` will be called when the clip is done:

```
private void play(final int audioResource) {
  mLastAudioResource = audioResource;
  mMediaPlayer = MediaPlayer.create(mContext, audioResource);
  mMediaPlayer.setOnCompletionListener(
      new OnCompletionListener() {
    @Override
    public void onCompletion(final MediaPlayer mediaPlayer) {
      mediaPlayer.release();
      if (mMediaPlayer == mediaPlayer) {
        mMediaPlayer = null;
      }
      takeAutoBranch();
    }
  });
  mMediaPlayer.start();
}
}
```

Now that we have written our supporting classes, we are ready to tackle the app's main class, including the computer vision functionality.

Capturing images and tracking faces in an activity

An Android app is a state machine in which each state is called an **activity**. An activity has a lifecycle. For example, it can be created, paused, resumed, and finished. During a transition between activities, the paused or finished activity can send data to the created or resumed activity. An app can define many activities and transition to them in any order. It can even transition to activities defined by the Android SDK or by other apps.

For more information about Android activities and their lifecycle, refer to the official documentation at http://developer.android.com/guide/components/activities.html.

For more information about OpenCV's Android and Java APIs (used throughout our activity class), refer to the official Javadocs at http://docs.opencv.org/java/. Unfortunately, at the time of writing this book, many of the comments in OpenCV's Javadocs are too closely based on the comments for C++. The class and method signatures in the Javadocs are correct, but in some cases, the comments are incorrect due to differences between the Java and C++ APIs.

OpenCV provides classes and interfaces that can be considered as add-ons to an activity's lifecycle. Specifically, we can use OpenCV callback methods to handle the following events:

- The OpenCV library is loaded.
- The camera preview starts.
- The camera preview stops.
- The camera preview captures a new frame.

Goldgesture uses just one activity called CameraActivity. As we saw earlier while implementing its layout in XML, CameraActivity uses a CameraBridgeViewBase object (more specifically, a JavaCameraView object) as its camera preview. CameraActivity implements an interface called CvCameraViewListener2, which provides callbacks for this camera preview. (Alternatively, an interface called CvCameraViewListener can serve this purpose. The difference between the two interfaces is that CvCameraViewListener2 allows us to specify a format for the captured image, whereas CvCameraViewListener does not.) The implementation of our class begins as follows:

```
package com.nummist.goldgesture;

// ...
// See code bundle for imports.
// ...

public final class CameraActivity extends Activity
implements CvCameraViewListener2 {

  // A tag for log output.
  private static final String TAG = "CameraActivity";
```

For readability and easy editing, we will use static final variables to store many parameters to our computer vision functions. You might wish to adjust these values based on experimentation. First, we have face detection parameters that should be familiar to you from last chapter's project:

```
// Parameters for face detection.
private static final double SCALE_FACTOR = 1.2;
private static final int MIN_NEIGHBORS = 3;
private static final int FLAGS = Objdetect.CASCADE_SCALE_IMAGE;
private static final double MIN_SIZE_PROPORTIONAL = 0.25;
private static final double MAX_SIZE_PROPORTIONAL = 1.0;
```

For the purpose of selecting features, we do not use the entire detected face. Rather, we use an inner portion that is less likely to contain any non-face background. Thus, we will define a proportion of the face that should be excluded from feature selection on each side:

```
// The portion of the face that is excluded from feature
// selection on each side.
// (We want to exclude boundary regions containing background.)
private static final double MASK_PADDING_PROPORTIONAL = 0.15;
```

For face tracking using optical flow, we will define a minimum and maximum number of features. If we fail to track at least the minimum number of features, we deem that the face has been lost. We will also define a minimum feature quality (relative to the quality of the best feature found), a minimum pixel distance between features, and a maximum acceptable error value while trying to match a new feature to an old feature. As we will see in a later section, these parameters pertain to OpenCV's `calcOpticalFlowPyrLK` function and its return values. The declarations are given in the following code:

```
// Parameters for face tracking.
private static final int MIN_FEATURES = 10;
private static final int MAX_FEATURES = 80;
private static final double MIN_FEATURE_QUALITY = 0.05;
private static final double MIN_FEATURE_DISTANCE = 4.0;
private static final float MAX_FEATURE_ERROR = 200f;
```

We will also define how much movement (as a proportion of the image size) and how many back and forth cycles are required before we deem that a nod or shake has occurred:

```
// Parameters for gesture detection
private static final double MIN_SHAKE_DIST_PROPORTIONAL = 0.04;
private static final double MIN_NOD_DIST_PROPORTIONAL = 0.005;
private static final double MIN_BACK_AND_FORTH_COUNT = 2;
```

Our member variables include the camera view, the dimensions of captured images, and the images at various stages of processing. The images are stored in OpenCV `Mat` objects, which are analogous to the NumPy arrays that we have seen in the Python bindings. OpenCV always captures images in landscape format, but we reorient them to portrait format, which is a more usual orientation for a picture of one's own face on a smartphone. Here are the relevant variable declarations:

```
// The camera view.
private CameraBridgeViewBase mCameraView;

// The dimensions of the image before orientation.
private double mImageWidth;
private double mImageHeight;

// The current gray image before orientation.
private Mat mGrayUnoriented;

// The current and previous equalized gray images.
private Mat mEqualizedGray;
private Mat mLastEqualizedGray;
```

As seen in the following code and comments, we also declare several member variables related to face detection and tracking:

```
// The mask, in which the face region is white and the
// background is black.
private Mat mMask;
private Scalar mMaskForegroundColor;
private Scalar mMaskBackgroundColor;

// The face detector, more detection parameters, and
// detected faces.
private CascadeClassifier mFaceDetector;
private Size mMinSize;
private Size mMaxSize;
private MatOfRect mFaces;

// The initial features before tracking.
private MatOfPoint mInitialFeatures;

// The current and previous features being tracked.
private MatOfPoint2f mFeatures;
```

```
private MatOfPoint2f mLastFeatures;

// The status codes and errors for the tracking.

private MatOfByte mFeatureStatuses;
private MatOfFloat mFeatureErrors;

// Whether a face was being tracked last frame.
private boolean mWasTrackingFace;

// Colors for drawing.
private Scalar mFaceRectColor;
private Scalar mFeatureColor;
```

We store instances of the classes that we defined earlier, namely
BackAndForthGesture and YesNoAudioTree:

```
// Gesture detectors.
private BackAndForthGesture mNodHeadGesture;
private BackAndForthGesture mShakeHeadGesture;

// The audio tree for the 20 questions game.
private YesNoAudioTree mAudioTree;
```

Our last member variable is an instance of an OpenCV class called
BaseLoaderCallback. It is responsible for loading the OpenCV library. We will
initialize an anonymous (inline) subclass with a custom callback method that
enables the camera preview (provided that the library loaded successfully).
The code for its implementation is as follows:

```
// The OpenCV loader callback.
private BaseLoaderCallback mLoaderCallback =
    new BaseLoaderCallback(this) {
  @Override
  public void onManagerConnected(final int status) {
    switch (status) {
      case LoaderCallbackInterface.SUCCESS:
        Log.d(TAG, "OpenCV loaded successfully");
        mCameraView.enableView();
        break;
      default:
        super.onManagerConnected(status);
        break;
    }
  }
};
```

Now, let's implement the standard lifecycle callbacks of an Android activity. First, when the activity is created, we will specify that we want to keep the screen on even when there is no touch interaction (since all interaction is via the camera). Moreover, we need to load the layout from the XML file, get a reference to the camera preview, and set this activity as the handler for the camera preview's events. This implementation is given in the following code:

```
@Override
protected void onCreate(final Bundle savedInstanceState) {
    super.onCreate(savedInstanceState);

    final Window window = getWindow();
    window.addFlags(
        WindowManager.LayoutParams.FLAG_KEEP_SCREEN_ON);

    setContentView(R.layout.activity_camera);
    mCameraView = (CameraBridgeViewBase)
        findViewById(R.id.camera_view);
    //mCameraView.enableFpsMeter();
    mCameraView.setCvCameraViewListener(this);
}
```

Note that we have not yet initialized most of our member variables. Instead, we do so once the camera preview has started.

When the activity is paused, we will disable the camera preview, stop the audio, and reset the gesture recognition data, as seen in the following code:

```
@Override
public void onPause() {
    if (mCameraView != null) {
        mCameraView.disableView();
    }
    if (mAudioTree != null) {
        mAudioTree.stop();
    }
    resetGestures();
    super.onPause();
}
```

When the activity resumes (including the first time it comes to the foreground after being created), we will start loading the OpenCV library:

```
@Override
public void onResume() {
    super.onResume();
```

```
OpenCVLoader.initAsync(OpenCVLoader.OPENCV_VERSION_2_4_5,
    this, mLoaderCallback);
}
```

When the activity is destroyed, we will clean things up in the same way as when the activity is paused:

```
@Override
public void onDestroy() {
  super.onDestroy();
  if (mCameraView != null) {
    mCameraView.disableView();
  }
  if (mAudioTree != null) {
    mAudioTree.stop();
  }
  resetGestures();
}
```

Now, let's turn our attention to the camera callbacks. When the camera preview starts (after the OpenCV library is loaded), we will initialize our remaining member variables. Many of these variables cannot be initialized earlier because they are OpenCV types and their constructors are implemented in the library that we just loaded. To begin, we will store the pixel dimensions that the camera is using:

```
@Override
public void onCameraViewStarted(final int width,
    final int height) {

  mImageWidth = width;
  mImageHeight = height;
```

Next, we will initialize our face detection variables, mostly via a helper method called initFaceDetector. The role of initFaceDetector includes loading the detector's cascade file, res/raw/lbpcascade_frontalface.xml. A lot of boilerplate code for file handling and error handling is involved in this task, so separating it into another function improves readability. We will examine the helper function's implementation later, but here is the call:

```
initFaceDetector();
mFaces = new MatOfRect();
```

As we did in the last chapter's project, we will determine the smaller of the two image dimensions and use it in proportional size calculations:

```
final int smallerSide;
if (height < width) {
  smallerSide = height;
} else {
  smallerSide = width;
}

final double minSizeSide =
    MIN_SIZE_PROPORTIONAL * smallerSide;
mMinSize = new Size(minSizeSide, minSizeSide);

final double maxSizeSide =
    MAX_SIZE_PROPORTIONAL * smallerSide;
mMaxSize = new Size(maxSizeSide, maxSizeSide);
```

We will initialize the matrices related to the features:

```
mInitialFeatures = new MatOfPoint();
mFeatures = new MatOfPoint2f(new Point());
mLastFeatures = new MatOfPoint2f(new Point());
mFeatureStatuses = new MatOfByte();
mFeatureErrors = new MatOfFloat();
```

We will specify colors (in RGB format, not BGR) for drawing a rectangle around the face and circles around the features:

```
mFaceRectColor = new Scalar(0.0, 0.0, 255.0);
mFeatureColor = new Scalar(0.0, 255.0, 0.0);
```

We will initialize variables related to nod and shake recognition:

```
final double minShakeDist =
    smallerSide * MIN_SHAKE_DIST_PROPORTIONAL;
mShakeHeadGesture = new BackAndForthGesture(minShakeDist);

final double minNodDist =
    smallerSide * MIN_NOD_DIST_PROPORTIONAL;
mNodHeadGesture = new BackAndForthGesture(minNodDist);
```

We will initialize and start the audio sequence:

```
mAudioTree = new YesNoAudioTree(this);
mAudioTree.start();
```

Finally, we will initialize the image matrices, most of which are transposed to be in portrait format:

```
mGrayUnoriented = new Mat(height, width, CvType.CV_8UC1);

// The rest of the matrices are transposed.

mEqualizedGray = new Mat(width, height, CvType.CV_8UC1);
mLastEqualizedGray = new Mat(width, height, CvType.CV_8UC1);

mMask = new Mat(width, height, CvType.CV_8UC1);
mMaskForegroundColor = new Scalar(255.0);
mMaskBackgroundColor = new Scalar(0.0);
}
```

When the camera view stops, we do not do anything. Here is the empty callback method:

```
@Override
public void onCameraViewStopped() {
}
```

When the camera captures a frame, we do all the real work, the computer vision. We will start by getting the color image (in RGBA format, not BGR), converting it to gray, reorienting it to portrait format, and equalizing it. Thus, the callback's implementation begins as follows:

```
@Override
public Mat onCameraFrame(final CvCameraViewFrame inputFrame) {
    final Mat rgba = inputFrame.rgba();

    // For processing, orient the image to portrait and equalize
    // it.
    Imgproc.cvtColor(rgba, mGrayUnoriented,
            Imgproc.COLOR_RGBA2GRAY);
    Core.transpose(mGrayUnoriented, mEqualizedGray);
    Core.flip(mEqualizedGray, mEqualizedGray, -1);
    Imgproc.equalizeHist(mEqualizedGray, mEqualizedGray);
```

Note that we get the RGBA image by calling `inputFrame.rgba()` and then we convert that image to grayscale. Alternatively, we could get the grayscale image directly by calling `inputFrame.gray()`. In our case, we want both the RGBA and grayscale images because we use the RGBA image for display and the grayscale image for detection and tracking.

Next, we will declare a list of features. A standard Java `List` is mutable whereas an OpenCV `Mat` is not, so we are going to need a `List` when we filter out features that did not track well. The declaration is as follows:

```
final List<Point> featuresList;
```

We will detect faces—a familiar task from the last chapter. Unlike in OpenCV's Python bindings, the structure to store the face rectangles is provided as an argument:

```
mFaceDetector.detectMultiScale(
    mEqualizedGray, mFaces, SCALE_FACTOR, MIN_NEIGHBORS,
    FLAGS, mMinSize, mMaxSize);
```

When at least one face is detected, we take the first detected face and draw a rectangle around it. We are detecting a face in portrait orientation but drawing to the original image in landscape orientation, so some conversion of coordinates is necessary. The code for this is as follows:

```
if (mFaces.rows() > 0) {

    // Get the first detected face.
    final double[] face = mFaces.get(0, 0);

    double minX = face[0];
    double minY = face[1];
    double width = face[2];
    double height = face[3];
    double maxX = minX + width;
    double maxY = minY + height;

    // Draw the face.
    Core.rectangle(
        rgba, new Point(mImageWidth-minY, mImageHeight-minX),
        new Point(mImageWidth-maxY, mImageHeight-maxX),
        mFaceRectColor);
```

Next, we will select the features within the inner part of the detected face. We will specify the region of interest by passing a mask to OpenCV's `goodFeaturesToTrack` function. A mask is an image that is white in the foreground (the inner part of the face) and black in the background. The following code finds the region of interest, creates the mask, and calls `goodFeaturesToTrack` with all relevant parameters:

```
// Create a mask for the face region.
double smallerSide;
if (height < width) {
  smallerSide = height;
} else {
  smallerSide = width;
}
double maskPadding =
    smallerSide * MASK_PADDING_PROPORTIONAL;
mMask.setTo(mMaskBackgroundColor);
Core.rectangle(
    mMask,
    new Point(minX + maskPadding,
              minY + maskPadding),
    new Point(maxX - maskPadding,
              maxY - maskPadding),
    mMaskForegroundColor, -1);

// Find features in the face region.
Imgproc.goodFeaturesToTrack(
    mEqualizedGray, mInitialFeatures, MAX_FEATURES,
    MIN_FEATURE_QUALITY, MIN_FEATURE_DISTANCE,
    mMask, 3, false, 0.04);
mFeatures.fromArray(mInitialFeatures.toArray());
featuresList = mFeatures.toList();
```

Note that we will copy the features into several variables: a matrix of initial features, a matrix of current features, and a mutable list of features that we will filter later.

Depending on whether we were already tracking a face, we will call a helper function to either initialize our data on gestures or update our data on gestures. We will also record that we are now tracking a face:

```
if (mWasTrackingFace) {
  updateGestureDetection();
} else {
  startGestureDetection();
}
mWasTrackingFace = true;
```

Alternatively, we might not have detected any face in this frame. Then, we will update any previously selected features using OpenCV's `calcOpticalFlowPyrLK` function to give us a matrix of error values, a matrix of status values, and a matrix of new features (`0` for an invalid feature, `1` for a valid feature). Being invalid typically means that the new feature is estimated to be outside the frame and thus it can no longer be tracked by optical flow. We will convert the new features to a list and filter out the ones that are invalid or have a high error value, as seen in the following code:

```
    } else {
      Video.calcOpticalFlowPyrLK(
          mLastEqualizedGray, mEqualizedGray, mLastFeatures,
          mFeatures, mFeatureStatuses, mFeatureErrors);

      // Filter out features that are not found or have high
      // error.
      featuresList = new LinkedList<Point>(mFeatures.toList());
      final LinkedList<Byte> featureStatusesList =
          new LinkedList<Byte>(mFeatureStatuses.toList());
      final LinkedList<Float> featureErrorsList =
          new LinkedList<Float>(mFeatureErrors.toList());
      for (int i = 0; i < featuresList.size();) {
        if (featureStatusesList.get(i) == 0 ||
            featureErrorsList.get(i) > MAX_FEATURE_ERROR) {
          featuresList.remove(i);
          featureStatusesList.remove(i);
          featureErrorsList.remove(i);
        } else {
          i++;
        }
      }
    }
```

If too few features remain after filtering, we will deem that the face is no longer tracked and we will discard all features. Otherwise, we will put the accepted features back in the matrix of current features and update our data on gestures:

```
    if (featuresList.size() < MIN_FEATURES) {
      // The number of remaining features is too low; we have
      // probably lost the target completely.

      // Discard the remaining features.
      featuresList.clear();
      mFeatures.fromList(featuresList);

      mWasTrackingFace = false;
    } else {
```

```
      mFeatures.fromList(featuresList);
      updateGestureDetection();
    }
  }
```

We will draw green circles around the current features. Again, we must convert coordinates from portrait format back to landscape format in order to draw on the original image:

```
// Draw the current features.
for (int i = 0; i< featuresList.size(); i++) {
  final Point p = featuresList.get(i);
  final Point pTrans = new Point(
      mImageWidth - p.y,
      mImageHeight - p.x);
  Core.circle(rgba, pTrans, 8, mFeatureColor);
}
```

At the end of the frame, the current equalized gray image and current features become the previous equalized gray image and previous features. Rather than copying these matrices, we swap the references:

```
// Swap the references to the current and previous images.
final Mat swapEqualizedGray = mLastEqualizedGray;
mLastEqualizedGray = mEqualizedGray;
mEqualizedGray = swapEqualizedGray;

// Swap the references to the current and previous features.
final MatOfPoint2f swapFeatures = mLastFeatures;
mLastFeatures = mFeatures;
mFeatures = swapFeatures;
```

We will horizontally flip the preview image to make it look like a mirror. Then, we will return it so that OpenCV can display it:

```
// Mirror (horizontally flip) the preview.
Core.flip(rgba, rgba, 1);

return rgba;
}
```

We have mentioned several helper functions, which we will examine now. When we start analyzing face motion, we will find the geometric mean of the features and use the mean's x and y coordinates, respectively, as the starting coordinates for shake and nod gestures, as done in the following code:

```
private void startGestureDetection() {

    double[] featuresCenter = Core.mean(mFeatures).val;

    // Motion in x may indicate a shake of the head.
    mShakeHeadGesture.start(featuresCenter[0]);

    // Motion in y may indicate a nod of the head.
    mNodHeadGesture.start(featuresCenter[1]);
}
```

 Remember that our `BackAndForthGesture` class uses one-dimensional positions. For an upright head, only the x coordinate is relevant to a shake gesture and only the y coordinate is relevant to a nod gesture.

Similarly, as we continue to analyze face motion, we will find the features' new geometric mean and use the mean's coordinates to update the shake and nod data. Based on the number of back and forth shaking or nodding motions, we can take a "yes" branch or a "no" branch in the question and answer tree. Alternatively, we can decide that the user's current gesture is ambiguous (both "yes" and "no"), in which case we will reset the data as shown in the following code:

```
private void updateGestureDetection() {

    final double[] featuresCenter = Core.mean(mFeatures).val;

    // Motion in x may indicate a shake of the head.
    mShakeHeadGesture.update(featuresCenter[0]);
    final int shakeBackAndForthCount =
        mShakeHeadGesture.getBackAndForthCount();
    //Log.i(TAG, "shakeBackAndForthCount=" +
    //        shakeBackAndForthCount);
    final boolean shakingHead =
        (shakeBackAndForthCount >=
        MIN_BACK_AND_FORTH_COUNT);

    // Motion in y may indicate a nod of the head.
    mNodHeadGesture.update(featuresCenter[1]);
```

```
    final int nodBackAndForthCount =
        mNodHeadGesture.getBackAndForthCount();
    //Log.i(TAG, "nodBackAndForthCount=" +
    //        nodBackAndForthCount);
    final boolean noddingHead =
        (nodBackAndForthCount >=
        MIN_BACK_AND_FORTH_COUNT);

    if (shakingHead && noddingHead) {
      // The gesture is ambiguous. Ignore it.
      resetGestures();
    } else if (shakingHead) {
      mAudioTree.takeNoBranch();
      resetGestures();
    } else if (noddingHead) {
      mAudioTree.takeYesBranch();
      resetGestures();
    }
  }
```

We will always reset the nod gesture data and the shake gesture data at the same time:

```
    private void resetGestures() {
      if (mNodHeadGesture != null) {
        mNodHeadGesture.resetCounts();
      }
      if (mShakeHeadGesture != null) {
        mShakeHeadGesture.resetCounts();
      }
    }
```

Our helper method to initialize the face detector is very similar to the method found in an official OpenCV sample project that performs face detection on Android. We will copy the cascade's raw data from the app bundle to a new file that is more accessible. Then, we will initialize a CascadeClassifier object using this file's path. If an error is encountered at any point, we will log it and close the app. Here is the method's implementation:

```
    private void initFaceDetector() {
      try {
        // Load cascade file from application resources.

        InputStream is = getResources().openRawResource(
            R.raw.lbpcascade_frontalface);
```

```
    File cascadeDir = getDir(

        "cascade", Context.MODE_PRIVATE);
    File cascadeFile = new File(
        cascadeDir, "lbpcascade_frontalface.xml");
    FileOutputStream os = new FileOutputStream(cascadeFile);

    byte[] buffer = new byte[4096];
    int bytesRead;
    while ((bytesRead = is.read(buffer)) != -1) {
      os.write(buffer, 0, bytesRead);
    }
    is.close();
    os.close();

    mFaceDetector = new CascadeClassifier(
        cascadeFile.getAbsolutePath());
    if (mFaceDetector.empty()) {
      Log.e(TAG, "Failed to load cascade");
      finish();
    } else {
      Log.i(TAG, "Loaded cascade from " +
        cascadeFile.getAbsolutePath());
    }

    cascadeDir.delete();

  } catch (IOException e) {
    e.printStackTrace();
    Log.e(TAG, "Failed to load cascade. Exception thrown: "
        + e);
    finish();
  }
 }
}
```

That's all the code! We are ready to test. Make sure your Android device has its sound turned on. Plug the device into a USB port and press the **Run** button (the play icon in green). The first time you run the project, you might see the **Run As** window, as shown in the following screenshot:

If you see this window, select **Android Application** and click on the **OK** button. Then, you might see another window, **Android Device Chooser**, as shown in the following screenshot:

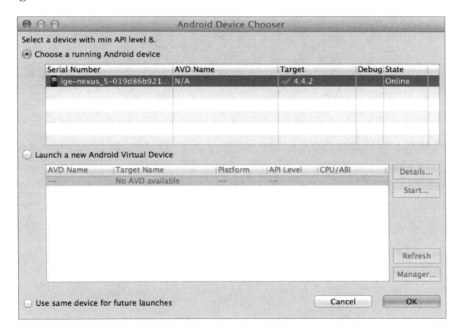

If you see this window, select your device and click on the **OK** button.

Soon, you should see the app's camera preview appear on your device as shown in the following screenshot. Nod or shake your head knowingly as the questions are asked.

Summary

Silence is golden—or perhaps gestures are. At least gestures can fill an awkward silence and control an app that whispers reminders in your earphones.

We have built our first Android app with OpenCV's Java bindings. We have also learned how to use optical flow to track the movement of an object after detection. Thus, we are able to recognize a gesture such as a head moving up and down in a nod.

Our next project deals with motion in three dimensions. We will build a system that estimates changes in distance in order to alert a driver when the car is being followed.

5

Equipping Your Car with a Rearview Camera and Hazard Detection

Comes the morning and the headlights fade away.

— The Living Daylights (1987)

James Bond is a car thief. The movies show that he has stolen many automobiles, often from innocent bystanders. We do not know whether these unfortunate people ever recovered their property, but even if they did, the damages from collisions, submersions, bullets, and rockets would have had a lasting impact on their insurance premiums. Bond has also stolen a propeller plane, a tank, and a moon buggy.

The man has been driving since the 1950s, and perhaps it is time that he stopped.

Be that as it may, we can break away from the bad, old Cold War days of indifference to collateral damage. With modern technology, we can provide a driver with timely information about others who are sharing the road. This information might make it easier to avoid collisions and to properly aim the vehicle's rocket launchers such that a chase scene can be conducted in an orderly manner, without flattening whole city blocks. Secret agents will not lose so many cars and, thus, will not feel compelled to steal so many.

Since driver assistance is a broad topic, let's focus on one scenario. Twilight and nighttime are difficult times for drivers, including secret agents. We might be blinded by the lack of natural light or the glare of headlights. However, we can make a computer vision system that sees headlights (or rear lights) clearly and can estimate the distance to them. It can also distinguish between lights of different colors, a feature that is relevant to identifying signals and types of vehicles. We will choose computationally inexpensive techniques, suitable for a low-powered computer—namely, Raspberry Pi—that we can plug into a car's cigarette lighter receptacle via an adapter. An LCD panel can display the relevant information along with a live rearview video feed that is less glaring than the real headlights.

This project presents us with several new topics and challenges, which are as follows:

- Detecting blobs of light and classifying their color
- Estimating the distance from the camera to a detected object whose real-world size is known
- Setting up a low-budget lab where we can experiment with lights of many colors
- Setting up a Raspberry Pi and peripherals in a car

Realistically, our quick, homemade project is not sufficiently robust to be relied upon as an automotive safety tool, so take it with a grain of salt. However, it is a fun introduction to analyzing signal lights and wiring up a custom in-car computer. The choice of Raspberry Pi as a platform challenges us to think about the car as an environment for rapid prototyping. We can plug in any standard peripherals including a webcam, keyboard, mouse, and even a monitor, which will give us a complete desktop Linux system with Python—on wheels! (Snakes in a car!) For more exotic projects, Pi is compatible with many electronics kits too! A smartphone or tablet is also a good alternative for use in a car—and is easier to power than a Pi with a monitor—but the Pi excels as a well-rounded prototyping tool.

Let the app be known as *The Living Headlights*.

 The completed project for this chapter can be downloaded from my website at `http://nummist.com/opencv/7376_05.zip`.

Planning The Living Headlights app

For this app, we will return to the cross-platform wxPython framework. Optionally, we can develop and test our wxPython application on a Windows, Mac, or Linux desktop or laptop before deploying it to our Raspberry Pi computer in the car. With the Raspbian operating system, Raspberry Pi can run wxPython just as any Linux desktop could.

The GUI for The Living Headlights includes a live video feed, a set of controls where the user can enter the true distance to the currently imaged headlights, and a label that initially displays a set of instructions, as seen in the following screenshot:

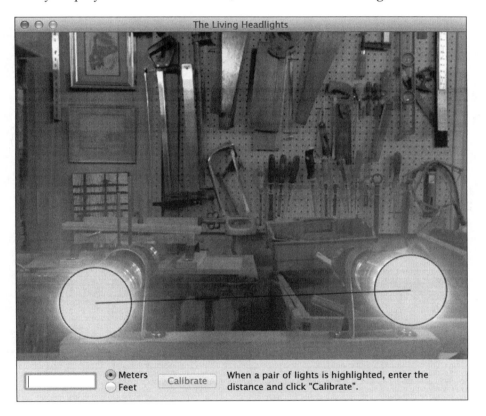

When a pair of headlights is detected, the user must perform a one-time calibration step. This consists of entering the true distance between the camera and headlights (specifically, the midpoint between the headlights) and then clicking on the **Calibrate** button. Thereafter, the app continuously updates and displays an estimate of the headlights' distance and color, as seen in the label at the bottom of the following screenshot:

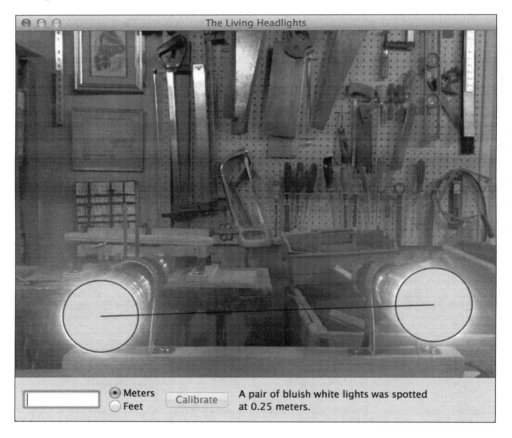

The calibration and the selected unit (meters or feet) are stored in a configuration file when the app closes. They are reloaded from this file when the app reopens.

Atop the video feed, colored circles are drawn to mark detected lights, and lines are drawn between pairs of detected lights whose colors match. Such a pair is considered to be a set of headlights.

Next, let's consider the techniques we will use to detect lights and classify their colors.

Detecting lights as blobs

To the human eye, light can appear both very bright and very colorful. Imagine a sunny landscape or a storefront lit by a neon sign; they are bright and colorful! However, a camera captures a range of contrast that is much narrower and not as intelligently selected such that the sunny landscape or neon-lit storefront can look washed-out. This problem of poorly controlled contrast is especially bad in cheap cameras and cameras that have small sensors, as webcams do. As a result, bright light sources tend to be imaged as big white blobs with thin rims of color. Moreover, these blobs tend to take the shape of the lens's iris, typically a polygon approximating a circle.

The thought of all lights becoming white and circular makes the world seem like a poorer place, if you ask me. Nonetheless, in computer vision, we can take advantage of such a predictable pattern. We can look for white blobs that are nearly circular, and we can infer their human-perceptible color from a sample that includes extra pixels around the rim.

Blob detection is actually a major branch of computer vision. Unlike face detectors (or other object detectors) that we have discussed in previous chapters, a blob detector is not trained. There is no concept of a reference image, so meaningful classifications, such as "This blob is a light" or "This blob is skin", are a step further. Classification goes beyond the ken of the blob detector itself. We explicitly define thresholds between non-lights and lights, and between different human-perceptible colors of lights, based on *a priori* knowledge about typical shapes and colors of light sources as imaged by a webcam.

 Other terms for a blob include a **connected component** and a **region**. However, in this book, we will call a blob a blob.

At its simplest, blob detection consists of five steps:

1. Partition the image into two or more colors. For example, this can be accomplished by **binary thresholding** (also called **binarization**), whereby all grayscale values above a threshold are converted to white, and all grayscale values below the threshold are converted to black.

2. Find the **contour** of each contiguously colored region—that is, each blob. The contour is a set of points describing the region's outline.

3. Merge the blobs that are deemed to be neighbors.

4. Optionally, determine each blob's **features** — higher-level measurements such as the center point, radius, and circularity. The usefulness of these features lies in their simplicity. For further blob-related computations and logic, we might not want to work with a complex representation such as a contour's many points.

5. Reject blobs that fail to meet certain measurable criteria.

OpenCV implements such a simple blob detector in a class called cv2. SimpleBlobDetector (appropriately enough). This class's constructor takes an instance of a helper class called cv2.SimpleBlobDetector_Params, which describes the criteria for accepting or rejecting a candidate blob. SimpleBlobDetector_Params has the following member variables:

- thresholdStep, minThreshold, and maxThreshold: The search for blobs is based on a series of binarized images (analogous to the series of scaled images that are searched by a Haar cascade detector, as described in *Chapter 3, Training a Smart Alarm to Recognize the Villain and His Cat*). The thresholds for binarization are based on the range and step size given by these variables. We use 8, 191, and 255.

- minRepeatability: This variable minus one is the minimum number of neighbors that a blob must have. We use two.

- minDistBetweenBlobs: Blobs must be at least this many pixels apart. Any closer blobs are counted as neighbors. We use a minimum distance calculated as 2 percent of the image's larger dimension (typically width).

- filterByColor: This can have two values, True or False and blobColor. If filterByColor is True, a blob's central pixel must exactly match blobColor. We use True and 255 (white), based on our assumption that light sources are white blobs.

- filterByArea (True or False), minArea, and maxArea: If filterByArea is True, a blob's area in pixels must fall within the given range. We use True and a range calculated as 0.5 percent to 10 percent of the image's larger dimension (typically width).

- filterByCircularity (True or False), minCircularity, and maxCircularity: If filterByCircularity is True, a blob's circularity must fall within the given range, where circularity is defined as 4 * PI * area / (perimeter ^ 2). A circle's circularity is 1.0 and a line's circularity is 0.0. For our approximately circular light sources, we use True and the range 0.7 to 1.0.

- `filterByInertia` (True or False), `minInertiaRatio`, and `maxInertiaRatio`: If `filterByInertia` is True, a blob's inertia ratio must fall within the given range. A relatively high inertia ratio implies that the blob is relatively elongated (and would thus require more torque to rotate along its longest axis). A circle's inertia ratio is `1.0` and a line's inertia ratio is `0.0`. We use `filterByInertia=False` (no filtering by inertia).

- `filterByConvexity` (True or False), `minConvexity`, and `maxConvexity`: If `filterByConvexity` is True, a blob's convexity must fall within the given range, where convexity is defined as `area / hullArea`. Here, `hullArea` refers to the area of the convex hull—the convex polygon surrounding all the points of the contour with the minimum area. Convexity is always more than 0.0 and not less than 1.0. A relatively high convexity implies that the contour is relatively smooth. We will use `filterByConvexity=False` (no filtering by convexity).

Although these parameters cover many useful criteria, they are designed for grayscale images and do not provide a practical means to filter or classify blobs based on separate criteria for hue, saturation, and luminosity. The suggested values in the preceding list are tuned to extract bright blobs of light. However, remember that we also want to classify such blobs by subtle variations in color, especially around the blob's edge.

Hue refers to a color's angle on the color wheel, where 0 degrees is red, 120 is green, and 240 is blue. The hue in degrees can be calculated from the RGB values by using the following formula:

*hue = (180 / PI) * atan2(sqrt(3) * (g - b), 2 * r - g - b)*

Saturation refers to a color's distance from grayscale. There are several alternative formulations of an RGB color's saturation. We will use the following formulation, which some authors call **chroma** instead of saturation:

saturation = max(r, g, b) – min(r, g, b)

We can classify a light source's human-perceptible color based on the average hue and saturation of the blob and some surrounding pixels. The combination of low saturation and a blue or yellow hue tends to suggest that the light will appear white to human vision. Other light sources might appear (in order of ascending hue) as red, orange/amber/yellow, green (a wide range from spring green to emerald), blue/purple (another wide range), or pink, to give just a few examples of possible names. Threshold values can be chosen based on trial and error.

With the preceding techniques, we can detect the location, pixel radius, and perceptual color of light sources. However, we need additional techniques to get an estimate of real distance between the camera and a pair of headlights. Let's turn our attention to this problem now.

Estimating distances (a cheap approach)

Suppose we have an object sitting in front of a pinhole camera. Regardless of the distance between the camera and object, the following equation holds true:

objectSizeInImage / focalLength = objectSizeInReality / distance

We might use any unit (such as pixels) in the equation's left-hand side and any unit (such as meters) in its right-hand side. (On each side of the equation, the division cancels the unit.) Moreover, we can define the object's size based on anything linear that we can detect in the image, such as the diameter of a detected blob or the width of a detected face rectangle.

Let's rearrange the equation to illustrate that the distance to the object is inversely proportional to the object's size in the image:

*distance = focalLength * objectSizeInReality / objectSizeInImage*

Let's assume that the object's real size and the camera's focal length are constant. Consider the following arrangement, which isolates the pair of constants on the right-hand side of the equation:

*distance * objectSizeInImage = focalLength * objectSizeInReality*

As the right-hand side of the equation is constant, so is the left. We can conclude that the following relationship holds true over time:

*newDist * newObjectSizeInImage = oldDist * oldObjectSizeInImage*

Let's solve the equation for the new distance:

*newDist = oldDist * oldObjectSizeInImage / newSizeInImage*

Now, let's think about applying this equation in software. To provide a ground truth, the user must take a single, true measurement of the distance to use as our *old* distance in all future calculations. Moreover, based on our detection algorithm, we know the object's old pixel size and its subsequent new pixel sizes, so we can compute the new distance anytime we have a detection result. Let's review the following assumptions for the camera:

1. There is no lens distortion; the pinhole camera model can be used here.

2. Focal length is constant; no zoom is applied.

3. The object is rigid; its real-world measurements do not change.

4. The camera is always viewing the same side of the object; the relative rotation of camera and object does not change.

One might wonder whether the first assumption is problematic, as webcams often have cheap wide-angle lenses with significant distortion. Despite lens distortion, does the object's size in the image remain inversely proportional to the real distance between the camera and object? The following paper reports experimental results for a lens that appears to distort very badly and an object that is located off-center (in an image region where distortion is likely to be especially bad):

M. N. A. Wahab, N. Sivadev, and K. Sundaraj. "Target distance estimation using monocular vision system for mobile robot", *IEEE Conference on Open Systems (ICOS) 2011 Proceedings*, vol. 11, no. 15, p. 25-28. September 2011.

Using exponential regression, the authors show that the following model is a good fit for the experimental data ($R^2 = 0.995$):

distanceInCentimeters = 4042 * (objectSizeInPixels ^ -1.2)

Note that the exponent is close to -1 and, thus, the statistical model is not far from the ideal inverse relationship that we would hope to find. Even the bad lens and off-center subject did not break our assumptions too horribly!

We can ensure that the second assumption (no zooming) holds true.

Let's consider the third and fourth assumptions (rigidity and constant rotation) in the case of a camera and object that are parts of two cars on a highway. Except in a crash, most of the car's exterior parts are rigid. Except when passing or pulling over, one car travels directly behind the other on a surface that is mostly flat and mostly straight. However, on a road that is hilly or has many turns, the assumptions start to fall apart. It becomes more difficult to predict which side of the object is currently being viewed. Thus, it is more difficult to say whether our reference measurements are applied to the side that is currently being viewed.

Of course, we need to define a generic piece of a car to be our "object". The headlights (and the space between them) are a decent choice, since we have a method for detecting them and the distance between headlights is *similar* across most models of cars. That being said, this distance is not *exactly equal* across models of cars, and this difference can be considered as a weakness in the choice of object, though the same is true for other car components too.

All distance estimation techniques in computer vision rely on some assumptions (or some calibration steps) relating to the camera, object, relationship between camera and object, and/or the lighting. For comparison, let's consider some of the common techniques:

- A **time-of-flight (ToF) camera** shines a light on objects and measures the intensity of reflected light. This intensity is used to estimate distance at each pixel based on the known falloff characteristics of the light source. Some ToF cameras, such as Microsoft Kinect, use an infrared light source. Other more expensive ToF cameras scan a scene with a laser or even use a grid of lasers. ToF cameras suffer from interference if other bright lights are being imaged, so they are poorly suited to our application.

- A **stereo camera** consists of two parallel cameras with a known, fixed distance between them. Each frame, a pair of images is captured, features are identified, and a **disparity** or pixel distance is calculated for each pair of corresponding features in the images. We can convert disparity to real distance, based on the cameras' known field of view and the known distance between them. For our application, stereo techniques would be feasible except that they are computationally expensive and also use a lot of input bus bandwidth for the pair of cameras. Optimizing these techniques for Raspberry Pi would be a big challenge.

- **Structure from motion (SfM)** techniques only need a single, regular camera but rely on moving the camera by known distances over time. For each pair of images taken from neighboring locations, disparities are calculated just as they are done for a stereo camera. While knowing the camera's movements, we must know the object's movements as well (or we must know that the object is stationary). Due to these limitations, SfM techniques are poorly suited to our application, where the camera and object are mounted on two freely moving vehicles.

- Various **3D feature tracking** techniques entail estimating the rotation of the object as well as its distance and other coordinates. The types of features might include edges and texture details. For our application, differences between models of cars make it difficult to define one set of features that is suitable for 3D tracking. Moreover, 3D tracking is computationally expensive, especially by the standards of a low-powered computer such as Raspberry Pi.

For more information on these techniques, refer to the following books, available from Packt Publishing:

- Kinect and other ToF cameras are covered in my book *OpenCV Computer Vision with Python*, specifically in *Chapter 5, Detecting Foreground/Background Regions and Depth.*

- 3D feature tracking and SfM are covered in *Mastering OpenCV with Practical Computer Vision Projects*, specifically in *Chapter 3, Markerless Augmented Reality*, and *Chapter 4, Exploring Structure from Motion Using OpenCV.*

- Stereo vision and 3D feature tracking are covered in Robert Laganière's book *OpenCV 2 Computer Vision Application Programming Cookbook*, specifically in *Chapter 9, Estimating Projective Relations in Images.*

On balance, the simplistic approach based on pixel distances being inversely proportional to real distances is a justifiable choice, given our application and our intent to support the Pi.

Implementing The Living Headlights app

The Living Headlights app will use the following files:

- `LivingHeadlights.py`: This contains our application class and its main function. This is a new file.

- `ColorUtils.py`: This contains the utility functions to convert colors to different representations. This is a new file.

- `GeomUtils.py`: This contains the utility functions for geometric calculations. Create a copy of or link to the version that we used in *Chapter 3, Training a Smart Alarm to Recognize the Villain and His Cat.*

- `PyInstallerUtils.py`: This contains the utility functions for accessing resources in a PyInstaller application bundle. Create a copy of or link to the version that we used in *Chapter 3, Training a Smart Alarm to Recognize the Villain and His Cat.*

- `ResizeUtils.py`: This contains the utility functions for resizing images, including camera capture dimensions. Create a copy of or link to the version that we used in *Chapter 3, Training a Smart Alarm to Recognize the Villain and His Cat.*

- `WxUtils.py`: This contains the utility functions for using OpenCV images in wxPython apps. Create a copy of or link to the version that we used in *Chapter 3, Training a Smart Alarm to Recognize the Villain and His Cat.*

Let's start with the creation of `ColorUtils.py`. We need functions to calculate a color's hue and saturation according to the formulae mentioned in the *Detecting lights as blobs* section. The module's implementation is done in the following code:

```
import math

def hueFromBGR(color):
  b, g, r = color
  # Note: sqrt(3) = 1.7320508075688772
  hue = math.degrees(math.atan2(
    1.7320508075688772 * (g - b), 2 * r - g - b))
  if hue < 0.0:
    hue += 360.0
  return hue

def saturationFromBGR(color):
  return max(color) - min(color)
```

If we want to convert an entire image (every pixel) to hue, saturation, and either luminosity or value, we can use OpenCV's `cvtColor` method:

- `hslImage = cv2.cvtColor(bgrImage, COLOR_BGR2HSL)`
- `hsvImage = cv2.cvtColor(bgrImage, COLOR_BGR2HSV)`

Refer to the following Wikipedia article for the definitions of saturation, luminosity, and value in HSV and HSL color models at `https://en.wikipedia.org/wiki/HSL_and_HSV`. Our definition of saturation is called chroma in the Wikipedia article and it differs from HSL saturation, which differs again from HSV saturation. Moreover, OpenCV represents hue in units of 2 degrees (in a range of 0 to 180) so that the hue channel fits inside a byte.

We will write our own conversion functions because, for our purposes, converting an entire image is unnecessary. We just need to convert a sample from each blob. Also, we prefer a more accurate floating-point representation instead of the byte-sized integer representation that OpenCV imposes.

We also need to modify `GeomUtils.py` by adding a function to calculate the Euclidean distance between two 2D points, such as the pixel coordinates of two headlights in an image. At the top of the file, let's add an import statement and implement the function thusly:

```
import math

def dist2D(p0, p1):
  deltaX = p1[0] - p0[0]
```

```
deltaY = p1[1] - p0[1]
return math.sqrt(deltaX * deltaX +
  deltaY * deltaY)
```

Distances (and other magnitudes) can also be calculated using NumPy's linalg.norm function, as seen in the following code:

```
dist = numpy.linalg.norm(a1 - a0)
```

Here, a0 and a1 can be of any size and shape. However, for a low-dimensional space such as 2D or 3D coordinate vectors, the overhead of using NumPy arrays is probably not worthwhile, so a utility function such as ours is a reasonable alternative.

The preceding code contains all the new utility functions. Now, let's create a file, LivingHeadlights.py, for the app's main class, LivingHeadlights. Like InteractiveRecognizer in *Chapter 3, Training a Smart Alarm to Recognize the Villain and His Cat*, LivingHeadlights is a class for a wxPython app that captures and processes images on a background thread (to avoid blocking the GUI on the main thread), allows a user to enter reference data, serializes its reference data when exiting, and deserializes its reference data when starting up again. This time, serialization/deserialization is accomplished using Python's cPickle module or, if cPickle is unavailable for any reason, the less optimized pickle module. Let's add the following import statements to the start of LivingHeadlights.py:

```
import numpy
import cv2
import os
import threading
import wx

try:
    import cPickle as pickle
except:
    import pickle

import ColorUtils
import GeomUtils
import PyInstallerUtils
import ResizeUtils
import WxUtils
```

Let's also define some BGR color values and names at the start of the module. We will classify each blob as one of these colors, depending on the hue and saturation:

```
COLOR_Red         = ((  0,   0, 255), 'red')
COLOR_YellowWhite = ((223, 247, 255), 'yellowish white')
COLOR_AmberYellow = ((  0, 191, 255), 'amber or yellow')
COLOR_Green       = ((128, 255, 128), 'green')
COLOR_BlueWhite   = ((255, 231, 223), 'bluish white')
COLOR_BluePurple  = ((255,  64,   0), 'blue or purple')
COLOR_Pink        = ((240, 128, 255), 'pink')
```

Now, let's begin implementing the class. The initializer takes several arguments relating to the configuration of the blob detector and the camera. Refer to the preceding section, *Detecting lights as blobs*, for explanations of the blob detection parameters supported by OpenCV's `SimpleBlobDetector` and `SimpleBlobDetector_Params` classes. The following is the class declaration and the declaration of the initializer:

```
class LivingHeadlights(wx.Frame):

    def __init__(self, configPath, thresholdStep=8.0,
        minThreshold=191.0, maxThreshold=255.0,
        minRepeatability=2,
        minDistBetweenBlobsProportional=0.02,
        minBlobAreaProportional=0.005,
        maxBlobAreaProportional=0.1,
        minBlobCircularity=0.7, cameraDeviceID=0,
        imageSize=(640, 480),
        title='The Living Headlights'):
```

We will start the initializer's implementation by setting a public Boolean variable indicating that the app should currently display a mirrored image, and a protected Boolean variable indicating that the app should currently be running (not preparing to quit):

```
        self.mirrored = True

        self._running = True
```

If there is any configuration file saved from a previous run of the app, we will deserialize the reference measurements (pixel distance between lights and real distance in meters between lights and camera) as well as the user's preferred unit of measurement (meters or feet):

```
        self._configPath = configPath
        self._pixelDistBetweenLights = None
        if os.path.isfile(configPath):
```

```
file = open(self._configPath, 'r')
self._referencePixelDistBetweenLights = \
    pickle.load(file)
self._referenceMetersToCamera = \
    pickle.load(file)
self._convertMetersToFeet = pickle.load(file)
else:
    self._referencePixelDistBetweenLights = None
    self._referenceMetersToCamera = None
    self._convertMetersToFeet = False
```

We will initialize a `VideoCapture` object and try to configure the size of the captured images. If the requested size is unsupported, we will fall back to the default size:

```
self._capture = cv2.VideoCapture(cameraDeviceID)
size = ResizeUtils.cvResizeCapture(
    self._capture, imageSize)
w, h = size
self._imageWidth, self._imageHeight = w, h
```

We will create a `SimpleBlobDetector_Params` object and `SimpleBlobDetector` object based on the arguments passed to the app's initializer:

```
minDistBetweenBlobs = \
    min(w, h) * \
    minDistBetweenBlobsProportional

area = w * h
minBlobArea = area * minBlobAreaProportional
maxBlobArea = area * maxBlobAreaProportional

detectorParams = cv2.SimpleBlobDetector_Params()

detectorParams.minDistBetweenBlobs = \
    minDistBetweenBlobs

detectorParams.thresholdStep = thresholdStep
detectorParams.minThreshold = minThreshold
detectorParams.maxThreshold = maxThreshold

detectorParams.minRepeatability = minRepeatability

detectorParams.filterByArea = True
detectorParams.minArea = minBlobArea
```

```
    detectorParams.maxArea = maxBlobArea

    detectorParams.filterByColor = True
    detectorParams.blobColor = 255

    detectorParams.filterByCircularity = True
    detectorParams.minCircularity = minBlobCircularity

    detectorParams.filterByInertia = False

    detectorParams.filterByConvexity = False

    self._detector = cv2.SimpleBlobDetector(
        detectorParams)
```

We will specify the style of the app's window and will initialize the base class,
wx.Frame:

```
    style = wx.CLOSE_BOX | wx.MINIMIZE_BOX | \
        wx.CAPTION | wx.SYSTEM_MENU | \
        wx.CLIP_CHILDREN
    wx.Frame.__init__(self, None, title=title,
            style=style, size=size)
    self.SetBackgroundColour(wx.Colour(232, 232, 232))
```

We will bind the *Esc* key to a callback that closes the app:

```
    self.Bind(wx.EVT_CLOSE, self._onCloseWindow)

    quitCommandID = wx.NewId()
    self.Bind(wx.EVT_MENU, self._onQuitCommand,
        id=quitCommandID)
    acceleratorTable = wx.AcceleratorTable([
      (wx.ACCEL_NORMAL, wx.WXK_ESCAPE,
       quitCommandID)
    ])
    self.SetAcceleratorTable(acceleratorTable)
```

We will create the GUI elements, including the bitmap, the text field for the reference
distance, radio buttons for the unit (meters or feet), and the **Calibrate** button. We will
also bind callbacks for various input events:

```
    self._staticBitmap = wx.StaticBitmap(self,
            size=size)
```

```
self._showImage(None)

self._calibrationTextCtrl = wx.TextCtrl(
    self, style=wx.TE_PROCESS_ENTER)
self._calibrationTextCtrl.Bind(
    wx.EVT_KEY_UP,
    self._onCalibrationTextCtrlKeyUp)

self._distanceStaticText = wx.StaticText(self)
if self._referencePixelDistBetweenLights is None:
  self._showInstructions()
else:
  self._clearMessage()

self._calibrationButton = wx.Button(
        self, label='Calibrate')
self._calibrationButton.Bind(
    wx.EVT_BUTTON, self._calibrate)
self._calibrationButton.Disable()

border = 12

metersButton = wx.RadioButton(self,
        label='Meters')
metersButton.Bind(wx.EVT_RADIOBUTTON,
        self._onSelectMeters)

feetButton = wx.RadioButton(self, label='Feet')
feetButton.Bind(wx.EVT_RADIOBUTTON,
        self._onSelectFeet)
```

We will ensure that the proper radio buttons start in a selected state, depending on the configuration data that we deserialized earlier:

```
if self._convertMetersToFeet:
  feetButton.SetValue(True)
else:
  metersButton.SetValue(True)
```

We will stack the radio buttons vertically using BoxSizer:

```
unitButtonsSizer = wx.BoxSizer(wx.VERTICAL)
unitButtonsSizer.Add(metersButton)
unitButtonsSizer.Add(feetButton)
```

We will line up all our controls horizontally, again using `BoxSizer`:

```
controlsSizer = wx.BoxSizer(wx.HORIZONTAL)
style = wx.ALIGN_CENTER_VERTICAL | wx.RIGHT
controlsSizer.Add(self._calibrationTextCtrl, 0,
        style, border)
controlsSizer.Add(unitButtonsSizer, 0, style,
        border)
controlsSizer.Add(self._calibrationButton, 0,
        style, border)
controlsSizer.Add(self._distanceStaticText, 0,
        wx.ALIGN_CENTER_VERTICAL)
```

To finish our layout, we will place the controls below the image:

```
rootSizer = wx.BoxSizer(wx.VERTICAL)
rootSizer.Add(self._staticBitmap)
rootSizer.Add(controlsSizer, 0,
        wx.EXPAND | wx.ALL, border)
self.SetSizerAndFit(rootSizer)
```

The last thing we will do in the initializer is start a background thread to capture and process images from the camera:

```
self._captureThread = threading.Thread(
    target=self._runCaptureLoop)
self._captureThread.start()
```

When closing the app, we will first ensure that the capture thread terminates itself, just as we did in `InteractiveRecognizer` in *Chapter 3, Training a Smart Alarm to Recognize the Villain and His Cat*. We will also use pickle or cPickle to serialize the reference measurements and preferred unit (meters or feet) to a file. Here is the implementation of the relevant callback:

```
def _onCloseWindow(self, event):
    self._running = False
    self._captureThread.join()
    configDir = os.path.dirname(self._configPath)
    if not os.path.isdir(configDir):
        os.makedirs(configDir)
    file = open(self._configPath, 'w')
    pickle.dump(self._referencePixelDistBetweenLights,
            file)
    pickle.dump(self._referenceMetersToCamera, file)
    pickle.dump(self._convertMetersToFeet, file)
    self.Destroy()
```

The callback associated with the escape button just closes the app, as follows:

```
def _onQuitCommand(self, event):
    self.Close()
```

When either of the radio buttons is selected, we will record the newly selected unit of measurement, as seen in these two callback methods:

```
def _onSelectMeters(self, event):
    self._convertMetersToFeet = False

def _onSelectFeet(self, event):
    self._convertMetersToFeet = True
```

Whenever a new character is entered in the text field, we will call a helper method to validate this text as potential input:

```
def _onCalibrationTextCtrlKeyUp(self, event):
    self._enableOrDisableCalibrationButton()
```

When the **Calibrate** button is clicked, we will parse the measurement from the text field, clear the text field, convert the measurement to meters if necessary, and store the value. The button's callback is implemented as follows:

```
def _calibrate(self, event):
    self._referencePixelDistBetweenLights = \
        self._pixelDistBetweenLights
    s = self._calibrationTextCtrl.GetValue()
    self._calibrationTextCtrl.SetValue('')
    self._referenceMetersToCamera = float(s)
    if self._convertMetersToFeet:
        self._referenceMetersToCamera *= 0.3048
```

Just like the Interactive Recognizer app in *Chapter 3, Training a Smart Alarm to Recognize the Villain and His Cat*, the background thread runs a loop that includes capturing an image, calling a helper method to process the image, and calling another helper method to display the image. Optionally, the image might be mirrored (flipped horizontally) before being displayed. Here is the loop's implementation:

```
def _runCaptureLoop(self):
    while self._running:
        success, image = self._capture.read()
        if image is not None:
            self._detectAndEstimateDistance(image)
            if (self.mirrored):
                image[:] = numpy.fliplr(image)
            wx.CallAfter(self._showImage, image)
```

The helper method used for processing the image is quite long. Let's look at it in several chunks. First, we will detect blobs in a gray version of the image and will initialize a dictionary that we will use to sort blobs by color:

```
def _detectAndEstimateDistance(self, image):

    grayImage = cv2.cvtColor(
        image, cv2.COLOR_BGR2GRAY)
    blobs = self._detector.detect(grayImage)
    blobsForColors = {}
```

For each blob, we will crop out a square region that is likely to include a white circle of light, plus some more saturated pixels around the edge:

```
for blob in blobs:

    centerXAsInt, centerYAsInt = \
        (int(n) for n in blob.pt)
    radiusAsInt = int(blob.size)

    minX = max(0, centerXAsInt - radiusAsInt)
    maxX = min(self._imageWidth,
        centerXAsInt + radiusAsInt)
    minY = max(0, centerYAsInt - radiusAsInt)
    maxY = min(self._imageHeight,
        centerYAsInt + radiusAsInt)

    region = image[minY:maxY, minX:maxX]
```

We will find the average hue and saturation of the region and, using these values, we will classify the blob as one of the colors that we defined at the top of this module:

```
    # Get the region's dimensions, which may
    # differ from the blob's diameter if the blob
    # extends past the edge of the image.
    h, w = region.shape[:2]

    meanColor = region.reshape(w * h, 3).mean(0)
    meanHue = ColorUtils.hueFromBGR(meanColor)
    meanSaturation = ColorUtils.saturationFromBGR(
        meanColor)

    if meanHue < 22.5 or meanHue > 337.5:
        color = COLOR_Red
```

```
  elif meanHue < 67.5:
    if meanSaturation < 25.0:
      color = COLOR_YellowWhite
    else:
      color = COLOR_AmberYellow
  elif meanHue < 172.5:
    color = COLOR_Green
  elif meanHue < 277.5:
    if meanSaturation < 25.0:
      color = COLOR_BlueWhite
    else:
      color = COLOR_BluePurple
  else:
    color = COLOR_Pink

  if color in blobsForColors:
    blobsForColors[color] += [blob]
  else:
    blobsForColors[color] = [blob]
```

> Depending on your camera's color rendition, you might need to tweak some of the hue and saturation thresholds.
>
> Note that our color-matching logic is based on perceptual (subjective) similarity and not on the geometric distance in any color space such as RGB, HSV, or HSL. Perceptually, a "green" light could be emerald green (geometrically close to cyan), neon green, or even spring green (geometrically close to yellow), but most people would never mistake a spring green light for an "amber" light, nor a yellowish orange light for a "red" light. Within the reddish and yellowish ranges, most people perceive more abrupt distinctions of color.

Finally, after classifying all blobs, we will call a helper method that handles the classification results and a helper method that can enable or disable the **Calibrate** button:

```
  self._processBlobsForColors(image, blobsForColors)
  self._enableOrDisableCalibrationButton()
```

Based on the color classification results, we want to highlight the blobs in certain colors, draw lines that connect pairs of like-colored blobs (if any), and display a message about the estimated distance to the first such pair of blobs. We will use the BGR color values and human-readable color names that we defined at the top of this module. The relevant code is as follows:

```
def _processBlobsForColors(self, image,
            blobsForColors):

    self._pixelDistBetweenLights = None

    for color in blobsForColors:

        prevBlob = None

        for blob in blobsForColors[color]:

            colorBGR, colorName = color

            centerAsInts = \
                tuple(int(n) for n in blob.pt)
            radiusAsInt = int(blob.size)

            # Fill the circle with the selected color.
            cv2.circle(image, centerAsInts,
                radiusAsInt, colorBGR,
                cv2.cv.CV_FILLED, cv2.CV_AA)
            # Outline the circle in black.
            cv2.circle(image, centerAsInts,
                radiusAsInt, (0, 0, 0), 1,
                cv2.CV_AA)

            if prevBlob is not None:

                if self._pixelDistBetweenLights is None:
                    self._pixelDistBetweenLights = \
                        GeomUtils.dist2D(blob.pt,
                            prevBlob.pt)
                    wx.CallAfter(self._showDistance,
                        colorName)

                prevCenterAsInts = \
```

```
        tuple(int(n) for n in prevBlob.pt)

        # Connect the current and previous
        # circle with a black line.
        cv2.line(image, prevCenterAsInts,
            centerAsInts, (0, 0, 0), 1,
            cv2.CV_AA)

        prevBlob = blob
```

Next, let's look at the helper method that enables or disables the **Calibrate** button. The button should be enabled only when a pixel distance between two lights is being measured and when a number (the real distance between the lights and camera) is in the text field. Here are the tests for these conditions:

```
def _enableOrDisableCalibrationButton(self):
  s = self._calibrationTextCtrl.GetValue()
  if len(s) < 1 or \
      self._pixelDistBetweenLights is None:
    self._calibrationButton.Disable()
  else:
    # Validate that the input is a number.
    try:
      float(s)
      self._calibrationButton.Enable()
    except:
      self._calibrationButton.Disable()
```

The helper method for displaying an image is the same as in our previous wxPython projects:

```
def _showImage(self, image):
  if image is None:
    # Provide a black bitmap.
    bitmap = wx.EmptyBitmap(self._imageWidth,
                self._imageHeight)
  else:
    # Convert the image to bitmap format.
    bitmap = WxUtils.wxBitmapFromCvImage(image)
  # Show the bitmap.
  self._staticBitmap.SetBitmap(bitmap)
```

Here is the helper method that shows the instructional message:

```
def _showInstructions(self):
    self._showMessage(
        'When a pair of lights is highlighted, '
        'enter the\ndistance and click '
        '"Calibrate".')
```

And here is the helper method that shows the estimated distance in either meters or feet:

```
def _showDistance(self, colorName):
    if self._referenceMetersToCamera is None:
        return
    value = self._referenceMetersToCamera * \
        self._referencePixelDistBetweenLights / \
        self._pixelDistBetweenLights
    if self._convertMetersToFeet:
        value /= 0.3048
        unit = 'feet'
    else:
        unit = 'meters'
    self._showMessage(
        'A pair of %s lights was spotted\nat '
        '%.2f %s.' % \
        (colorName, value, unit))
```

When the message is cleared, we will leave a newline character so that the label still has the same height as when it was populated:

```
def _clearMessage(self):
    # Insert an endline for consistent spacing.
    self._showMessage('\n')
```

Showing a message simply entails changing the text of the StaticText object, as seen in the following helper method:

```
def _showMessage(self, message):
    self._distanceStaticText.SetLabel(message)
```

The class is complete. Now, we just need the following main function (similar to our main functions for previous wxPython apps) to specify a file path for serialization/ deserialization and to launch the app:

```
def main():
    app = wx.App()
    configPath = PyInstallerUtils.pyInstallerResourcePath(
```

```
        'config.dat')
    livingHeadlights = LivingHeadlights(configPath)
    livingHeadlights.Show()
    app.MainLoop()

if __name__ == '__main__':
    main()
```

That is the whole implementation of The Living Headlights app! This project's code is short, but we have some unusual requirements for setup and testing. Let's turn to these tasks now.

Testing The Living Headlights app at home

Do not run out onto the highway at night to point your laptop's webcam into the headlights! We can devise more convenient and safer ways to test The Living Headlights, even if you have no car or do not drive.

A pair of LED flashlights is a good proxy for a pair of headlights. A flashlight with many LEDs (for example, 19) is preferable because it creates a denser circle of light that is more likely to be detected as exactly one blob. To ensure that the distance between the two flashlights remains constant, we can attach them to a rigid object, such as a board, using brackets, clamps, or tape. Here is an image of my flashlight holder, seen from the side:

The next image shows a frontal view of the flashlight holder, including a decorative grill:

Set up the lights in front of the webcam (parallel to the webcam's lens), run the app, and make sure that the lights are being detected. Then, using a tape measure, find the distance between the webcam and the center point between the front of the lights, as seen in the following image:

Type the distance in the text field and click on **Calibrate**. Then, move the lights nearer to the camera or farther from the camera (but keep them parallel to the camera's lens). Check that the app is updating the distance estimate appropriately.

To simulate colored car lights, place a thick piece of colored glass in front of the flashlights, as close to the light source as possible. Stained glass (the kind used in church windows) works well and you can find it in craft supply stores. Colored lens filters for photography or videography should also work. They are widely available, new or used, from camera stores. Colored acetate or other thin materials do not work well, as the LED lights are very intense. Here is an image of my lighting setup with an orange or amber colored stained glass filter:

Here is a screenshot showing the app's analysis of the same lighting setup:

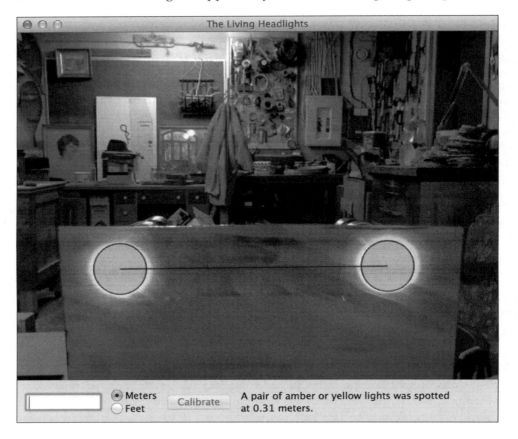

Check that the app is reporting an appropriate color for the detected lights. Depending on your particular camera's color rendition, you might find that you need to adjust some of the hue and saturation thresholds in your detectAndEstimateDistance method. You might also want to experiment with adjusting the attributes of your SimpleBlobDetector_Params object (in the initializer) to see their effects on the detection of lights and other blobs.

Once we are satisfied that the app is working well with our homemade apparatus, we can step up to a more realistic level of testing!

Testing The Living Headlights app in a car

While choosing the hardware for our setup in a car, we must consider two questions:

- Can the car's outlets power the hardware?
- Can the hardware fit conveniently in the car?

A Raspberry Pi draws power via its micro USB port. It needs a 5V, 700mA power source. We can satisfy this power requirement by plugging a USB adapter into the car's cigarette lighter receptacle and then connecting it to the Raspberry Pi via a USB to micro USB cable, as seen in the following image:

Normally, the cigarette lighter receptacle is a 12V power source, so it can power a variety of devices via an adapter. You could even power a chain of devices, and Raspberry Pi need not be the first device in the chain. Later in this section, we will discuss the example of Raspberry Pi drawing power from a 5V outlet on an HDMIPi display, which is in turn drawing power from a cigarette lighter receptacle via an adapter.

Standard USB peripherals, such as a webcam, mouse, and keyboard, can draw enough power from Raspberry Pi's USB ports. Although Raspberry Pi only has two USB ports, we can use a USB splitter to power a webcam, mouse, and keyboard simultaneously. Alternatively, some keyboards have a built-in touchpad that we can use as a mouse. Another option is to simply make do with only using two peripherals at a time and swapping one of them for the third peripheral as needed. In any case, once the app is started and calibrated (and once we are driving!), we do not want to use the keyboard or mouse input anymore.

The webcam should sit against the inside of the car's rear window. The webcam's lens should be as close to the window as possible to reduce the visibility of grime, moisture, and reflections (for example, the reflection of the webcam's "on" light). If the Raspberry Pi lies just behind the car's front seats, the webcam cable should be able to reach the back window while the power cable should still reach the USB adapter in the cigarette lighter receptacle. If not, use a longer USB to micro USB cable for the power and, if necessary, position the Pi farther back in the car. Alternatively, use a webcam with a longer cable. The following image shows the suggested positioning of the Pi:

Similarly, the next image shows the suggested positioning of the camera:

Now we have come to the hard part: the display. For video output, Raspberry Pi supports HDMI (as found in new TVs and many new monitors) and composite RCA (as found in old TVs). For other common connectors, we can use an adapter, such as HDMI to DVI or HDMI to VGA. Raspberry Pi also has limited support (via third-party kernel extensions) for video output via DSI or SPI (as found in cellphone displays and prototyping kits).

 Do not use a CRT television or monitor in a vehicle or in any context where it is liable to be bumped. A CRT might implode if the glass is damaged. Instead, use an LCD television or monitor.

A small display is desirable because it can be more conveniently mounted on the dashboard and it consumes less power. A few displays might be able to draw enough power from the cigarette lighter receptacle via a 5V or 12V adapter. For example, HDMIPi (a 9 inch, 1280 x 800 display, in beta at the time of writing this book) will work with a 12V, 1A power source or perhaps even a power source with lesser specifications, according to beta testers' reports. HDMIPi also promises to include a 5V outlet, making it possible for Raspberry Pi to draw power from the display. For more information, refer to the HDMIPi product site (`http://hdmipi.com/`) and Kickstarter page (`https://www.kickstarter.com/projects/697708033/hdmipi-affordable-9-high-def-screen-for-the-raspbe`).

Typically, though, a display needs a much higher voltage and wattage than the cigarette lighter receptacle can supply. Conveniently, some cars have an electrical outlet that resembles a wall socket, with the standard voltage for the type of socket but a lower maximum wattage. My car has a 110V, 150W outlet for two-pronged North American plugs (NEMA 1-15P). As seen in the following image, I use an extension cord to convert the two-pronged connection to a three-pronged connection (NEMA 5-15P) that my monitor cables use:

I tried plugging in three different monitors (one at a time, of course), with the following results:

- HP Pavilion 25xi (25 inch, 1920 x 1080): Does not turn on. Presumably, it requires a higher wattage.

- HP w2207 (22 inch, 1680 x 1050, 19.8 lbs.): Does not turn on but its weight and sturdy hinge make it useful as a flail to beat off hijackers, just in case the rocket launchers fail.

- Xplio XP22WD (22 inch, 1440 x 900): Turns on and works!

If you are unable to power a monitor from any of your car's outlets, an alternative is to use a battery block to power the monitor. Another alternative is to use a laptop or netbook as a substitute for the entire Pi-based system.

The XP22WD's ports are seen in the following image. To connect from Raspberry Pi, I am using an HDMI to DVI cable because the monitor does not have an HDMI port:

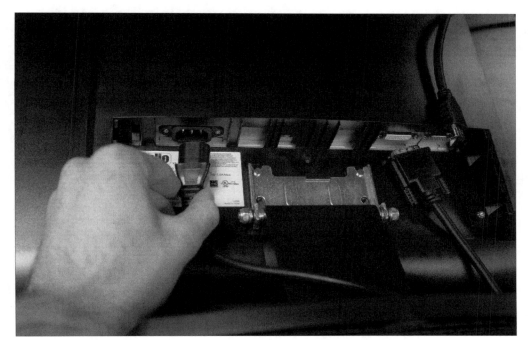

I admit that all my monitors are too big to mount on a dashboard! However, for testing the system in my driveway, I am content to have a monitor that sits on the front passenger seat, as seen in the following image:

Voilà! A car can power Raspberry Pi, peripherals, and a desktop monitor! As soon as the car is turned on, our system boots and then it runs exactly as we would expect of a Linux desktop. We can launch The Living Headlights app from the command line or from an IDE such as Geany. Our app's behavior on Raspberry Pi should be identical to its behavior on a conventional desktop system, except that on Pi we will experience a lower frame rate and greater lag.

Now that the app is running in a car, do not forget to recalibrate it so that it estimates distances based on the size of real headlights and not the size of our flashlight rig!

Summary

This chapter has provided you an opportunity to scale down the complexity of our algorithms in order to support low-powered hardware. We have also played with colorful lights, a homemade toy car, a puzzle of adapters, and a real car!

There is much room to extend the functionality of The Living Headlights. We could take an average of multiple reference measurements or store different reference measurements for different colors of lights. Across multiple frames, we could analyze patterns of flashing colored lights to judge whether the vehicle behind us is a police car or a road maintenance truck, or is signaling to turn. We could try to detect the flash of rocket launchers, though testing it might be problematic.

The next chapter's project is not something a driver should use! We are going to amplify our perception of motion so that we can even check a person's pulse in real time!

6
Seeing a Heartbeat with a Motion Amplifying Camera

Remove everything that has no relevance to the story. If you say in the first chapter that there is a rifle hanging on the wall, in the second or third chapter it absolutely must go off. If it's not going to be fired, it shouldn't be hanging there.

— Anton Chekhov

King Julian: I don't know why the sacrifice didn't work. The science seemed so solid.

— Madagascar: Escape 2 Africa (2008)

Despite their strange design and mysterious engineering, Q's gadgets always prove useful and reliable. Bond has such faith in the technology that he never even asks how to charge the batteries.

One of the inventive ideas in the Bond franchise is that even a lightly equipped spy should be able to see and photograph concealed objects, anyplace, anytime. Let's consider a timeline of a few relevant gadgets in the movies:

- 1967 (*You Only Live Twice*): An X-ray desk scans guests for hidden firearms.
- 1979 (*Moonraker*): A cigarette case contains an X-ray imaging system that is used to reveal the tumblers of a safe's combination lock.
- 1989 (*License to Kill*): A Polaroid camera takes X-ray photos. Oddly enough, its flash is a visible, red laser.

- 1995 (*GoldenEye*): A tea tray contains an X-ray scanner that can photograph documents beneath the tray.

- 1999 (*The World is Not Enough*): Bond wears a stylish pair of blue-lensed glasses that can see through one layer of clothing to reveal concealed weapons. According to the *James Bond Encyclopedia* (2007), which is an official guide to the movies, the glasses display infrared video after applying special processing to it. Despite using infrared, they are commonly called X-ray specs, a misnomer.

These gadgets deal with unseen wavelengths of light (or radiation) and are broadly comparable to real-world devices such as airport security scanners and night vision goggles. However, it remains difficult to explain how Bond's equipment is so compact and how it takes such clear pictures in diverse lighting conditions and through diverse materials. Moreover, if Bond's devices are active scanners (meaning they emit X-ray radiation or infrared light), they will be clearly visible to other spies using similar hardware.

To take another approach, what if we avoid unseen wavelengths of light but instead focus on unseen frequencies of motion? Many things move in a pattern that is too fast or too slow for us to easily notice. Suppose that a man is standing in one place. If he shifts one leg more than the other, perhaps he is concealing a heavy object, such as a gun, on the side that he shifts more. We also might fail to notice deviations from a pattern. Suppose the same man has been looking straight ahead but suddenly, when he believes no one is looking, his eyes dart to one side. Is he watching someone?

We can make motions of a certain frequency more visible by repeating them, like a delayed afterimage or a ghost, with each repetition being more faint (less opaque) than the last. The effect is analogous to an echo or a ripple, and it is achieved using an algorithm called **Eulerian video magnification**.

By applying this technique, we will build a desktop app that allows us to simultaneously see the present and selected slices of the past. The idea of experiencing multiple images simultaneously is, to me, quite natural because for the first 26 years of my life, I had strabismus—commonly called a *lazy eye*—that caused double vision. A surgeon corrected my eyesight and gave me depth perception but, in memory of strabismus, I would like to name this application Lazy Eyes.

Let's take a closer look—or two or more closer looks—at the fast-paced, moving world that we share with all the other secret agents.

[The completed project for this chapter can be downloaded from my website at http://nummist.com/opencv/7376_06.zip.]

Planning the Lazy Eyes app

Of all our apps, Lazy Eyes has the simplest user interface. It just shows a live video feed with a special effect that highlights motion. The parameters of the effect are quite complex and, moreover, modifying them at runtime would have a big effect on performance. Thus, we do not provide a user interface to reconfigure the effect, but we do provide many parameters in code to allow a programmer to create many variants of the effect and the app.

The following is a screenshot illustrating one configuration of the app. This image shows me eating cake. My hands and face are moving often and we see an effect that looks like light and dark waves rippling around the places where moving edges have been. (The effect is more graceful in a live video than in a screenshot.)

 For more screenshots and an in-depth discussion of the parameters, refer to the section *Configuring and testing the app for various motions*, later in this chapter.

Regardless of how it is configured, the app loops through the following actions:

1. Capturing an image.

2. Copying and downsampling the image while applying a blur filter and optionally an edge finding filter. We will downsample using so-called **image pyramids**, which will be discussed in *Compositing two images using image pyramids*, later in this chapter. The purpose of downsampling is to achieve a higher frame rate by reducing the amount of image data used in subsequent operations. The purpose of applying a blur filter and optionally an edge finding filter is to create haloes that are useful in amplifying motion.

3. Storing the downsampled copy in a history of frames, with a timestamp. The history has a fixed capacity and once it is full, the oldest frame is overwritten to make room for the new one.

4. If the history is not yet full, we continue to the next iteration of the loop.

5. Decomposing the history into a list of frequencies describing fluctuations (motion) at each pixel. The decomposition function is called a **Fast Fourier Transform**. We will discuss this in the *Extracting repeating signals from video using the Fast Fourier Transform* section, later in this chapter.

6. Setting all frequencies to zero except a certain chosen range that interests us. In other words, filter out the data on motions that are faster or slower than certain thresholds.

7. Recomposing the filtered frequencies into a series of images that are motion maps. Areas that are still (with respect to our chosen range of frequencies) become dark, and areas that are moving might remain bright. The recomposition function is called an **Inverse Fast Fourier Transform (IFFT)**, and we will discuss it later alongside the FFT.

8. Upsampling the latest motion map (again using image pyramids), intensifying it, and overlaying it additively atop the original camera image.

9. Showing the resulting composite image.

There it is — a simple plan that requires a rather nuanced implementation and configuration. Let's prepare ourselves by doing a little background research.

Understanding what Eulerian video magnification can do

Eulerian video magnification is inspired by a model in fluid mechanics called **Eulerian specification of the flow field**. Let's consider a moving, fluid body, such as a river. The Eulerian specification describes the river's velocity at a given position and time. The velocity would be fast in the mountains in springtime and slow at the river's mouth in winter. Also, the velocity would be slower at a silt-saturated point at the river's bottom, compared to a point where the river's surface hits a rock and sprays. An alternative to the Eulerian specification is the Lagrangian specification, which describes the position of a given particle at a given time. A given bit of silt might make its way down from the mountains to the river's mouth over a period of many years and then spend eons drifting around a tidal basin.

 For a more formal description of the Eulerian specification, the Lagrangian specification, and their relationship, refer to this Wikipedia article `http://en.wikipedia.org/wiki/Lagrangian_and_Eulerian_specification_of_the_flow_field`.

The Lagrangian specification is analogous to many computer vision tasks, in which we model the motion of a particular object or feature over time. However, the Eulerian specification is analogous to our current task, in which we model any motion occurring in a particular position and a particular window of time. Having modeled a motion from an Eulerian perspective, we can visually exaggerate the motion by overlaying the model's results for a blend of positions and times.

Let's set a baseline for our expectations of Eulerian video magnification by studying other people's projects:

- Michael Rubenstein's webpage at MIT (`http://people.csail.mit.edu/mrub/vidmag/`) gives an abstract and demo videos of his team's pioneering work on Eulerian video magnification.

- Bryce Drennan's Eulerian-magnification library (`https://github.com/brycedrennan/eulerian-magnification`) implements the algorithm using NumPy, SciPy, and OpenCV. This implementation is good inspiration for us, but it is designed to process prerecorded videos and is not sufficiently optimized for real-time input.

Now, let's discuss the functions that are building blocks of these projects and ours.

Extracting repeating signals from video using the Fast Fourier Transform (FFT)

An audio signal is typically visualized as a bar chart or wave. The bar chart or wave is high when the sound is loud and low when it is soft. We recognize that a repetitive sound, such as a metronome's beat, makes repetitive peaks and valleys in the visualization. When audio has multiple channels (being a stereo or surround sound recording), each channel can be considered as a separate signal and can be visualized as a separate bar chart or wave.

Similarly, in a video, every channel of every pixel can be considered as a separate signal, rising and falling (becoming brighter and dimmer) over time. Imagine that we use a stationary camera to capture a video of a metronome. Then, certain pixel values rise and fall at a regular interval as they capture the passage of the metronome's needle. If the camera has an attached microphone, its signal values rise and fall at the same interval. Based on either the audio or the video, we can measure the metronome's frequency—its **beats per minute (bpm)** or its beats per second (Hertz or Hz). Conversely, if we change the metronome's bpm setting, the effect on both the audio and the video is predictable. From this thought experiment, we can learn that a signal—be it audio, video, or any other kind—can be expressed as a function of time and, *equivalently*, a function of frequency.

Consider the following pair of graphs. They express the same signal, first as a function of time and then as a function of frequency. Within the time domain, we see one wide peak and valley (in other words, a tapering effect) spanning many narrow peaks and valleys. Within the frequency domain, we see a low-frequency peak and a high-frequency peak.

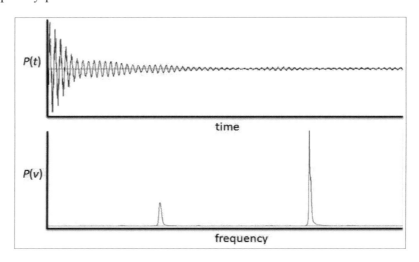

The transformation from the time domain to the frequency domain is called the Fourier transform. Conversely, the transformation from the frequency domain to the time domain is called the inverse Fourier transform. Within the digital world, signals are discrete, not continuous, and we use the terms **discrete Fourier transform (DFT)** and **inverse discrete Fourier transform (IDFT)**. There is a variety of efficient algorithms to compute the DFT or IDFT and such an algorithm might be described as a Fast Fourier Transform or an Inverse Fast Fourier Transform.

 For algorithmic descriptions, refer to the following Wikipedia article: `http://en.wikipedia.org/wiki/Fast_Fourier_transform`.

The result of the Fourier transform (including its discrete variants) is a function that maps a frequency to an amplitude and phase. The **amplitude** represents the magnitude of the frequency's contribution to the signal. The **phase** represents a temporal shift; it determines whether the frequency's contribution starts on a high or a low. Typically, amplitude and phase are encoded in a complex number, $a+bi$, where $amplitude=sqrt(a\text{^}2+b\text{^}2)$ and $phase=atan2(a,b)$.

 For an explanation of complex numbers, refer to the following Wikipedia article: `http://en.wikipedia.org/wiki/Complex_number`.

The FFT and IFFT are fundamental to a field of computer science called **digital signal processing**. Many signal processing applications, including Lazy Eyes, involve taking the signal's FFT, modifying or removing certain frequencies in the FFT result, and then reconstructing the filtered signal in the time domain using the IFFT. For example, this approach enables us to amplify certain frequencies while leaving others unchanged.

Now, where do we find this functionality?

Choosing and setting up an FFT library

Several Python libraries provide FFT and IFFT implementations that can process NumPy arrays (and thus OpenCV images). Here are the five major contenders:

- **NumPy**: This provides FFT and IFFT implementations in a module called `numpy.fft` (for more information, refer to `http://docs.scipy.org/doc/numpy/reference/routines.fft.html`). The module also offers other signal processing functions to work with the output of the FFT.

- **SciPy**: This provides FFT and IFFT implementations in a module called `scipy.fftpack` (for more information refer to `http://docs.scipy.org/doc/scipy/reference/fftpack.html`). This SciPy module is closely based on the `numpy.fft` module, but adds some optional arguments and dynamic optimizations based on the input format. The SciPy module also adds more signal processing functions to work with the output of the FFT.

- **OpenCV**: This has implementations of FFT (`cv2.dft`) and IFT (`cv2.idft`). An official tutorial provides examples and a comparison to NumPy's FFT implementation at `http://docs.opencv.org/doc/tutorials/core/discrete_fourier_transform/discrete_fourier_transform.html`. OpenCV's FFT and IFT interfaces are not directly interoperable with the `numpy.fft` and `scipy.fftpack` modules that offer a broader range of signal processing functionality. (The data is formatted very differently.)

- **PyFFTW**: This is a Python wrapper (`https://hgomersall.github.io/pyFFTW/`) around a C library called the **Fastest Fourier Transform in the West (FFTW)** (for more information, refer to `http://www.fftw.org/`). FFTW provides multiple implementations of FFT and IFFT. At runtime, it dynamically selects implementations that are well optimized for given input formats, output formats, and system capabilities. Optionally, it takes advantage of multithreading (and its threads might run on multiple CPU cores, as the implementation releases Python's Global Interpreter Lock or GIL). PyFFTW provides optional interfaces matching NumPy's and SciPy's FFT and IFFT functions. These interfaces have a low overhead cost (thanks to good caching options that are provided by PyFFTW) and they help to ensure that PyFFTW is interoperable with a broader range of signal processing functionality as implemented in `numpy.fft` and `scipy.fftpack`.

- **Reinka**: This is a Python library for GPU-accelerated computations using either PyCUDA (`http://mathema.tician.de/software/pycuda/`) or PyOpenCL (`http://mathema.tician.de/software/pyopencl/`) as a backend. Reinka (`http://reikna.publicfields.net/en/latest/`) provides FFT and IFFT implementations in a module called `reikna.fft`. Reinka internally uses PyCUDA or PyOpenCL arrays (not NumPy arrays), but it provides interfaces for conversion from NumPy arrays to these GPU arrays and back. The converted NumPy output is compatible with other signal processing functionality as implemented in `numpy.fft` and `scipy.fftpack`. However, this compatibility comes at a high overhead cost due to locking, reading, and converting the contents of the GPU memory.

NumPy, SciPy, OpenCV, and PyFFTW are open-source libraries under the BSD license. Reinka is an open-source library under the MIT license.

I recommend PyFFTW because of its optimizations and its interoperability (at a low overhead cost) with all the other functionality that interests us in NumPy, SciPy, and OpenCV. For a tour of PyFFTW's features, including its NumPy- and SciPy-compatible interfaces, refer to the official tutorial at `https://hgomersall.github.io/pyFFTW/sphinx/tutorial.html`.

Depending on our platform, we can set up PyFFTW in one of the following ways:

- In Windows, download and run a binary installer from `https://pypi.python.org/pypi/pyFFTW`. Choose the installer for either a 32-bit Python 2.7 or 64-bit Python 2.7 (depending on whether your Python installation, not necessarily your system, is 64-bit).

- In Mac with MacPorts, run the following command in Terminal:

```
$ sudo port install py27-pyfftw
```

- In Ubuntu 14.10 (Utopic) and its derivatives, including Linux Mint 14.10, run the following command in Terminal:

```
$ sudo apt-get install python-fftw3
```

  In Ubuntu 14.04 and earlier versions (and derivatives thereof), do not use this package, as its version is too old. Instead, use the PyFFTW source bundle, as described in the last bullet of this list.

- In Debian Jessie, Debian Sid, and their derivatives, run the following command in Terminal:

```
$ sudo apt-get install python-pyfftw
```

  In Debian Wheezy and its derivatives, including Raspbian, this package does not exist. Instead, use the PyFFTW source bundle, as described in the next bullet.

- For any other system, download the PyFFTW source bundle from `https://pypi.python.org/pypi/pyFFTW`. Decompress it and run the `setup.py` script inside the decompressed folder.

 Some old versions of the library are called PyFFTW3. We do not want PyFFTW3. However, on Ubuntu 14.10 and its derivatives, the packages are misnamed such that `python-fftw3` is really the most recent packaged version (whereas `python-fftw` is an older PyFFTW3 version).

We have our FFT and IFFT needs covered by FFTW (and if we were cowboys instead of secret agents, we could say, "Cover me!"). For additional signal processing functionality, we will use SciPy, which can be set up in the way described in *Chapter 1, Preparing for the Mission, Setting up a development machine*.

Signal processing is not the only new material that we must learn for Lazy Eyes, so let's now look at other functionality that is provided by OpenCV.

Compositing two images using image pyramids

Running an FFT on a full-resolution video feed would be slow. Also, the resulting frequencies would reflect localized phenomena at each captured pixel, such that the motion map (the result of filtering the frequencies and then applying the IFFT) might appear noisy and overly sharpened. To address these problems, we want a cheap, blurry downsampling technique. However, we also want the option to enhance edges, which are important to our perception of motion.

Our need for a blurry downsampling technique is fulfilled by a **Gaussian image pyramid**. A **Gaussian filter** blurs an image by making each output pixel a weighted average of many input pixels in the neighborhood. An image pyramid is a series in which each image is half the width and height of the previous image. The halving of image dimensions is achieved by **decimation**, meaning that every other pixel is simply omitted. A Gaussian image pyramid is constructed by applying a Gaussian filter before each decimation operation.

Our need to enhance edges in downsampled images is fulfilled by a **Laplacian image pyramid**, which is constructed in the following manner. Suppose we have already constructed a Gaussian image pyramid. We take the image at level i+1 in the Gaussian pyramid, upsample it by duplicating the pixels, and apply a Gaussian filter to it again. We then subtract the result from the image at level i in the Gaussian pyramid to produce the corresponding image at level i of the Laplacian pyramid. Thus, the Laplacian image is the difference between a blurry, downsampled image and an even blurrier image that was downsampled, downsampled again, and upsampled.

You might wonder how such an algorithm is a form of edge finding. Consider that edges are areas of local contrast, while non-edges are areas of local uniformity. If we blur a uniform area, it is still uniform—zero difference. If we blur a contrasting area, it becomes more uniform—nonzero difference. Thus, the difference can be used to find edges.

The Gaussian and Laplacian image pyramids are described in detail in the journal article downloadable from `http://web.mit.edu/persci/people/adelson/pub_pdfs/RCA84.pdf`.

This article is written by E. H. Adelson, C. H. Anderson, J. R. Bergen, P. J. Burt, and J. M. Ogden on "Pyramid methods in image processing, *RCA Engineer*, vol. 29, no. 6, November/December 1984.

Besides using image pyramids to downsample the FFT's input, we also use them to upsample the most recent frame of the IFFT's output. This upsampling step is necessary to create an overlay that matches the size of the original camera image so that we can composite the two. Like in the construction of the Laplacian pyramid, upsampling consists of duplicating pixels and applying a Gaussian filter.

OpenCV implements the relevant downsizing and upsizing functions as `cv2.pyrDown` and `cv2.pyrUp`. These functions are useful in compositing two images in general (whether or not signal processing is involved) because they enable us to soften differences while preserving edges. The OpenCV documentation includes a good tutorial on this topic at `http://docs.opencv.org/trunk/doc/py_tutorials/py_imgproc/py_pyramids/py_pyramids.html`.

Now, we are armed with the knowledge to implement Lazy Eyes!

Implementing the Lazy Eyes app

Let's create a new folder for Lazy Eyes and, in this folder, create copies of or links to the `ResizeUtils.py` and `WxUtils.py` files from any of our previous Python projects such as the project *The Living Headlights* in *Chapter 5, Equipping Your Car with a Rearview Camera and Hazard Detection*. Alongside the copies or links, let's create a new file, `LazyEyes.py`. Edit it and enter the following import statements:

```
import collections
import numpy
import cv2
import threading
import timeit
import wx

import pyfftw.interfaces.cache
from pyfftw.interfaces.scipy_fftpack import fft
from pyfftw.interfaces.scipy_fftpack import ifft
```

```
from scipy.fftpack import fftfreq

import ResizeUtils
import WxUtils
```

Besides the modules that we have used in previous projects, we are now using the standard library's `collections` module for efficient collections and `timeit` module for precise timing. Also for the first time, we are using signal processing functionality from PyFFTW and SciPy.

Like our other Python applications, Lazy Eyes is implemented as a class that extends `wx.Frame`. Here are the declarations of the class and its initializer:

```
class LazyEyes(wx.Frame):

   def __init__(self, maxHistoryLength=360,
      minHz=5.0/6.0, maxHz=1.0,
      amplification=32.0, numPyramidLevels=2,
      useLaplacianPyramid=True,
      useGrayOverlay=True,
      numFFTThreads = 4, numIFFTThreads=4,
      cameraDeviceID=0, imageSize=(480, 360),
      title='Lazy Eyes'):
```

The initializer's arguments affect the app's frame rate and the manner in which motion is amplified. These effects are discussed in detail in the section *Configuring and testing the app for various motions*, later in this chapter. The following is just a brief description of the arguments:

- `maxHistoryLength` is the number of frames (including the current frame and preceding frames) that are analyzed for motion.

- `minHz` and `maxHz`, respectively, define the slowest and fastest motions that are amplified.

- `amplification` is the scale of the visual effect. A higher value means motion is highlighted more brightly.

- `numPyramidLevels` is the number of pyramid levels by which frames are downsampled before signal processing is done. Remember that each level corresponds to downsampling by a factor of 2. Our implementation assumes `numPyramidLevels>0`.

   If `useLaplacianPyramid` is `True`, frames are downsampled using a Laplacian pyramid before the signal processing is done. The implication is that only edge motion is highlighted. Alternatively, if `useLaplacianPyramid` is `False`, a Gaussian pyramid is used, and the motion in all areas is highlighted.

- If useGrayOverlay is True, frames are converted to grayscale before the signal processing is done. The implication is that motion is only highlighted in areas of grayscale contrast. Alternatively, if useGrayOverlay is False, motion is highlighted in areas that have contrast in any color channel.

- numFFTThreads and numIFFTThreads, respectively, are the numbers of threads used in FFT and IFFT computations.

- cameraDeviceID and imageSize are our usual capture parameters.

The initializer's implementation begins in the same way as our other Python apps. It sets flags to indicate that the app is running and (by default) should be mirrored. It creates the capture object and configures its resolution to match the requested width and height if possible. Failing that, the device's default capture resolution is used. The relevant code is as follows:

```
self.mirrored = True

self._running = True

self._capture = cv2.VideoCapture(cameraDeviceID)
size = ResizeUtils.cvResizeCapture(
    self._capture, imageSize)
w, h = size
self._imageWidth = w
self._imageHeight = h
```

Next, we will determine the shape of the history of frames. It has at least 3 dimensions: a number of frames, a width, and height for each frame. The width and height are downsampled from the capture width and height based on the number of pyramid levels. If we are concerned about the color motion and not just the grayscale motion, the history also has a fourth dimension, consisting of 3 color channels. Here is the code to calculate the history's shape:

```
self._useGrayOverlay = useGrayOverlay
if useGrayOverlay:
  historyShape = (maxHistoryLength,
          h >> numPyramidLevels,
          w >> numPyramidLevels)
else:
  historyShape = (maxHistoryLength,
          h >> numPyramidLevels,
          w >> numPyramidLevels, 3)
```

Note the use of >>, the right bit shift operator, to reduce the dimensions by a power of 2. The power is equal to the number of pyramid levels.

We will store the specified maximum history length. For the frames in the history, we will create a NumPy array of the shape that we just determined. For timestamps of the frames, we will create a **deque (double-ended queue)**, a type of collection that allows us to cheaply add or remove elements from either end:

```
self._maxHistoryLength = maxHistoryLength
self._history = numpy.empty(historyShape,
             numpy.float32)
self._historyTimestamps = collections.deque()
```

We will store the remaining arguments because later, in each frame, we will pass them to the pyramid functions and signal the processing functions:

```
self._numPyramidLevels = numPyramidLevels
self._useLaplacianPyramid = useLaplacianPyramid

self._minHz = minHz
self._maxHz = maxHz
self._amplification = amplification

self._numFFTThreads = numFFTThreads
self._numIFFTThreads = numIFFTThreads
```

> To ensure meaningful error messages and early termination in the case of invalid arguments, we could add code such as the following for each argument:
> ```
> assert numPyramidLevels > 0, \
>     'numPyramidLevels must be positive.'
> ```
> For brevity, such assertions are omitted from our code samples.

We call the following two functions to tell PyFFTW to cache its data structures (notably, its NumPy arrays) for a period of at least 1.0 second from their last use. (The default is 0.1 seconds.) Caching is a critical optimization for the PyFFTW interfaces that we are using, and we will choose a period that is more than long enough to keep the cache alive from frame to frame:

```
pyfftw.interfaces.cache.enable()
pyfftw.interfaces.cache.set_keepalive_time(1.0)
```

The initializer's implementation ends with code to set up a window, event bindings, a bitmap, layout, and background thread—all familiar tasks from our previous Python projects:

```
style = wx.CLOSE_BOX | wx.MINIMIZE_BOX | \
    wx.CAPTION | wx.SYSTEM_MENU | \
```

```
        wx.CLIP_CHILDREN
wx.Frame.__init__(self, None, title=title,
        style=style, size=size)

self.Bind(wx.EVT_CLOSE, self._onCloseWindow)

quitCommandID = wx.NewId()
self.Bind(wx.EVT_MENU, self._onQuitCommand,
    id=quitCommandID)
acceleratorTable = wx.AcceleratorTable([
  (wx.ACCEL_NORMAL, wx.WXK_ESCAPE,
   quitCommandID)
])
self.SetAcceleratorTable(acceleratorTable)

self._staticBitmap = wx.StaticBitmap(self,
                 size=size)
self._showImage(None)

rootSizer = wx.BoxSizer(wx.VERTICAL)
rootSizer.Add(self._staticBitmap)
self.SetSizerAndFit(rootSizer)

self._captureThread = threading.Thread(
    target=self._runCaptureLoop)
self._captureThread.start()
```

We must modify our usual _onCloseWindow callback to disable PyFFTW's cache.
Disabling the cache ensures that resources are freed and that PyFFTW's threads
terminate normally. The callback's implementation is given in the following code:

```
def _onCloseWindow(self, event):
  self._running = False
  self._captureThread.join()
  pyfftw.interfaces.cache.disable()
  self.Destroy()
```

The *Esc* key is bound to our usual _onQuitCommand callback, which just closes
the app:

```
def _onQuitCommand(self, event):
  self.Close()
```

The loop running on our background thread is similar to the one in our other Python apps. In each frame, it calls a helper function, `_applyEulerianVideoMagnification`. Here is the loop's implementation.

```
def _runCaptureLoop(self):
  while self._running:
    success, image = self._capture.read()
    if image is not None:
      self._applyEulerianVideoMagnification(
          image)
      if (self.mirrored):
        image[:] = numpy.fliplr(image)
      wx.CallAfter(self._showImage, image)
```

The `_applyEulerianVideoMagnification` helper function is quite long so we will consider its implementation in several chunks. First, we will create a timestamp for the frame and copy the frame to a format that is more suitable for processing. Specifically, we will use a floating point array with either one gray channel or 3 color channels, depending on the configuration:

```
def _applyEulerianVideoMagnification(self, image):

  timestamp = timeit.default_timer()

  if self._useGrayOverlay:
    smallImage = cv2.cvtColor(
        image, cv2.COLOR_BGR2GRAY).astype(
            numpy.float32)
  else:
    smallImage = image.astype(numpy.float32)
```

Using this copy, we will calculate the appropriate level in the Gaussian or Laplacian pyramid:

```
# Downsample the image using a pyramid technique.
i = 0
while i < self._numPyramidLevels:
  smallImage = cv2.pyrDown(smallImage)
  i += 1
if self._useLaplacianPyramid:
  smallImage[:] -= \
    cv2.pyrUp(cv2.pyrDown(smallImage))
```

For the purposes of the history and signal processing functions, we will refer to this pyramid level as "the image" or "the frame".

Next, we will check the number of history frames that have been filled so far. If the history has more than one unfilled frame (meaning the history will still not be full after adding this frame), we will append the new image and timestamp and then return early, such that no signal processing is done until a later frame:

```
historyLength = len(self._historyTimestamps)

if historyLength < self._maxHistoryLength - 1:

    # Append the new image and timestamp to the
    # history.
    self._history[historyLength] = smallImage
    self._historyTimestamps.append(timestamp)

    # The history is still not full, so wait.
    return
```

If the history is just one frame short of being full (meaning the history will be full after adding this frame), we will append the new image and timestamp using the code given as follows:

```
if historyLength == self._maxHistoryLength - 1:
    # Append the new image and timestamp to the
    # history.
    self._history[historyLength] = smallImage
    self._historyTimestamps.append(timestamp)
```

If the history is already full, we will drop the oldest image and timestamp and append the new image and timestamp using the code given as follows:

```
else:
    # Drop the oldest image and timestamp from the
    # history and append the new ones.
    self._history[:-1] = self._history[1:]
    self._historyTimestamps.popleft()
    self._history[-1] = smallImage
    self._historyTimestamps.append(timestamp)

    # The history is full, so process it.
```

The history of image data is a NumPy array and, as such, we are using the terms "append" and "drop" loosely. NumPy arrays are immutable, meaning they cannot grow or shrink. Moreover, we are not recreating this array because it is large and reallocating it each frame would be expensive. We are just overwriting data within the array by moving the old data leftward and copying the new data in.

Based on the timestamps, we will calculate the average time per frame in the history, as seen in the following code:

```
# Find the average length of time per frame.
startTime = self._historyTimestamps[0]
endTime = self._historyTimestamps[-1]
timeElapsed = endTime - startTime
timePerFrame = \
    timeElapsed / self._maxHistoryLength
#print 'FPS:', 1.0 / timePerFrame
```

We will proceed with a combination of signal processing functions, collectively called a temporal bandpass filter. This filter blocks (zeros out) some frequencies and allows others to pass (remain unchanged). Our first step in implementing this filter is to run the `pyfftw.interfaces.scipy_fftpack.fft` function using the history and a number of threads as arguments. Also, with the argument `axis=0`, we will specify that the history's first axis is its time axis:

```
# Apply the temporal bandpass filter.
fftResult = fft(self._history, axis=0,
        threads=self._numFFTThreads)
```

We will pass the FFT result and the time per frame to the `scipy.fftpack.fftfreq` function. This function returns an array of midpoint frequencies (Hz in our case) corresponding to the indices in the FFT result. (This array answers the question, "Which frequency is the midpoint of the bin of frequencies represented by index i in the FFT?".) We will find the indices whose midpoint frequencies lie closest (minimum absolute value difference) to our initializer's `minHz` and `maxHz` parameters. Then, we will modify the FFT result by setting the data to zero in all ranges that do not represent the frequencies of interest:

```
frequencies = fftfreq(
    self._maxHistoryLength, d=timePerFrame)
lowBound = (numpy.abs(
    frequencies - self._minHz)).argmin()
highBound = (numpy.abs(
```

```
        frequencies - self._maxHz)).argmin()
fftResult[:lowBound] = 0j
fftResult[highBound:-highBound] = 0j
fftResult[-lowBound:] = 0j
```

> The FFT result is symmetrical: `fftResult[i]` and `fftResult[-i]` pertain to the same bin of frequencies. Thus, we will modify the FFT result symmetrically.
>
> Remember, the Fourier transform maps a frequency to a complex number that encodes an amplitude and phase. Thus, while the indices of the FFT result correspond to frequencies, the values contained at those indices are complex numbers. Zero as a complex number is written in Python as `0+0j` or `0j`.

Having thus filtered out the frequencies that do not interest us, we will finish applying the temporal bandpass filter by passing the data to the `pyfftw.interfaces.scipy_fftpack.ifft` function:

```
ifftResult = ifft(fftResult, axis=0,
        threads=self._numIFFTThreads)
```

From the IFFT result, we will take the most recent frame. It should somewhat resemble the current camera frame, but should be black in areas that do not exhibit recent motion matching our parameters. We will multiply this filtered frame so that the non-black areas become bright. Then, we will upsample it (using a pyramid technique) and add the result to the current camera frame so that areas of motion are lit up. Here is the relevant code, which concludes the `_applyEulerianVideoMagnification` method:

```
# Amplify the result and overlay it on the
# original image.
overlay = numpy.real(ifftResult[-1]) * \
        self._amplification
i = 0
while i < self._numPyramidLevels:
  overlay = cv2.pyrUp(overlay)
  i += 1
if self._useGrayOverlay:
  overlay = cv2.cvtColor(overlay,
            cv2.COLOR_GRAY2BGR
cv2.convertScaleAbs(image + overlay, image)
```

To finish the implementation of the LazyEyes class, we will display the image in the same manner as we have done in our other Python apps. Here is the relevant method:

```
def _showImage(self, image):
  if image is None:
    # Provide a black bitmap.
    bitmap = wx.EmptyBitmap(self._imageWidth,
               self._imageHeight)
  else:
    # Convert the image to bitmap format.
    bitmap = WXUtils.wxBitmapFromCvImage(image)
  # Show the bitmap.
  self._staticBitmap.SetBitmap(bitmap)
```

Our module's main function just instantiates and runs the app, as seen in the following code:

```
def main():
  app = wx.App()
  lazyEyes = LazyEyes()
  lazyEyes.Show()
  app.MainLoop()

if __name__ == '__main__':
  main()
```

That's all! Run the app and stay quite still while it builds up its history of frames. Until the history is full, the video feed will not show any special effect. At the history's default length of 360 frames, it fills in about 20 seconds on my machine. Once it is full, you should see ripples moving through the video feed in areas of recent motion — or perhaps all areas if the camera is moved or the lighting or exposure is changed. The ripples will gradually settle and disappear in areas of the scene that become still, while new ripples will appear in new areas of motion. Feel free to experiment on your own. Now, let's discuss a few recipes for configuring and testing the parameters of the LazyEyes class.

Configuring and testing the app for various motions

Currently, our main function initializes the LazyEyes object with the default parameters. By filling in the same parameter values explicitly, we would have this statement:

```
lazyEyes = LazyEyes(maxHistoryLength=360,
         minHz=5.0/6.0, maxHz=1.0,
```

```
amplification=32.0,
numPyramidLevels=2,
useLaplacianPyramid=True,
useGrayOverlay=True,
numFFTThreads = 4,
numIFFTThreads=4,
imageSize=(480, 360))
```

This recipe calls for a capture resolution of 480 x 360 and a signal processing resolution of 120 x 90 (as we are downsampling by 2 pyramid levels or a factor of 4). We are amplifying the motion only at frequencies of 0.833 Hz to 1.0 Hz, only at edges (as we are using the Laplacian pyramid), only in grayscale, and only over a history of 360 frames (about 20 to 40 seconds, depending on the frame rate). Motion is exaggerated by a factor of 32. These settings are suitable for many subtle upper-body movements such as a person's head swaying side to side, shoulders heaving while breathing, nostrils flaring, eyebrows rising and falling, and eyes scanning to and fro. For performance, the FFT and IFFT are each using 4 threads.

Here is a screenshot of the app that runs with these default parameters. Moments before taking the screenshot, I smiled like a comic theater mask and then I recomposed my normal expression. Note that my eyebrows and moustache are visible in multiple positions, including their current, low positions and their previous, high positions. For the sake of capturing the motion amplification effect in a still image, this gesture is quite exaggerated. However, in a moving video, we can see the amplification of more subtle movements too.

Here is a less extreme example where my eyebrows appear very tall because I raised and lowered them:

The parameters interact with each other in complex ways. Consider the following relationships between these parameters:

- Frame rate is greatly affected by the size of the input data for the FFT and IFFT functions. The size of the input data is determined by maxHistoryLength (where a shorter length provides less input and thus a faster frame rate), numPyramidLevels (where a greater level implies less input), useGrayOverlay (where True means less input), and imageSize (where a smaller size implies less input).

- Frame rate is also greatly affected by the level of multithreading of the FFT and IFFT functions, as determined by numFFTThreads and numIFFTThreads (a greater number of threads is faster up to some point).

- Frame rate is slightly affected by useLaplacianPyramid (False implies a faster frame rate), as the Laplacian algorithm requires extra steps beyond the Gaussian image.

- Frame rate determines the amount of time that maxHistoryLength represents.

- Frame rate and `maxHistoryLength` determine how many repetitions of motion (if any) can be captured in the `minHz` to `maxHz` range. The number of captured repetitions, together with `amplification`, determines how greatly a motion or a deviation from the motion will be amplified.

- The inclusion or exclusion of noise is affected by `minHz` and `maxHz` (depending on which frequencies of noise are characteristic of the camera), `numPyramidLevels` (where more implies a less noisy image), `useLaplacianPyramid` (where `True` is less noisy), `useGrayOverlay` (where `True` is less noisy), and `imageSize` (where a smaller size implies a less noisy image).

- The inclusion or exclusion of motion is affected by `numPyramidLevels` (where fewer means the amplification is more inclusive of small motions), `useLaplacianPyramid` (`False` is more inclusive of motion in non-edge areas), `useGrayOverlay` (`False` is more inclusive of motion in areas of color contrast), `minHz` (where a lower value is more inclusive of slow motion), `maxHz` (where a higher value is more inclusive of fast motion), and `imageSize` (where bigger size is more inclusive of small motions).

- Subjectively, the visual effect is always best when the frame rate is high, noise is excluded, and small motions are included. Again subjectively, other conditions for including or excluding motion (edge versus non-edge, grayscale contrast versus color contrast, and fast versus slow) are application-dependent.

Let's try our hand at reconfiguring Lazy Eyes, starting with the `numFFTThreads` and `numIFFTThreads` parameters. We want to determine the numbers of threads that maximize Lazy Eyes' frame rate on your machine. The more CPU cores you have, the more threads you can gainfully use. However, experimentation is the best guide to pick a number. To get a log of the frame rate in Lazy Eyes, uncomment the following line in the `_applyEulerianVideoMagnification` method:

```
print 'FPS:', 1.0 / timePerFrame
```

Run `LazyEyes.py` from the command line. Once the history fills up, the history's average FPS will be printed to the command line in every frame. Wait until this average FPS value stabilizes. It might take a minute for the average to adjust to the effect of the FFT and IFFT functions that begin running once the history is full. Take note of the FPS value, close the app, adjust the thread count parameters, and test again. Repeat until you feel that you have enough data to pick good numbers of threads to use on your hardware.

By activating additional CPU cores, multithreading can cause your system's temperature to rise. As you experiment, monitor your machine's temperature, fans, and CPU usage statistics. If you become concerned, reduce the number of FFT and IFFT threads. Having a suboptimal frame rate is better than overheating of your machine.

Now, experiment with other parameters to see how they affect FPS. The `numPyramidLevels`, `useGrayOverlay`, and `imageSize` parameters should all have a large effect. For subjectively good visual results, try to maintain a frame rate above 10 FPS. A frame rate above 15 FPS is excellent. When you are satisfied that you understand the parameters' effects on frame rate, comment out the following line again because the print statement is itself an expensive operation that can reduce frame rate:

```
#print 'FPS:', 1.0 / timePerFrame
```

Let's try another recipe. Although our default recipe accentuates motion at edges that have high grayscale contrast, this next recipe accentuates motion in all areas (edge or non-edge) that have high contrast (color or grayscale). By considering 3 color channels instead of one grayscale channel, we are tripling the amount of data being processed by the FFT and IFFT. To offset this change, we will cut each dimension of the capture resolution to two third times its default value, thus reducing the amount of data to 2/3 * 2/3 = 4/9 times the default amount. As a net change, the FFT and IFFT process 3 * 4/9 = 4/3 times the default amount of data, a relatively small change. The following initialization statement shows our new recipe's parameters:

```
lazyEyes = LazyEyes(useLaplacianPyramid=False,
        useGrayOverlay=False,
        imageSize=(320, 240))
```

Note that we are still using the default values for most parameters. If you have found non-default values that work well for `numFFTThreads` and `numIFFTThreads` on your machine, enter them as well.

Here are the screenshots to show our new recipe's effect. This time, let's look at a non-extreme example first. I was typing on my laptop when this was taken. Note the haloes around my arms, which move a lot when I type, and a slight distortion and discoloration of my left cheek (viewer's left in this mirrored image). My left cheek twitches a little when I think. Apparently, it is a tic—already known to my friends and family but rediscovered by me with the help of computer vision!

If you are viewing the color version of this image in the e-book, you should see that the haloes around my arms take a green hue from my shirt and a red hue from the sofa. Similarly, the haloes on my cheek take a magenta hue from my skin and a brown hue from my hair.

Now, let's consider a more fanciful example. If we were Jedi instead of secret agents, we might wave a steel ruler in the air and pretend it was a lightsaber. While testing the theory that Lazy Eyes could make the ruler *look like a real lightsaber*, I took the following screenshot. The image shows two pairs of light and dark lines in two places where I was waving the lightsaber ruler. One of the pairs of lines passes through each of my shoulders. The Light Side (light line) and the Dark Side (dark line) show opposite ends of the ruler's path as I waved it. The lines are especially clear in the color version in the e-book.

Finally, the moment for which we have all been waiting is ... a recipe for amplifying a heartbeat! If you have a heart rate monitor, start by measuring your heart rate. Mine is approximately 87 bpm as I type these words and listen to inspiring ballads by the Canadian folk singer Stan Rogers. To convert bpm to Hz, divide the bpm value by 60 (the number of seconds per minute), giving *(87 / 60) Hz = 1.45 Hz* in my case. The most visible effect of a heartbeat is that a person's skin changes color, becoming more red or purple when blood is pumped through an area. Thus, let's modify our second recipe, which is able to amplify color motions in non-edge areas. Choosing a frequency range centered on 1.45 Hz, we have the following initializer:

```
lazyEyes = LazyEyes(minHz=1.4, maxHz=1.5,
        useLaplacianPyramid=False,
        useGrayOverlay=False,
        imageSize=(320, 240))
```

Customize `minHz` and `maxHz` based on your own heart rate. Also, specify `numFFTThreads` and `numIFFTThreads` if non-default values work best for you on your machine.

Even amplified, a heartbeat is difficult to show in still images; it is much clearer in the live video while running the app. However, take a look at the following pair of screenshots. My skin in the left-hand side screenshot is more yellow (and lighter) while in the right-hand side screenshot it is more purple (and darker). For comparison, note that there is no change in the cream-colored curtains in the background.

Three recipes are a good start—certainly enough to fill an episode of a cooking show on TV. Go observe some other motions in your environment, try to estimate their frequencies, and then configure Lazy Eyes to amplify them. How do they look with grayscale amplification versus color amplification? Edge (Laplacian) versus area (Gaussian)? Different history lengths, pyramid levels, and amplification multipliers?

Check the book's support page, http://www.nummist.com/opencv, for additional recipes and feel free to share your own by mailing me at josephhowse@nummist.com.

Seeing things in another light

Although we began this chapter by presenting Eulerian video magnification as a useful technique for visible light, it is also applicable to other kinds of light or radiation. For example, a person's blood (in veins and bruises) is more visible when imaged in **ultraviolet** (**UV**) or in **near infrared** (**NIR**) than in visible light. (Skin is more transparent to UV and NIR). Thus, a UV or NIR video is likely to be a better input if we are trying to magnify a person's pulse.

Here are some examples of NIR and UV cameras that might provide useful results, though I have not tested them:

- The Pi NoIR camera (`http://www.raspberrypi.org/products/pi-noir-camera/`) is a consumer grade NIR camera with a MIPI interface. Here is a time lapse video showing the Pi NoIR renders outdoor scenes at `https://www.youtube.com/watch?v=LLA9KHNvUK8`. The camera is designed for Raspberry Pi, and on Raspbian it has V4L-compatible drivers that are directly compatible with OpenCV's `VideoCapture` class. (For instructions on setting up the drivers, refer to the section *Setting up the Raspberry Pi Camera Module* in *Chapter 1, Preparing for the Mission*.) Some Raspberry Pi clones might have drivers for it too. Unfortunately, Raspberry Pi is too slow to run Eulerian video magnification in real time. However, streaming the Pi NoIR input from Raspberry Pi to a desktop, via Ethernet, might allow for a real-time solution.

- The Agama V-1325R (`http://www.agamazone.com/products_v1325r.html`) is a consumer grade NIR camera with a USB interface. It is officially supported on Windows and Mac. Users report that it also works on Linux. It includes four NIR LEDs, which can be turned on and off via the vendor's proprietary software on Windows.

- Artray offers a series of industrial grade NIR cameras called InGaAs (`http://www.artray.us/ingaas.html`), as well as a series of industrial grade UV cameras (`http://www.artray.us/usb2_uv.html`). The cameras have USB interfaces. Windows drivers and an SDK are available from the vendor. A third-party project called OpenCV ARTRAY SDK (for more information refer to `https://github.com/eiichiromomma/CVMLAB/wiki/OpenCV-ARTRAY-SDK`) aims to provide interoperability with at least OpenCV's C API.

Good luck and good hunting in the invisible light!

Summary

This chapter has introduced you to the relationship between computer vision and digital signal processing. We have considered a video feed as a collection of many signals—one for each channel value of each pixel—and we have understood that repetitive motions create wave patterns in some of these signals. We have used the Fast Fourier Transform and its inverse to create an alternative video stream that only sees certain frequencies of motion. Finally, we have superimposed this filtered video atop the original to amplify the selected frequencies of motion. There, we summarized Eulerian video magnification in 100 words!

Our implementation adapts Eulerian video magnification to real time by running the FFT repeatedly on a sliding window of recently captured frames rather than running it once on an entire prerecorded video. We have considered optimizations such as limiting our signal processing to grayscale, recycling large data structures rather than recreating them, and using several threads.

After experiencing the slow but suspenseful work of studying subtle motions, let's finish this book with panache! Our next and final project is an action-packed physics simulation that makes drawings bounce off the page!

7

Creating a Physics Simulation Based on a Pen and Paper Sketch

James Bond lives in a nightmarish world where laws are written at the point of a gun

— Yuri Zhukov, Pravda, 30 September 1965

Bond: Just a moment. Three measures of Gordon's, one of vodka, half a measure of Kina Lillet. Shake it very well until it's ice-cold, then add a large thin slice of lemon peel. Got it?

— Casino Royale, Chapter 7: Rouge et Noir (1953)

James Bond is a precise man. Like a physicist, he seems to see order in a world where others see chaos. Another mission, another romance, another shaken drink, another crashing car or helicopter or skier, and another gunshot do not change the way the world works or the way the Cold War worked. He seems to take comfort in this consistency.

A psychologist might say that Bond has a habit of re-enacting an unhappy childhood, which the novels reveal to us in brief glimpses. The boy lacked a permanent home. His father was an international arms dealer for the Vickers company, so the family moved often for work. When James was 11, his parents died in a mountain climbing accident — the first of many dramatic, untimely deaths in the Bond saga. An aunt in Kent, England took in the orphaned James, but the next year he was sent to board at Eton College. There, the lonesome boy became infatuated with a maid, got into trouble over it, and was expelled — the first of his many short-lived and fraught romances. Next, he was sent even further from family, to Fettes College in Scotland. The pattern of displacement and trouble was set. By 16, he was trying to live the life of a playboy in Paris. By 20, he was a dropout from the University of Geneva, and he was off to join the Royal Navy at the height of the Second World War.

Amid all that upheaval, Bond did manage to learn a thing or two. He is clever, not just with his eyebrow-raising witty remarks, but also with his fast solutions to puzzles that involve mechanics, kinematics, or physics. He is never caught flat-footed (though he is sometimes caught in other ways).

The moral of the story is that a secret agent must practice his physics even under the most trying of circumstances. An app can help with that.

When I think about problems of geometry or physics, I like to draw them with pen and paper. However, I also like to see animations. Our app, *Rollingball*, will allow us to combine these two media. It will use computer vision to detect simple geometric shapes that the user can draw on paper. Then, based on the detected shapes, the app will create a physics simulation that the user can watch. The user can also influence the simulation by tilting the device to alter the simulated direction of gravity. The experience is like designing and playing one's own version of a ball-in-a-maze puzzle, a fine toy for aspiring secret agents.

Building games is fun — but it is not *all* fun and games! We have a new list of skills to master in this chapter:

- Detecting linear and circular edges using the Hough transform
- Detecting solid circles as blobs
- Using OpenCV in the Unity game engine
- Building a Unity game for Android
- Converting coordinates from OpenCV's space to Unity's space, and creating 3D objects in Unity, based on our detection results in OpenCV
- Customizing the appearance and physics behavior of 3D objects in Unity using shaders, materials, and physics materials
- Drawing lines and rectangles explicitly using OpenGL calls from Unity

With these goals in mind, let's get ready to play ball!

 The completed project for this chapter can be downloaded from my website at http://nummist.com/opencv/7376_07.zip. The download does not include the OpenCV for Unity plugin, which must be licensed and added to the project as described in the *Setting up OpenCV for Unity* section.

Planning the Rollingball app

Rollingball will be a mobile app. We will develop it in the Unity game engine using a third-party plugin called OpenCV for Unity. The app will be compatible with both Android and iOS. Our build instructions will focus on Android, but we will also provide a few notes for readers who are experienced with the iOS build process (on Mac).

 For instructions on setting up Unity and finding relevant documentation and tutorials, please refer back to the *Unity* section in *Chapter 1, Preparing for the Mission*. At the time of writing, Unity's supported development environments are Windows and Mac, but sadly not Linux.

Using the mobile device's camera, Rollingball will scan two types of primitive shapes: circles and lines. The user will start by drawing any combination of these primitive shapes. For example, refer to the following photograph:

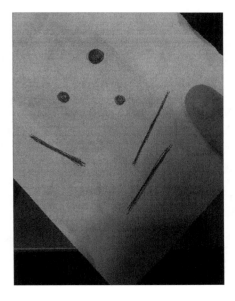

Here we have three circles and three lines drawn on the facing side of the paper. The reverse side also has some shapes drawn or printed on it, but these shapes are only faintly visible, so our detector should ignore them. The edges of the paper and some elements of the background can be considered as clearly visible lines, so our detector should detect them.

Rollingball is a simple app with only one Android activity or one iOS view controller. A live video feed fills most of the background. When circles or lines are detected, they are highlighted in red, as seen in the following screenshot:

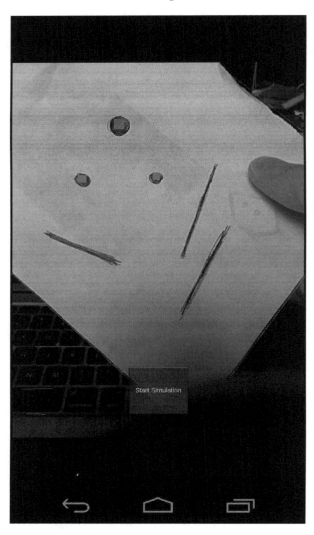

Note that some lines, especially the drawn lines, are detected multiple times because they are not perfectly straight nor are they perfectly continuous.

The user may press a button to start the physics simulation. During the simulation, the video pauses, the detector stops running, and the red-highlighted areas are replaced with cyan balls and lines. The lines are stationary but the balls fall freely and may bounce off each other and off the lines. Real-world gravity, as measured by the mobile device's gravity sensor, is used to control the simulated direction of gravity. However, the simulation is two-dimensional, and gravity is flattened such that it points toward an edge of the screen. The following screenshot shows the simulated balls after they have fallen partway down the page:

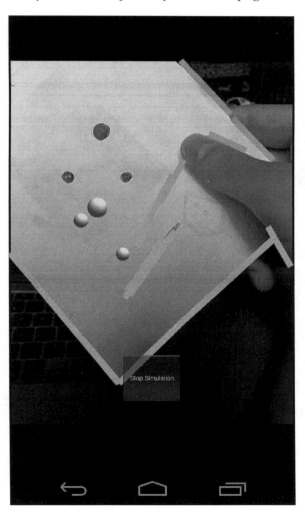

The user may press the button again to clear all the simulated objects and resume the live video and detection. The cycle can continue indefinitely with the user choosing to simulate different drawings or different views of the same drawing.

Now, let's consider the techniques to detect circles and lines.

Detecting circles and lines

From The Living Headlights (our project in *Chapter 5, Equipping Your Car with a Rearview Camera and Hazard Detection*), we are already familiar with one technique to detect circles. We treated the problem as a special case of blob detection and we used an OpenCV class, SimpleBlobDetector, which allows us to specify many detection criteria such as a blob's size, color, and circularity (or noncircularity, that is linearity).

A blob is a shape filled with a solid (or nearly solid) color. This definition implies that many circular or linear objects are not detectable as blobs. In the following photo we see a sunlit desk with a china teapot, china bowl, and pewter bowl:

The bowls and the lid of the teapot have approximately circular outlines in this top-down view. However, they are unlikely to pass the detection as blobs because the interior of each shape is multicolored, especially in uneven light.

Blob detection starts with a simple threshold filter (marking bright regions as white and dark regions as black); a more general approach to shape detection should start with an edge finding filter (marking edge regions as white and interior regions as black) and then a thresholding process. We define an edge as the discontinuity between neighboring regions of different brightness. Thus, an edge pixel has darker neighbors on one side and brighter neighbors on the opposite side. An edge-finding filter subtracts the neighbor values from one side and adds them from the opposite side in order to measure how strongly a pixel exhibits this edge-like contrast in a given direction. To achieve a measurement that is independent of edges' direction, we can apply multiple filters (each oriented for edges of a different direction) and treat each filter's output as a dimension of a vector whose magnitude represents the overall "edginess" of the pixel. A set of such measurements for all pixels is sometimes called the **derivative** of the image. Having computed the image's derivative, we select a threshold value based on the minimum contrast that we require in an edge. A high threshold accepts only high-contrast edges, while a lower threshold also accepts lower-contrast edges.

A popular edge-finding technique is the Canny algorithm. OpenCV's implementation, the `Imgproc.Canny` function, performs both filtering and thresholding. As arguments, it takes a grayscale image, an output image, a low threshold value, and a high threshold value. The low threshold should accept all pixels that *might be* part of a good edge. The high threshold should accept only pixels that *definitely are* part of a good edge. From the set whose members *might be* edge pixels, the Canny algorithm accepts only the members that connect to *definite* edge pixels. The double criteria help to ensure that we can accept thin extremities of a major edge while rejecting edges that are altogether faint. For example, a pen stroke or the curb of a road extending into the distance can be a major edge with thin extremities.

Having identified edge pixels, we can count how many of them are intersected by a given primitive shape. The greater the number of intersections, the more confident we can be that the given primitive shape correctly represents an edge in the image. Each intersection is called a **vote**, and a shape needs a specified number of votes to be accepted as a real edge's shape. Out of all the possible primitive shapes (of a given kind) in the image, we will consider an evenly spaced representative sample. We do so by specifying a step size for the shapes' geometric parameters. (For example, a line's parameters are a point and angle, while a circle's parameters are a center point and radius.) This sample of possible shapes is called a **grid**, the individual shapes in it are called **cells**, and the votes are said to be cast in cells. This process—tallying the matches between actual edge pixels and a sample of possible shapes—is the core of a technique called the **Hough transform**, which has various specializations such as **Hough line detection** and **Hough circle detection**.

Hough line detection has two implementations in OpenCV: `Imgproc.HoughLines`, which is based on the original Hough transform, and `Imgproc.HoughLinesP`, which is based on a probabilistic variant of the Hough transform. `Imgproc.HoughLines` does an exhaustive count of intersections for all possible lines of a given pair of step sizes in pixels and in radians. `Imgproc.HoughLinesP` is usually faster (particularly in images with a few long line segments) as it takes possible lines in a random order and discards some possible lines after finding a good line in a region. `Imgproc.HoughLines` expresses each line as a distance from the origin and an angle, whereas `Imgproc.HoughLinesP` expresses each line as two points—the endpoints of a detected segment of the line—which is a more useful representation since it gives us the option to treat the detection results as line segments rather than indefinitely long lines. For both the functions, the arguments include the image (which should be preprocessed with Canny or a similar algorithm), the step sizes in pixels and radians, and the minimum number of intersections required to accept a line. The arguments to `Imgproc.HoughLinesP` also include a minimum length between endpoints and a maximum gap, where a gap consists of non-edge pixels between edge pixels that intersect the line.

Hough circle detection has one implementation in OpenCV, `Imgproc.HoughCircles`, which is based on a variant of the Hough transform that makes use of gradient information at edges. This function's arguments include the image (preprocessed with Canny or a similar algorithm), a step size in pixels, a minimum distance between detected circles' centers, and minimum and maximum radii.

 For more details on the Canny algorithm, the Hough transform, and OpenCV's implementations of them, refer to *Chapter 7, Extracting Lines, Contours, and Components* in Robert Laganière's book, *OpenCV 2 Computer Vision Application Programming Cookbook* (Packt Publishing, 2011).

Despite using a more efficient algorithm than the original Hough transform, `Imgproc.HoughCircles` is a computationally expensive function, so we do not actually use it in Rollingball. Instead, we assume that the user will draw circles in a solid color and we will apply blob detection, which is cheaper. For line detection, we will use the `Imgproc.HoughLinesP` function, which is not as expensive as OpenCV's other Hough detectors.

Having chosen algorithms and their OpenCV implementations, let's set up the plugin that will let us easily access this functionality in Unity.

Setting up OpenCV for Unity

Unity provides a cross-platform framework for scripting games in high-level languages such as C#. However, it also supports platform-specific plugins in languages such as C, C++, Objective-C (for Mac and iOS), and Java (for Android). Developers can publish these plugins (and other assets) on the Unity Asset Store. Many published plugins represent a large amount of high-quality work, and buying one might be more economical than writing your own.

OpenCV for Unity, by Enox Software (https://github.com/EnoxSoftware/), is a $75 plugin at the time of writing. It offers a C# API that is closely based on OpenCV's official Java (Android) bindings. However, the plugin wraps OpenCV's C++ libraries and is compatible with Android, iOS, Windows, and Mac. It is reliable, in my experience, and it saves us a lot of work that we would otherwise put into custom C++ code and C# wrappers. Moreover, it comes with several valuable samples.

> Although OpenCV for Unity supports Android, iOS, Windows, and Mac, there are other OpenCV C# bindings that support a different set of platforms, including Linux. These alternatives are not designed with Unity in mind, so getting them to work in a Unity project might prove difficult or even impractical. Generally, they support .NET and Mono. The OpenCvSharp binding (https://github.com/shimat/opencvsharp) is an up-to-date, open-source binding, whereas Emgu CV (http://www.emgu.com) is a commercially supported binding . Have a look.

Let's go shopping. Open Unity and create a new project, as described in *Chapter 1, Preparing for the Mission*, of this book. From the menu bar, select **Asset Store** under **Window**. If you have not already created a Unity account, follow the prompts to create one. Once you log into the store, you should see the **Asset Store** window. Enter OpenCV for Unity in the search bar in the upper-right corner.

Click on the **OpenCV for Unity** link among the search results. You should see something similar to the following screenshot:

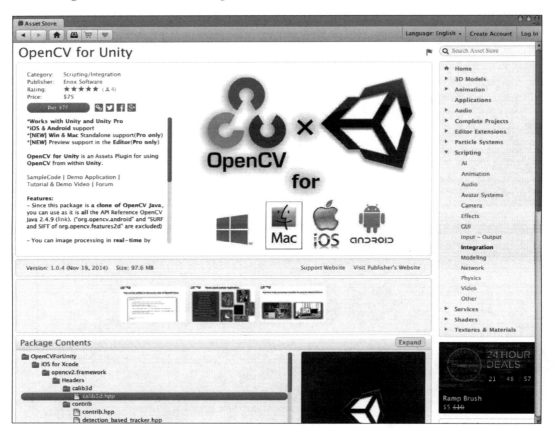

Click on the **Buy** button and complete the transaction as directed. Click on the **Download** button and wait for the download to complete. Click on the **Import** button. You should now see the **Importing package** window, as shown in the next screenshot:

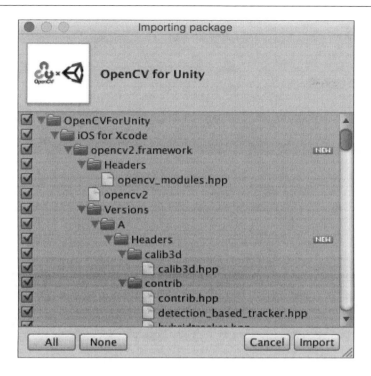

This is a list of all the files in the bundle that we just purchased. Ensure that all their checkboxes are checked, and then click on the **Import** button. Soon, you should see all the files in the **Project** pane of the Unity Editor.

The bundle includes further setup instructions and helpful links in the OpenCVForUnity/ReadMe.pdf file. Read the ReadMe! To run Rollingball on Android, we need to copy libopencvforunity.so and opencvforunity.jar from OpenCVForUnity/Plugins/Android to Plugins/Android. Also, to run one of OpenCV for Unity's samples, we must copy assets/haarcascade_frontalface_alt.xml from AOpenCVForUnity/Plugins/Android to Assets/Plugins/Android. Refer to the ReadMe's similar instructions for iOS if you wish to build for that platform.

 Throughout this chapter, paths are relative to the project's Assets folder unless otherwise specified.

Next let's try the samples.

Configuring and building the Unity project

Unity supports many target platforms. Switching to a new target is easy as long as our plugins support it. We just need to set a few build configuration values, some of which are shared across multiple targets and some of which are platform-specific.

From the menu bar, select **Preferences** under **Unity**, which should bring up the **Unity Preferences** window. Click on the **External Tools** tab and set **Android SDK Location** to be the base path to your Android SDK installation. (We referred to this location as <android_sdk> in the *Tegra Android Developer Pack* section of *Chapter 1*, *Preparing for the Mission*.) Recent versions of Unity support API level 9 (Android 2.3) and newer versions, so you probably already have an appropriate API version installed with your Android SDK. Now, the window should look similar to the following screenshot:

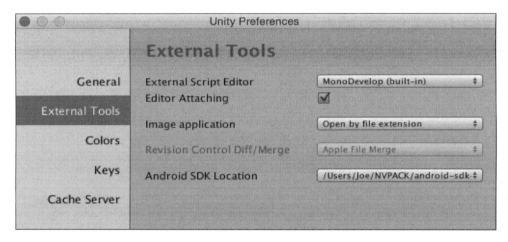

Now, from the menu bar, select **Build Settings** under **File**. The **Build Settings** window should appear. Drag all of the sample scene files, such as Samples/OpenCVForUnitySample.unity and Samples/ComicFilterSample/ComicFilterSample.unity, from the **Project** pane to the **Scenes In Build** list in the **Build Settings** window. Ensure that **OpenCVForUnitySample.unity** is the first scene in the list. (Drag-and-drop list items to reorder them.) Also ensure that all the scenes' checkboxes are checked. Click on the **Android** platform and then the **Switch Platform** button. The window should now look like what is shown in the following screenshot:

Click on the **Player Settings...** button. A list of settings should appear in the **Inspector** pane of the Unity Editor. Fill out a **Company Name**, such as Nummist Media Corporation Limited, and a **Product Name**, such as Rollingball. Click on **Resolution and Presentation** to expand it and then, for **Default Orientation**, select **Portrait**. Click on **Other Settings** to expand it and then fill out a **Bundle Identifier**, such as com.nummist.rollingball.

Ensure that an Android device is plugged in and that USB debugging is enabled on the device. Go back to the **Build Settings** window and click on **Build and Run**. Specify a path for the build. It is good practice to separate the build path from the Unity project folder, just as you would normally separate builds from source code. Once the build begins, a progress bar should appear. Watch the **Console** pane of the Unity Editor to be sure that no build errors occur. When the build is finished, it is copied onto the Android device and then it runs.

Enjoy the OpenCV for Unity samples! If you like, browse their source code and scenes in the Unity Editor. Next, we have our own scene to build!

Creating the Rollingball scene in Unity

Let's create a directory, `Rollingball`, to contain our application-specific code and assets. Right-click on the **Project** pane and choose **Folder** under **Create** from the context menu. Rename the new folder `Rollingball`. Create a subfolder, `Rollingball/Scenes`, in a similar way.

From the menu bar, select **New Scene** under **File** and then select **Save Scene as...** under **File**. Save the scene as `Rollingball/Scenes/Rollingball.unity`.

By default, our newly created scene contains just a camera—that is, the virtual world's camera, not a capture device. We are going to add three more objects in the following way:

1. From the menu bar, navigate to **Game Object | Create Other | Quad**. An object called **Quad** should appear in the **Hierarchy** pane. Rename **Quad** to `VideoRenderer`. This object is going to represent the live video feed.

2. From the menu bar, navigate to **Game Object | Create Other | Directional Light**. An object, **Directional light**, should appear in the **Hierarchy** pane. It will illuminate the balls and lines in our physics simulation.

3. From the menu bar, select **Create Empty** under **Game Object**. An object called **GameObject** should appear in the **Hierarchy** pane. Rename **GameObject** to `QuitOnAndroidBack`. Later, it will hold a script component that responds to the standard back button on Android.

 Objects in **Hierarchy** are called **game objects**, and the sections that are visible in their **Inspector** panes are called **components**.

Drag **Main Camera** onto **VideoRenderer** in order to make the former a child of the latter. A child moves, rotates, and scales up or down when its parent does. The relevance is that we want our camera to maintain a predictable relationship to the live video background.

 Parent-child relationships in **Hierarchy** do not represent object-oriented inheritance or, in other words, a child does not have an "is a" relationship with its parent. Rather, a parent has a one-to-many "has a" relationship with its children.

With the new objects created and **Main Camera** reparented, **Hierarchy** should look like what is shown in the following screenshot:

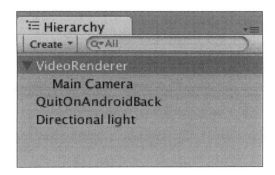

VideoRenderer and **Main Camera** will be configured in code based on the properties of the mobile device's video camera. However, let's set some reasonable defaults. Select **VideoRenderer** in **Hierarchy** and then, in the **Inspector** pane, edit its **Transform** properties to match the following screenshot:

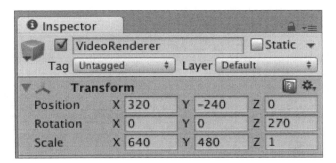

Similarly, select **Main Camera** and edit its **Transform** and **Camera** properties to match the following screenshot:

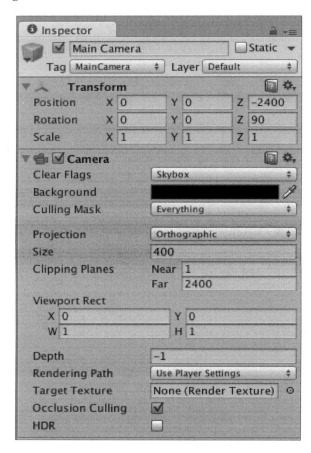

Note that we have configured an orthographic projection, meaning that objects' pixel size is constant, regardless of their distance from the camera. This configuration is appropriate for a 2D game or simulation such as Rollingball.

These four objects are the foundation of our scene. The rest of the project involves attaching custom properties to these objects and using C# scripts to control them and to create new objects around them.

Creating Unity assets and adding them to the scene

Custom properties and behaviors in a Unity project are defined through various types of files that are generically called **Assets**. Our project has four remaining questions and requirements that we must address by creating and configuring assets:

1. What is the appearance of the surfaces in the scene—namely, the video feed, the detected circles and lines, and the simulated balls and lines? We need to write **Shader** code and create **Material** configurations to define the appearance of these surfaces.

2. How bouncy are the balls? We need to create a **Physics Material** configuration to answer this all-important question.

3. Which objects represent a simulated ball and simulated line? We need to create and configure **Prefab** objects that the simulation can instantiate.

4. How does it all behave? We need to write Unity **Scripts**—specifically, code that subclasses a Unity class called MonoBehaviour—in order to control objects in the scene at various stages in their life cycle.

The following subsections tackle these requirements one by one.

Writing shaders and creating materials

A shader is a set of functions that run on the GPU. Although such functions can be applied to general-purpose computing, typically they are used for graphics rendering—that is, to define the color of output pixels on the screen based on the inputs that describe lighting, geometry, surface texture, and perhaps other variables such as time. Unity comes with many shaders for common styles of 3D and 2D rendering. We can also write our own shader.

For in-depth tutorials on shader scripting in Unity, refer to the *Unity Shaders and Effects Cookbook* by Kenny Lammers (Packt Publishing, 2013).

Let's create a folder, Rollingball/Shaders, and then create a shader in it (by clicking on **Shader** under **Create** in the **Project** pane's context menu). Rename the shader DrawSolidColor. Double-click on it to edit it and replace the contents with the following code:

```
Shader "Draw/Solid Color" {
  Properties {
    _Color ("Main Color", Color) = (1.0, 1.0, 1.0, 1.0)
  }
  SubShader {
    Pass { Color [_Color] }
  }
}
```

This humble shader has one parameter, a color. The shader renders pixels in this color regardless of conditions such as lighting. For the purposes of **Inspector** GUI, the shader's name is **Draw | Solid Color** and its parameter's name is **Main Color**.

A material has a shader and a set of parameter values for the shader. The same shader can be used by multiple materials, which might use different parameter values. Let's create a material that draws solid red. We will use this material to highlight detected circles and lines.

Create a new folder, Rollingball/Materials, and then create a material in it (by clicking on **Material** under **Create** in the context menu). Rename the material *DrawSolidRed*. Select it and, in **Inspector**, set its shader to **Draw/Solid Color** and its **Main Color** to the RGBA value for red (255, 0, 0, 255). **Inspector** should now look like what is shown in the following screenshot:

 If a shader's parameters, such as **Main Color**, are not visible in the material's **Inspector**, click on the ball next to the shader's name to expand the list of parameters.

We are going to create two more materials using shaders that come with Unity. First, create a material named **Cyan** and configure it so that its shader is **Diffuse** and its **Main Color** is cyan (0, 255, 255, 255). Leave the **Base (RBG)** texture as **None**. We will apply this material to the simulated balls and lines. Its Inspector should look like this:

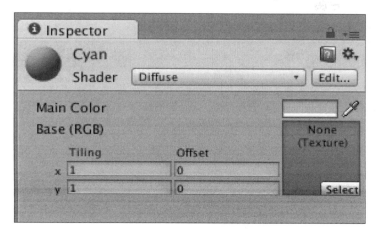

Now, create a material named **Video** and configure it so that its shader is **Unlit/Texture**. Leave the **Base (RBG)** texture as **None(Texture)**. Later, via code, we will assign the video texture to this material. Drag the **Video** material (from the **Project** pane) to **VideoRenderer** (in the **Hierarchy** pane) in order to assign the material to the quad. Select **VideoRenderer** and confirm that its **Inspector** includes the material component that is shown in the following screenshot:

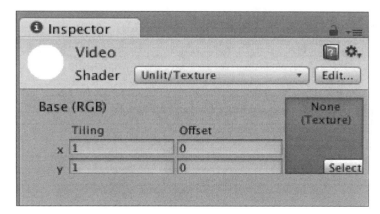

We will assign the remaining materials once we create prefabs and scripts.

Now that we have made materials for rendering, let's look at the analogous concept of physics materials.

Creating physics materials

Although Unity's rendering pipeline can run custom functions that we write in shaders, its physics pipeline runs fixed functions. Nonetheless, we can configure the parameters of those functions via physics materials.

 Unity's physics engine is based on NVIDIA PhysX with custom patches. PhysX supports GPU acceleration via CUDA on Windows. However, currently, Unity only uses PhysX's CPU implementation, which is completely cross-platform.

Let's create a folder, `Rollingball/Physics Materials`, and in it create a physics material (by clicking on **Physics Material** under **Create** in the context menu). Rename the physics material as `Bouncy`. Select it and note that it has the following properties in **Inspector**:

- **Dynamic Friction**: This is the ratio between the force that presses two objects together (for example, gravity) and the frictional force that resists continued motion along the surface.

- **Static Friction**: This is the ratio between the force that presses two objects together (for example, gravity) and the frictional force that resists initial motion along the surface. Refer to Wikipedia (`https://en.wikipedia.org/wiki/Friction#Approximate_coefficients_of_friction`) for sample values. For static friction, a value of 0.04 is like Teflon on Teflon, a value of 1.0 is like rubber on concrete, and a value of 1.05 is like copper on cast iron.

- **Bounciness**: This shows the proportion of an object's kinetic energy that it retains while bouncing off another surface. Here, a value of 0 means that the object does not bounce. A value of 1 means that it bounces without loss of energy. A value greater than 1 means that it (unrealistically) gains energy while bouncing.

- **Friction Combine**: When objects collide, which friction value affects this object? The options are **Average**, **Minimum**, **Multiply**, and **Maximum**.

- **Bounce Combine**: When objects collide, which bounciness value affects this object? The options are **Average**, **Minimum**, **Multiply**, and **Maximum**.

- **Friction Direction 2**: This represents a direction that exhibits different friction characteristics than other directions do. Such friction characteristics are said to be anisotropic (dependent on direction). If this parameter is set to the zero vector, anisotropic friction is disabled.

- **Dynamic Friction 2**: This is the dynamic friction along **Friction Direction 2**.

- **Static Friction 2**: This is the static friction along **Friction Direction 2**.

Careful! Are those physics materials explosive?

A physics simulation is said to *explode* when values grow continually and overflow the system's floating-point numeric limits. For example, if a collision's combined bounciness is greater than 1 and the collision occurs repeatedly, then over time the forces tend toward infinity. Ka-boom! We broke the physics engine.

Even without weird physics materials, numeric problems arise in scenes of an extremely large or small scale. For example, consider a multiplayer game that uses input from the Global Positioning System (GPS) such that objects in a Unity scene are positioned according to players' real-world longitude and latitude. The physics simulation cannot handle a human-sized object in this scene because the object and the forces acting on it are so small that they vanish inside the margin of floating-point error. This is a case where the simulation *implodes* (rather than explodes).

Let's set **Bounciness** to 1 (very bouncy!) and leave the other values at their defaults. Later, you can adjust everything to your taste if you wish. **Inspector** should look like this:

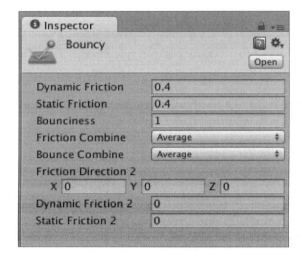

Our simulated lines will use default physics parameters, so they do not need a physics material.

Now that we have our rendering materials and physics materials, let's create prefabs for an entire simulated ball and an entire simulated line.

Creating prefabs

A prefab is an object that is not itself part of a scene but is designed to be copied into scenes during editing or at runtime. It can be copied many times to make many objects in the scene. At runtime, the copies have no special connection to the prefab or each other and all copies can behave independently. Although the role of a prefab is sometimes likened to the role of a class, a prefab is not a type.

Even though prefabs are not part of a scene, they are created and typically edited via a scene. Let's create a sphere in the scene by navigating to **Game Object | Create Other | Sphere** from the menu bar. An object named **Sphere** should appear in **Hierarchy**. Rename it as SimulatedCircle. Drag each of the following assets from the **Project** pane onto **SimulatedCircle** in **Hierarchy**:

- **Cyan** (in Rollingball/Materials)
- **Bouncy** (in Rollingball/PhysicsMaterials)

Now select **SimulatedCircle** and, in the **Rigidbody** section of **Inspector**, expand the **Constraints** field and check **Z** under **Freeze Position**. The effect of this change is to constrain the sphere's motion to two dimensions. Confirm that **Inspector** looks like this:

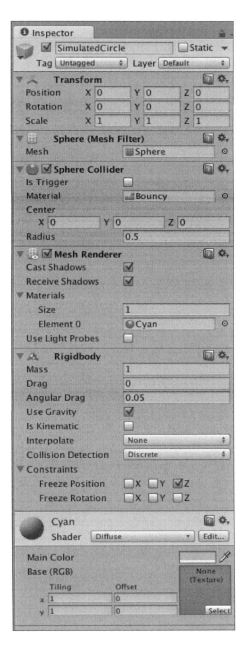

Create a folder, Rollingball/Prefabs, and drag **SimulatedCircle** from **Hierarchy** into the folder in the **Project** pane. A prefab, also named **SimulatedCircle**, should appear in the folder. Meanwhile, the name of the **SimulatedCircle** object in **Hierarchy** should turn blue to indicate that the object has a prefab connection. Changes to the object in the scene can be applied back to the prefab by clicking on the **Apply** button in the scene object's **Inspector**. Conversely, changes to the prefab (at edit time, not at runtime) are automatically applied to instances in scenes except for properties in which an instance has unapplied changes.

Now, let's follow similar steps to create a prefab of a simulated line. Create a cube in the scene by navigating to **Game Object | Create Other | Cube** from the menu bar. An object named **Cube** should appear in **Hierarchy**. Rename it as *SimulatedLine*. Drag **Cyan** from the **Project** pane onto **SimulatedLine** in **Hierarchy**. Select **SimulatedLine** and, in the **Rigidbody** section of its **Inspector**, tick the **Is Kinematic** checkbox, which means that the object is not moved by the physics simulation (even though it is part of the simulation for the purpose of other objects colliding with it). Recall that we want the lines to be stationary. They are just obstacles for the falling balls. **Inspector** should now look like this:

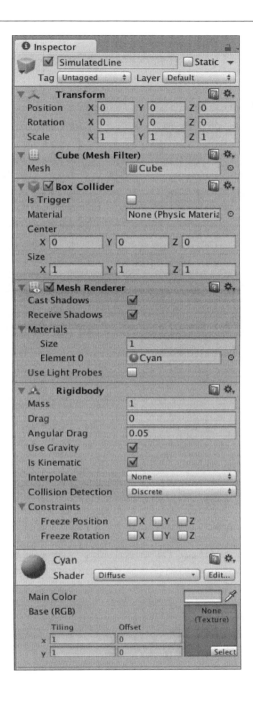

Let's clean up our scene by deleting the instances of the prefabs from **Hierarchy** (but we want to keep the prefabs themselves in the **Project** pane). Now, let's turn our attention to the writing of scripts, which among other things, are able to copy prefabs at runtime.

Writing our first Unity script

As mentioned earlier, a Unity script is a subclass of MonoBehaviour. A MonoBehaviour object can obtain references to objects in **Hierarchy** and components that we attach to these objects in **Inspector**. A MonoBehaviour object also has its own **Inspector** where we can assign additional references, including references to **Project** assets such as prefabs. At runtime, Unity sends messages to all MonoBehaviour objects when certain events occur. A subclass of MonoBehaviour can implement callbacks for any of these messages. MonoBehaviour supports more than 60 standard message callbacks. Here are some examples:

- Awake: This is called during initialization.
- Start: This is called after Awake but before the first call to Update, which is explained in the following bullet point.
- Update: This callback is called with every frame.
- OnGUI: This is called when the GUI overlay is ready for rendering instructions and the GUI events are ready to be handled.
- OnPostRender: This is called after the scene is rendered. This is an appropriate callback in which to implement post-processing effects.
- OnDestroy: This is called when the script is about to be deleted.

> For more information on the standard message callbacks, and the arguments that some callbacks' implementations may optionally take, refer to the official documentation at http://docs.unity3d.com/ScriptReference/MonoBehaviour.html. Also note that we can send custom messages to all MonoBehaviour objects using the SendMessage method.

Implementations of these and Unity's other callbacks can be private, protected, or public. Unity calls them regardless of protection level.

To summarize, then, scripts are the glue—the game logic—that connects runtime events to various objects that we see in **Project**, **Hierarchy**, and **Inspector**.

Let's create a folder, `Rollingball/Scripts`, and in it create a script (by clicking on **C#Script** under **Create** in the context menu). Rename the script `QuitOnAndroidBack` and double-click on it to edit it. Replace its contents with the following code:

```
using UnityEngine;


namespace com.nummist.rollingball {

  public sealed class QuitOnAndroidBack : MonoBehaviour {

    void Update() {
      if (Input.GetKeyUp(KeyCode.Escape)) {
        Application.Quit();
      }
    }
  }
}
```

We are using a namespace, `com.nummist.rollingball`, to keep our code organized and to avoid potential conflicts between our type names and type names in other parties' code. Namespaces in C# are like packages in Java. Our class is called `QuitOnAndroidBack`. It extends Unity's `MonoBehaviour` class. We use the `sealed` modifier (similar to Java's `final` modifier) to indicate that we do not intend to create subclasses of `QuitOnAndroidBack`.

 Note that `MonoBehaviour` uses the UK English spelling of "behaviour".

Thanks to Unity's callback system, the script's `Update` method gets called in every frame. It checks whether the user has pressed a key (or button) that is mapped to the `Escape` keycode. On Android, the standard back button is mapped to `Escape`. When the key (or button) is pressed, the application quits.

Save the script and drag it from the **Project** pane to the **QuitOnAndroidBack** object in **Hierarchy**. Click on the **QuitOnAndroidBack** object and confirm that its **Inspector** looks like this:

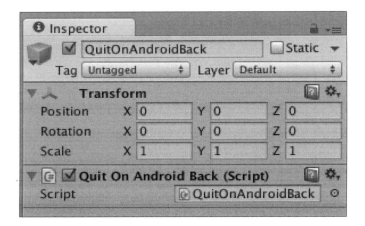

That was an easy script, right? The next one is a bit trickier—but more fun—because it handles everything *except* quitting.

Writing the main Rollingball script

Let's create a folder, **Rollingball/Scripts**, and in it create a script (by clicking on **C# Script** under **Create** in the context menu). Rename the script `DetectAndSimulate` and double-click on it to edit it. Delete its default contents and begin the code with the following import statements:

```
using UnityEngine;
using System.Collections;
using System.Collections.Generic;
using System.IO;

using OpenCVForUnity;
```

Next, let's declare our namespace and class with the following code:

```
namespace com.nummist.rollingball {

    [RequireComponent (typeof(Camera))]
    public sealed class DetectAndSimulate : MonoBehaviour {
```

Note that the class has an attribute, `[RequireComponent (typeof(Camera))]`, which means that the script can only be attached to a game object that has a camera (a game-world camera, not a video camera). We will specify this requirement because we are going to highlight the detected shapes via an implementation of the standard `OnPostRender` callback, and this callback only gets called for scripts attached to a game object with a camera.

`DetectAndSimulate` needs to store representations of circles and lines in both 2D screen space and 3D world space. These representations do not need to be visible to any other class in our application, so it is appropriate to define their types as private inner structs. Our `Circle` type stores 2D coordinates that represent the circle's center in screen space, a float representing its radius in screen space, and 3D coordinates representing the circle's center in world space. A constructor accepts all these values as arguments. Here is the `Circle` type's implementation:

```
struct Circle {

    public Vector2 screenPosition;
    public float screenDiameter;
    public Vector3 worldPosition;

    public Circle(Vector2 screenPosition,
        float screenDiameter,
        Vector3 worldPosition) {
        this.screenPosition = screenPosition;
        this.screenDiameter = screenDiameter;
        this.worldPosition = worldPosition;
    }
}
```

We will define another inner struct, `Line`, to store two sets of 2D coordinates representing endpoints in screen space and two sets of 3D coordinates representing the same endpoints in world space. A constructor accepts all these values as arguments. Here is the implementation of `Line`:

```
struct Line {

    public Vector2 screenPoint0;
    public Vector2 screenPoint1;
    public Vector3 worldPoint0;
    public Vector3 worldPoint1;

    public Line(Vector2 screenPoint0,
        Vector2 screenPoint1,
        Vector3 worldPoint0,
```

```
        Vector3 worldPoint1) {
        this.screenPoint0 = screenPoint0;
        this.screenPoint1 = screenPoint1;
        this.worldPoint0 = worldPoint0;
        this.worldPoint1 = worldPoint1;
    }
}
```

Next, we will define member variables that are editable in **Inspector**. Such a variable is marked with the [SerializeField] attribute, which means that Unity serializes the variable despite it being non-public. (Alternatively, public variables are also editable in **Inspector**.) The following four variables describe our preferences for camera input, including the direction the camera faces, its resolution, and its frame rate:

```
[SerializeField] bool useFrontFacingCamera = false;
[SerializeField] int preferredCaptureWidth = 640;
[SerializeField] int preferredCaptureHeight = 480;
[SerializeField] int preferredFPS = 15;
```

At runtime, the camera devices and modes available to us might differ from these preferences.

We will also make several more variables editable in **Inspector** — namely, a reference to the video background's renderer, a reference to the material for highlighting detected shapes, a factor for adjusting the scale of the simulation's gravity, references to the simulated shapes' prefabs, and a font size for the button:

```
[SerializeField] Renderer videoRenderer;

[SerializeField] Material drawPreviewMaterial;

[SerializeField] float gravityScale = 8f;

[SerializeField] GameObject simulatedCirclePrefab;
[SerializeField] GameObject simulatedLinePrefab;

[SerializeField] int buttonFontSize = 24;
```

We also have a number of member variables that do not need to be editable in **Inspector**. Among them are references to the game world's camera, a reference to the real-world camera's video texture, matrices to store images and intermediate processing results, and measurements relating to camera images, the screen, simulated objects, and the button:

```
Camera _camera;

WebCamTexture webCamTexture;
Color32[] colors;
Mat rgbaMat;
Mat grayMat;
Mat cannyMat;

float screenWidth;
float screenHeight;
float screenPixelsPerImagePixel;
float screenPixelsYOffset;

float raycastDistance;
float lineThickness;
UnityEngine.Rect buttonRect;
```

We will store a blob detector, a matrix of blob representations in OpenCV's format, and a list of circle representations in our own `Circle` format:

```
FeatureDetector blobDetector;
MatOfKeyPoint blobs = new MatOfKeyPoint();
List<Circle> circles = new List<Circle>();
```

Similarly, we will store a matrix of Hough line representations in OpenCV's format, and a list of line representations in our own `Line` format:

```
Mat houghLines = new Mat();
List<Line> lines = new List<Line>();
```

We will hold a reference to the gyroscope input device, and we will store the magnitude of gravity to be used in our physics simulation:

```
Gyroscope gyro;
float gravityMagnitude;
```

We (and the Unity API) are using the terms "gyroscope" and "gyro" loosely. We are referring to a fusion of motion sensors that might or might not include a real gyroscope. A gyroscope can be simulated, albeit poorly, using other real sensors such as an accelerometer and/or gravity sensor.

Unity provides a property, `SystemInfo.supportsGyroscope`, to indicate whether the device has a real gyroscope. However, this information does not concern us. We just use Unity's `Gyroscope.gravity` property, which can be derived from a real gravity sensor or can be simulated using other real sensors such as an accelerometer and/or gyroscope. Unity Android apps are configured by default to require an accelerometer, so we can safely assume that at least a simulated gravity sensor is available.

We will keep track of a list of simulated objects and provide a property, `simulating`, that is `true` when the list is non-empty:

```
List<GameObject> simulatedObjects =
  new List<GameObject>();
bool simulating {
  get {
    return simulatedObjects.Count > 0;
  }
}
```

Now, let's turn our attention to methods. We will implement the standard `Start` callback. The implementation begins by getting a reference to the attached camera, getting a reference to the gyro, and computing the magnitude of the game world's gravity, as seen in the following code:

```
void Start() {

  // Cache the reference to the game world's
  // camera.
  _camera = camera;

  gyro = Input.gyro;
  gravityMagnitude = Physics.gravity.magnitude *
    gravityScale;
```

MonoBehaviour provides getters for many components that might be attached to the same game object as the script. (Such components would appear alongside the script in **Inspector**). For example, the camera getter returns a Camera object (or null if none is present). These getters are expensive because they use introspection. Thus, if you need to refer to a component repeatedly, it is more efficient to store the reference in a member variable using a statement such as _camera = camera;, as shown in the preceding code.

The implementation of Start proceeds by finding a camera that faces the required direction (either front or rear, depending on the value of the useFrontFacingCamera field, above). If no suitable camera is found, the method returns early, as seen in the following code:

```
// Try to find a (physical) camera that faces
// the required direction.
WebCamDevice[] devices = WebCamTexture.devices;
int numDevices = devices.Length;
for (int i = 0; i < numDevices; i++) {
  WebCamDevice device = devices[i];
  if (device.isFrontFacing ==
        useFrontFacingCamera) {
    string name = device.name;
    Debug.Log("Selecting camera with " +
        "index " + i + " and name " +
        name);
    webCamTexture = new WebCamTexture(
        name, preferredCaptureWidth,
        preferredCaptureHeight,
        preferredFPS);
    break;
  }
}

if (webCamTexture == null) {
  // No camera faces the required direction.
  // Give up.
  Debug.LogError("No suitable camera found");
  Destroy(this);
  return;
}
```

> Throughout our implementation of `DetectAndSimulate`, when we encounter an unrecoverable runtime problem, we call `Destroy(this);`, thereby deleting the instance of the script and preventing further messages from reaching its callbacks.

The `Start` callback concludes by activating the camera and gyroscope (including the gravity sensor) and launching a helper coroutine called `Init`:

```
// Ask the camera to start capturing.
webCamTexture.Play();

if (gyro != null) {
  gyro.enabled = true;
}

// Wait for the camera to start capturing.
// Then, initialize everything else.
StartCoroutine(Init());
}
```

> A coroutine is a method that does not necessarily run to completion in one frame. Rather, it can `yield` for one or more frames in order to wait for a certain condition to be fulfilled or just to make something happen after a defined delay. Note that a coroutine runs on the main thread.

Our `Init` coroutine begins by waiting for the camera to capture the first frame. Then, we determine the frame's dimensions and we create OpenCV matrices to match these dimensions. Here is the first part of the method's implementation:

```
IEnumerator Init() {

  // Wait for the camera to start capturing.
  while (!webCamTexture.didUpdateThisFrame) {
    yield return null;
  }

  int captureWidth = webCamTexture.width;
  int captureHeight = webCamTexture.height;
  float captureDiagonal = Mathf.Sqrt(
    captureWidth * captureWidth +
    captureHeight * captureHeight);
  Debug.Log("Started capturing frames at " +
```

```
  captureWidth + "x" + captureHeight);

colors = new Color32[
  captureWidth * captureHeight];

rgbaMat = new Mat(captureHeight, captureWidth,
  CvType.CV_8UC4);
grayMat = new Mat(captureHeight, captureWidth,
  CvType.CV_8UC1);
cannyMat = new Mat(captureHeight, captureWidth,
  CvType.CV_8UC1);
```

The coroutine proceeds by configuring the game world's orthographic camera and video quad to match the capture resolution and to render the video texture:

```
transform.localPosition =
  new Vector3(0f, 0f, -captureWidth);
_camera.nearClipPlane = 1;
_camera.farClipPlane = captureWidth + 1;
_camera.orthographicSize =
  0.5f * captureDiagonal;
raycastDistance = 0.5f * captureWidth;

Transform videoRendererTransform =
  videoRenderer.transform;
videoRendererTransform.localPosition =
  new Vector3(captureWidth / 2,
  -captureHeight / 2, 0f);
videoRendererTransform.localScale =
  new Vector3(captureWidth,
  captureHeight, 1f);

videoRenderer.material.mainTexture =
  webCamTexture;
```

The device's screen and captured camera images likely have different resolutions. Moreover, remember that our application is configured for portrait orientation (in **Player Settings**). This orientation affects screen coordinates but not the coordinates in camera images, which will remain in landscape orientation. Thus, we need to calculate conversion factors between image coordinates and screen coordinates, as seen in the following code:

```
// Calculate the conversion factors between
// image and screen coordinates.
// Note that the image is landscape but the
```

```
    // screen is portrait.
    screenWidth = (float)Screen.width;
    screenHeight = (float)Screen.height;
    screenPixelsPerImagePixel =
      screenWidth / captureHeight;
    screenPixelsYOffset =
      0.5f * (screenHeight - (screenWidth *
      captureWidth / captureHeight));
```

Our conversions will be based on fitting the video background to the width of the portrait screen, while either letterboxing or cropping the video at the top and bottom if necessary.

The thickness of simulated lines and the dimensions of the button are based on screen resolution, as seen in the following code, which concludes the `Init` coroutine:

```
    lineThickness = 0.01f * screenWidth;

    buttonRect = new UnityEngine.Rect(
      0.4f * screenWidth,
      0.75f * screenHeight,
      0.2f * screenWidth,
      0.1f * screenHeight);

    InitBlobDetector();
  }
```

Our `InitBlobDetector` helper method serves to create a blob detector and set its blob detection parameters. The method begins by calling a factory method for a detector and validating that the returned detector is non-null, as seen in the following code:

```
    void InitBlobDetector() {

      // Try to create the blob detector.
      blobDetector = FeatureDetector.create(
          FeatureDetector.SIMPLEBLOB);
      if (blobDetector == null) {
        Debug.LogError(
            "Unable to create blob detector");
        Destroy(this);
        return;
      }
```

Unlike the Python API that we used for blob detection in *Chapter 5, Equipping Your Car with a Rearview Camera and Hazard Detection*, the OpenCV for Unity API requires the detector's parameters to be read from a YAML configuration file. (The official OpenCV Java API has the same limitation.) However, I prefer to keep the parameter values in the source code in case we ever decide that we want to compute them based on runtime data such as capture resolution. To work around the API's limitation, we can construct a string of parameters in YAML format and then save it to a temporary file. The YAML format is very simple. The first line declares the YAML version and each subsequent line consists of a variable name, a colon, and the variable's value. Let's continue with the method's implementation by declaring the following string:

```
        // The blob detector's parameters as a verbatim
        // string literal.
        // Do not indent the string's contents.
        string blobDetectorParams = @"%YAML:1.0
thresholdStep: 10.0
minThreshold: 50.0
maxThreshold: 220.0
minRepeatability: 2
minDistBetweenBlobs: 10.0
filterByColor: False
blobColor: 0
filterByArea: True
minArea: 50.0
maxArea: 5000.0
filterByCircularity: True
minCircularity: 0.8
maxCircularity: 3.4028234663852886e+38
filterByInertia: False
minInertiaRatio: 0.1
maxInertiaRatio: 3.4028234663852886e+38
filterByConvexity: False
minConvexity: 0.95
maxConvexity: 3.4028234663852886e+38
";
```

Now, let's try to save the string of parameters to a temporary file. If the file cannot be saved, the method returns early. Otherwise, the detector reads the parameters back from the file. Finally, the file is deleted. Here is the code, which concludes the `InitBlobDetector` method:

```
        // Try to write the blob detector's parameters
        // to a temporary file.
        string path = Application.persistentDataPath +
```

```
    "/blobDetectorParams.yaml";
  File.WriteAllText(path, blobDetectorParams);
  if (!File.Exists(path)) {
    Debug.LogError(
      "Unable to write blob " +
      "detector's parameters to " +
       path);
    Destroy(this);
    return;
  }

  // Read the blob detector's parameters from the
  // temporary file.
  blobDetector.read(path);

  // Delete the temporary file.
  File.Delete(path);
}
```

We will implement the standard Update callback by processing gravity sensor input and processing camera input, provided that certain conditions are met. At the beginning of the method, if OpenCV objects are not yet initialized, the method returns early. Otherwise, the game world's direction of gravity is updated based on the real-world direction of gravity, as detected by the device's gravity sensor. Here is the first part of the method's implementation:

```
void Update() {

  if (rgbaMat == null) {
    // Initialization is not yet complete.
    return;
  }

  if (gyro != null) {
    // Align the game-world gravity to real-world
    // gravity.
    Vector3 gravity = gyro.gravity;
    gravity.z = 0f;
    gravity = gravityMagnitude *
      gravity.normalized;
    Physics.gravity = gravity;
  }
```

Next, if there is no new camera frame ready or if the simulation is currently running, the method returns early. Otherwise, we will convert the frame to OpenCV's format, convert it to gray, find edges, and call the two helper methods, `UpdateCircles` and `UpdateLines`, to perform shape detection. Here is the relevant code, which concludes the `Update` method:

```
if (!webCamTexture.didUpdateThisFrame) {
  // No new frame is ready.
  return;
}

if (simulating) {
  // No new detection results are needed.
  return;
}

// Convert the RGBA image to OpenCV's format using
// a utility function from OpenCV for Unity.
Utils.WebCamTextureToMat(webCamTexture,
 rgbaMat, colors);

// Convert the OpenCV image to gray and
// equalize it.
Imgproc.cvtColor(rgbaMat, grayMat,
  Imgproc.COLOR_RGBA2GRAY);
Imgproc.Canny(grayMat, cannyMat, 50.0, 200.0);
Imgproc.equalizeHist(grayMat, grayMat);

UpdateCircles();
UpdateLines();
}
```

Our `UpdateCircles` helper method begins by performing blob detection. We will clear the list of any previously detected circles. Then, we will iterate over the blob detection results. Here is the opening of the method's implementation:

```
void UpdateCircles() {

  // Detect blobs.
  blobDetector.detect(grayMat, blobs);

  //
  // Calculate the circles' screen coordinates
```

```
// and world coordinates.
//

// Clear the previous coordinates.
circles.Clear();

// Iterate over the blobs.
KeyPoint[] blobsArray = blobs.toArray();
int numBlobs = blobsArray.Length;
for (int i = 0; i < numBlobs; i++) {
```

We will use a helper method, `ConvertToScreenPosition`, to convert the circle's center point from image space to screen space. We will also convert its diameter:

```
    // Convert blobs' image coordinates to
    // screen coordinates.
    KeyPoint blob = blobsArray[i];
    Point imagePoint = blob.pt;
    Vector2 screenPosition =
        ConvertToScreenPosition(
            (float)imagePoint.x,
            (float)imagePoint.y);
    float screenDiameter =
        blob.size *
        screenPixelsPerImagePixel;
```

We will use another helper method, `ConvertToWorldPosition`, to convert the circle's center point from screen space to world space. We will also convert its diameter. Having done our conversions, we will instantiate `Circle` and add it to the list. Here is the code that completes the `UpdateCircles` method:

```
    // Convert screen coordinates to world
    // coordinates based on raycasting.
    Vector3 worldPosition =
        ConvertToWorldPosition(
            screenPosition);

    Circle circle = new Circle(
        screenPosition, screenDiameter,
        worldPosition);
    circles.Add(circle);
    }
}
```

Our `UpdateLines` helper method begins by performing probabilistic Hough line detection with step sizes of one pixel and one degree. For each line, we require at least 50 detected intersections with edge pixels, a length of at least 50 pixels, and no gaps of more than 10 pixels. We will clear the list of any previously detected lines. Then, we will iterate over the results of the Hough line detection. Here is the first part of the method's implementation:

```
void UpdateLines() {

    // Detect lines.
    Imgproc.HoughLinesP(cannyMat, houghLines, 1.0,
            Mathf.PI / 180.0, 50,
            50.0, 10.0);

    //
    // Calculate the lines' screen coordinates and
    // world coordinates.
    //

    // Clear the previous coordinates.
    lines.Clear();

    // Iterate over the lines.
    int numHoughLines = houghLines.cols() *
            houghLines.rows() *
            houghLines.channels();
    int[] houghLinesArray = new int[numHoughLines];
    houghLines.get(0, 0, houghLinesArray);
    for (int i = 0; i < numHoughLines; i += 4) {
```

We will use our `ConvertToScreenPosition` helper method to convert the line's endpoints from image space to screen space:

```
        // Convert lines' image coordinates to
        // screen coordinates.
        Vector2 screenPoint0 =
            ConvertToScreenPosition(
                houghLinesArray[i],
                houghLinesArray[i + 1]);
        Vector2 screenPoint1 =
            ConvertToScreenPosition(
                houghLinesArray[i + 2],
                houghLinesArray[i + 3]);
```

Similarly, we will use our `ConvertToWorldPosition` helper method to convert the line's endpoints from screen space to world space. Having done our conversions, we will instantiate `Line` and add it to the list. Here is the code that completes the `UpdateLines` method:

```
    // Convert screen coordinates to world
    // coordinates based on raycasting.
    Vector3 worldPoint0 =
        ConvertToWorldPosition(screenPoint0);

    Vector3 worldPoint1 =
        ConvertToWorldPosition(screenPoint1);


    Line line = new Line(
        screenPoint0, screenPoint1,
        worldPoint0, worldPoint1);
    lines.Add(line);
  }
}
```

Our `ConvertToScreenPosition` helper method takes account of the fact that our screen coordinates are in portrait format, whereas our image coordinates are in the landscape format. The conversion from image space to screen space is implemented as follows:

```
Vector2 ConvertToScreenPosition(float imageX,
                float imageY) {
  float screenX = screenWidth - imageY *
        screenPixelsPerImagePixel;
  float screenY = screenHeight - imageX *
        screenPixelsPerImagePixel -
        screenPixelsYOffset;
  return new Vector2(screenX, screenY);
}
```

Our `ConvertToWorldPosition` helper method uses Unity's built-in raycasting functionality and our specified target distance, `raycastDistance`, to convert the given 2D screen coordinates to 3D world coordinates:

```
Vector3 ConvertToWorldPosition(
    Vector2 screenPosition) {
  Ray ray = _camera.ScreenPointToRay(
      screenPosition);
  return ray.GetPoint(raycastDistance);
}
```

We will implement the standard `OnPostRender` callback by checking whether any simulated balls or lines are present and, if not, by calling a helper method, `DrawPreview`. The code is as follows:

```
void OnPostRender() {
  if (!simulating) {
    DrawPreview();
  }
}
```

The `DrawPreview` helper method serves to show the positions and dimensions of detected circles and lines, if any. To avoid unnecessary draw calls, the method returns early if there are no objects to draw, as seen in the following code:

```
void DrawPreview() {

  // Draw 2D representations of the detected
  // circles and lines, if any.

  int numCircles = circles.Count;
  int numLines = lines.Count;
  if (numCircles < 1 && numLines < 1) {
    return;
  }
```

Having determined that there are detected shapes to draw, the method proceeds by configuring the OpenGL context to draw in screen space using `drawPreviewMaterial`. This setup is seen in the following code:

```
GL.PushMatrix();
if (drawPreviewMaterial != null) {
  drawPreviewMaterial.SetPass(0);
}
GL.LoadPixelMatrix();
```

If there are any detected circles, we will do one draw call to highlight them all. Specifically, we will tell OpenGL to begin drawing quads, we will feed it the screen coordinates of squares that approximate the circles, and then we will tell it to stop drawing quads. Here is the code:

```
if (numCircles > 0) {
  // Draw the circles.
  GL.Begin(GL.QUADS);
  for (int i = 0; i < numCircles; i++) {
    Circle circle = circles[i];
    float centerX =
```

```
        circle.screenPosition.x;
      float centerY =
        circle.screenPosition.y;
      float radius =
        0.5f * circle.screenDiameter;
      float minX = centerX - radius;
      float maxX = centerX + radius;
      float minY = centerY - radius;
      float maxY = centerY + radius;
      GL.Vertex3(minX, minY, 0f);
      GL.Vertex3(minX, maxY, 0f);
      GL.Vertex3(maxX, maxY, 0f);
      GL.Vertex3(maxX, minY, 0f);
    }
    GL.End();
  }
```

Similarly, if there are any detected lines, we perform one draw call to highlight them all. Specifically, we will tell OpenGL to begin drawing lines, we will feed it the lines' screen coordinate, and then we will tell it to stop drawing lines. Here is the code, which completes the `DrawPreview` method:

```
  if (numLines > 0) {
    // Draw the lines.
    GL.Begin(GL.LINES);
    for (int i = 0; i < numLines; i++) {
      Line line = lines[i];
      GL.Vertex(line.screenPoint0);
      GL.Vertex(line.screenPoint1);
    }
    GL.End();
  }

  GL.PopMatrix();
}
```

We will implement the standard `OnGUI` callback by drawing a button. Depending on whether simulated balls and lines are already present, the button displays either **Stop Simulation** or **Start Simulation**. When the button is clicked a helper method is called—either `StopSimulation` or `StartSimulation`. Here is the code for `OnGUI`:

```
  void OnGUI() {
    GUI.skin.button.fontSize = buttonFontSize;
    if (simulating) {
      if (GUI.Button(buttonRect,
```

```
        StopSimulation();
    }
} else {
    if (GUI.Button(buttonRect,
            "Start Simulation")) {
        StartSimulation();
    }
}
}
```

The StartSimulation helper method begins by pausing the video feed and placing copies of simulatedCirclePrefab atop the detected circles. Each instance is scaled to match a detected circle's diameter. Here is the first part of the method:

```
void StartSimulation() {

    // Freeze the video background
    webCamTexture.Pause();

    // Create the circles' representation in the
    // physics simulation.
    int numCircles = circles.Count;
    for (int i = 0; i < numCircles; i++) {
        Circle circle = circles[i];
        GameObject simulatedCircle =
            (GameObject)Instantiate(
                simulatedCirclePrefab);
        Transform simulatedCircleTransform =
            simulatedCircle.transform;
        simulatedCircleTransform.position =
            circle.worldPosition;
        simulatedCircleTransform.localScale =
            circle.screenDiameter *
            Vector3.one;
        simulatedObjects.Add(simulatedCircle);
    }
```

The method finishes by placing copies of simulatedLinePrefab atop the detected lines. Each instance is scaled to match a detected line's length. Here is the rest of the method:

```
    // Create the lines' representation in the
    // physics simulation.
    int numLines = lines.Count;
```

```
    for (int i = 0; i < numLines; i++) {
      Line line = lines[i];
      GameObject simulatedLine =
          (GameObject)Instantiate(
              simulatedLinePrefab);
      Transform simulatedLineTransform =
          simulatedLine.transform;
      float angle = -Vector2.Angle(
          Vector2.right, line.screenPoint1 -
              line.screenPoint0);
      Vector3 worldPoint0 = line.worldPoint0;
      Vector3 worldPoint1 = line.worldPoint1;
      simulatedLineTransform.position =
          0.5f * (worldPoint0 + worldPoint1);
      simulatedLineTransform.eulerAngles =
          new Vector3(0f, 0f, angle);
      simulatedLineTransform.localScale =
          new Vector3(
              Vector3.Distance(
                  worldPoint0,
                  worldPoint1),
              lineThickness,
              lineThickness);
      simulatedObjects.Add(simulatedLine);
    }
  }
```

The StopSimulation helper method simply serves to resume the video feed, delete all simulated balls and lines, and clear the list that contained these simulated objects. With the list empty, the conditions for the detectors to run (in the Update method) are fulfilled again. StopSimulation is implemented like this:

```
void StopSimulation() {

  // Unfreeze the video background.
  webCamTexture.Play();

  // Destroy all objects in the physics simulation.
  int numSimulatedObjects =
      simulatedObjects.Count;
  for (int i = 0; i < numSimulatedObjects; i++) {
    GameObject simulatedObject =
```

```
          simulatedObjects[i];
        Destroy(simulatedObject);
      }
      simulatedObjects.Clear();
  }
```

When the script's instance is destroyed (at the end of the scene), we will ensure that the webcam and gyroscope are released, as seen in the following code:

```
void OnDestroy() {
  if (webCamTexture != null) {
    webCamTexture.Stop();
  }
  if (gyro != null) {
    gyro.enabled = false;
  }
  }
}
}
```

Save the script and drag it from the **Project** pane to the **Main Camera** object in **Hierarchy**. Click on the **Main Camera** object and, in the **Detect And Simulate (Script)** section of its **Inspector**, drag the following objects to the following fields:

- Drag **VideoRenderer** (from **Hierarchy**) to the **Video Renderer** field (in **Inspector**)

- Drag **DrawSolidRed** (from `Rollingball/Materials` in the **Project** pane) to the **Draw Preview Material** field (in **Inspector**)

- Drag **SimulatedCircle** (from `Rollingball/Prefabs` in the **Project** pane) to the **Simulated Circle Prefab** field (in **Inspector**)

- Drag **SimulatedLine** (from `Rollingball/Prefabs` in the **Project** pane) to the **Simulated Line Prefab** field (in **Inspector**)

After these changes, the script's section in **Inspector** should look like this:

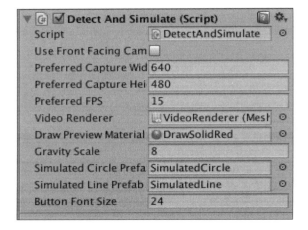

Our scene is complete! All that remains is to configure, build, and test it.

Tidying up and testing

Let's return to the **Build Settings** window (**Build Settings…** under **File**). We no longer want OpenCV for Unity demos in our build. Remove them by either unchecking them or selecting and deleting them (*Del* on Windows or *cmd + delete* on Mac). Then, add the **Rollingball** scene by clicking on the **Add Current** button. Click on the **Build and Run** button, overwrite any previous build, and let the good times roll!

> If you are building for iOS, remember to follow the additional instructions in OpenCVForUnity/ReadMe.pdf. Particularly, ensure that OpenCVForUnity/iOS for Xcode/opencv2. framework is added to the project.

Test the app by drawing and scanning dots and lines of various sizes and with various styles of pen strokes. Also try scanning some things that are not drawings. Feel free to go back to the code, edit the detectors' parameters, rebuild, and see how the sensitivity has changed.

Summary

This chapter has really rounded out our experience and drawn a line under our accomplishments. We learned to detect primitive shapes using the Hough transform. Then, we used OpenCV and Unity together to turn a pen and paper drawing into a physics toy. We have surpassed the things that even Q could make a pen do!

At this proud moment, however, our adventure must reach its conclusion. We might meet again. Look out for future books, webcasts, and presentations, to be announced on my website at `http://nummist.com/opencv`. Also, e-mail me at `josephhowse@nummist.com` to report issues, ask questions, and tell me how you are using OpenCV.

The book is ending now and I am waiting to find out whether I disappear into the sunset with a femme fatale or whether I have a melancholy debriefing with M.

Index

Javadocs
  URL 148

K

kittydar
  URL 122

L

Laplacian image pyramid 210
Lazy Eyes app
  configuring, for various motions 220-227
  implementing 211-220
  light, things viewing in 228
  planning 203
  testing, for various motions 220-227
  two images compositing, image pyramids
      used 210, 211
lights
  detecting, as blobs 170, 171
Living Headlights app
  distances, estimating 172-175
  implementing 175-189
  lights, detecting as blobs 169-171
  planning 167, 168
  testing, at home 189-192
  testing, in car 193-198
Living Headlights app, files
  ColorUtils.py 175
  GeomUtils.py 175
  LivingHeadlights.py 175
  PyInstallerUtils.py 175
  ResizeUtils.py 175
  WxUtils.py 175
Local Binary Pattern
      Histograms (LBPH) 79, 80
Local Binary Patterns (LBP) 79
Lucas-Kanade method
  URL 127
Luxocator app
  building, for distribution 71-74
  classifier, training with
      reference images 52, 53
  histograms, comparing 46-52
  histograms, creating 46-52
  histograms, storing 46-52

images, acquiring from Bing
      Image Search 55-60
images, acquiring from Web 53-55
images, preparing 60-62
integration, in GUI 63-71
planning 44, 45
resources, preparing 60-63

M

Mac
  about 15, 16
  Homebrew used 18, 19
  MacPorts used 16-18
machine learning 77
MacPorts
  URL 17
Marsboard A20
  URL 41
materials, Rollingball app
  writing 247-250
MediaPlayer class
  URL 144
Moiré 61

N

NoIR
  URL 39
NoIR renders outdoor scenes
  URL 228
NumPy
  URL 11, 207

O

Odroid U3
  URL 41
OpenCV
  books, URL 41
  dependencies, URL 22
  documentation, finding 40, 41
  documentation, URL 61, 211
  forum, URL 41
  on Windows, binary installers used 12
  on Windows, CMake used 12-15
  on Windows, compilers used 12-15

U

Unity
about 34
assets, adding to scene 247
assets, creating 247
Rollingball scene, creating 244-246
Unity project
building 242, 243
configuring 242-244
Unity script, Rollingball app
writing 256-258
unsupervised learning 77
USB Video Class (UVC) Linux driver 9

V

vote 237

W

Win32 Disk Imager
URL 35
Windows
about 80
development machine, setting up 10-12
wxPython
URL 11, 64

X

Xcode
URL 15

Thank you for buying
OpenCV for Secret Agents

About Packt Publishing

Packt, pronounced 'packed', published its first book, *Mastering phpMyAdmin for Effective MySQL Management*, in April 2004, and subsequently continued to specialize in publishing highly focused books on specific technologies and solutions.

Our books and publications share the experiences of your fellow IT professionals in adapting and customizing today's systems, applications, and frameworks. Our solution-based books give you the knowledge and power to customize the software and technologies you're using to get the job done. Packt books are more specific and less general than the IT books you have seen in the past. Our unique business model allows us to bring you more focused information, giving you more of what you need to know, and less of what you don't.

Packt is a modern yet unique publishing company that focuses on producing quality, cutting-edge books for communities of developers, administrators, and newbies alike. For more information, please visit our website at www.packtpub.com.

About Packt Open Source

In 2010, Packt launched two new brands, Packt Open Source and Packt Enterprise, in order to continue its focus on specialization. This book is part of the Packt Open Source brand, home to books published on software built around open source licenses, and offering information to anybody from advanced developers to budding web designers. The Open Source brand also runs Packt's Open Source Royalty Scheme, by which Packt gives a royalty to each open source project about whose software a book is sold.

Writing for Packt

We welcome all inquiries from people who are interested in authoring. Book proposals should be sent to author@packtpub.com. If your book idea is still at an early stage and you would like to discuss it first before writing a formal book proposal, then please contact us; one of our commissioning editors will get in touch with you.

We're not just looking for published authors; if you have strong technical skills but no writing experience, our experienced editors can help you develop a writing career, or simply get some additional reward for your expertise.

Instant OpenCV Starter

ISBN: 978-1-78216-881-2   Paperback: 56 pages

Get started with OpenCV using practical, hands-on projects

1. Learn something new in an Instant! A short, fast, focused guide delivering immediate results.

2. Step by step installation of OpenCV in Windows and Linux.

3. Examples and code based on real-life implementation of OpenCV to help the reader understand the importance of this technology.

4. Codes and algorithms with detailed explanations.

OpenCV Essentials

ISBN: 978-1-78398-424-4   Paperback: 214 pages

Acquire, process, and analyze visual content to build full-fledged imaging applications using OpenCV

1. Create OpenCV programs with a rich user interface.

2. Develop real-world imaging applications using free tools and libraries.

3. Understand the intricate details of OpenCV and its implementation using easy-to-follow examples.

Please check **www.PacktPub.com** for information on our titles

OpenCV 2 Computer Vision Application Programming Cookbook

ISBN: 978-1-84951-324-1   Paperback: 304 pages

Over 50 recipes to master this library of programming functions for real-time computer vision

1. Teaches you how to program computer vision applications in C++ using the different features of the OpenCV library.

2. Demonstrates the important structures and functions of OpenCV in detail with complete working examples.

3. Describes fundamental concepts in computer vision and image processing.

Mastering OpenCV with Practical Computer Vision Projects

ISBN: 978-1-84951-782-9   Paperback: 340 pages

Step-by-step tutorials to solve common real-world computer vision problems for desktop or mobile, from augmented reality and number plate recognition to face recognition and 3D head tracking

1. Allows anyone with basic OpenCV experience to rapidly obtain skills in many computer vision topics, for research or commercial use.

2. Each chapter is a separate project covering a computer vision problem, written by a professional with proven experience on that topic.

3. All projects include a step-by-step tutorial and full source-code, using the C++ interface of OpenCV.

Please check **www.PacktPub.com** for information on our titles

Made in the USA
San Bernardino, CA
22 March 2015